"As one of Canada's most astute and provocative media observers, Marc Edge analyzes the political economy trends underlying the corporate media's growing democratic deficit—and suggests what we might do about it."

Robert A. Hackett
Simon Fraser University

"Marc Edge offers well-informed analyses and criticisms of the commercial media system in Canada. Anybody who wants to think seriously about how money, consolidation, and cross-ownership have shaped the media environment should read *The News We Deserve*. His detailed and provocative analysis is must-read stuff for anyone seeking to better understand the media in Canada."

Dwayne Winseck
Carleton University and Canadian Media Concentration Research Project

The News We Deserve

The News
We Deserve

The Transformation of Canada's Media Landscape

Marc Edge

 NEW STAR BOOKS • VANCOUVER • 2016

NEW STAR BOOKS LTD.
newstarbooks.com • info@newstarbooks.com

#107–3477 Commercial St   1574 Gulf Road, #1517
Vancouver, BC   Point Roberts, WA 98281
V5N 4E8 CANADA   USA

The publisher acknowledges the financial support of the Canada Council for the Arts, the Government of Canada through the Canada Book Fund, the British Columbia Arts Council, and the Province of British Columbia through the Book Publishing Tax Credit.

Cataloguing information for this book is available from Library and Archives Canada, collectionscanada.gc.ca

Printed & bound in Canada on 100% post-consumer recycled paper by Imprimerie Gauvin, Gatineau, QC

ISBN 978-1-55420-121-1
Cover design by Oliver McPartlin
Typeset by New Star Books
First printing, November 2016

Contents

For *Markenurh*, aboard which,
at Riversbend Marina,
I have written all of my books.

Foreword by Vincent Mosco

Over the past two decades, Marc Edge has justifiably earned a reputation as a leading voice in Canadian media and journalism studies. It is no exaggeration to conclude that this has been a period of intense upheaval and crisis in Canadian media during which many of Edge's worst fears have been realized. However, *The News We Deserve* amounts to more than an expert chronicle of the decline and fall of Canada's once internationally respected print and electronic communication systems. It is as much a set of hopeful visions of what journalism excellence and a media service committed to the public interest and democracy can be, when it is properly managed and regulated. Striking the right balance between media criticism and proposals for change is difficult but essential and Edge's book is, among other things, an excellent guide to getting this right. His approach is to focus on the corrosive consequences of concentrated media ownership on democracy and the public sphere and to shine a light on attempts to challenge it with oppositional and alternative media. This makes Edge a consummate political economist.

Over the years Edge has demonstrated considerable strength in two areas of the political economy of communication. First, he is one of the foremost scholars of media ownership in Canada. Edge's book *Asper Nation* is an excellent exemplar because it brilliantly dissects the family's rise to prominence in Canadian media, displaying the ability to sustain an in-depth treatment of one of the central issues of political economic analysis: the consequences of media concentration for democracy. Focusing on the structure and operation of power, *Asper Nation* combines all of the key elements of political economy. It demonstrates the ability to work with primary documents to chart the development of the Asper's media holdings. Building on this historical analysis, Edge is able to situate the family's ascent within the social totality of Canadian media across the major sectors of print, broadcasting and new media. The book also assesses media concentration within a moral philosophical context that gives prominence to the value of democracy or full citizen involvement in political decision-making. Finally, *Asper Nation* makes the case for political and policy activism to counteract the disturbing growth of media concentration in Canada.

Edge has also demonstrated strength in the analysis of alternative and oppositional media. For example, Catherine McKercher and I accepted a co-authored article from Edge for a special themed issue of the *Canadian Journal of Communication* on the topic of media labour. His excellent contribution focused on the importance of making use of the media in labour disputes with an assessment of a newspaper produced by striking media workers at a British Columbia daily. The article described the challenges faced by strike newspapers and the potential for incorporating this longstanding practice into contemporary media struggles. In this regard Edge's research contributes to overcoming a blindspot in media analysis, the systematic study of media labour.

The News We Deserve richly embodies Edge's commitment to political economy research in Canada and particularly to the roots of the current crisis, the unprecedented power that a handful of companies wield over both traditional and new media. My introduction to Canadian media corresponds with an event that, as Edge recognizes, shone a bright light on the origins of today's crisis. The 1981 report of the Royal Commission on Newspapers was prompted by one outrageous event — the simultaneous closing by two different companies of newspapers in Ottawa and Winnipeg, giving each other a monopoly in these cities—and by years of concern over growing media concentration. It was an extraordinary document, in part because in the year after the Commission was called, it published numerous volumes examining the industry. At the time I was an American scholar asked to review the report for the *Journal of Communication*. The scope of the research and recommendations was remarkable, as was the extent of publicity the documents garnered. Sadly, as Edge has demonstrated, aside from educating the Canadian public about the extent of the problem, the report led to no policy action because a Conservative government swept into power and paid it little attention.

The long, slow decline signaled by the Royal Commission accelerated soon thereafter and Edge has been one of its leading storytellers. Print media in most cities is dominated by one company, Postmedia, which is nearing bankruptcy and mostly owned by US hedge funds that have bent the rules intended to restrict foreign ownership. Two companies, Rogers and Bell, rule broadcasting, telecommunications, and internet service provision, enabling a degree of concentration that would not be permitted in the US or in most other developed countries. Edge is particularly good at documenting the ties between Canada's media giants, pliable government agencies, and schools of journalism and communication across Canada. The nation's chief broadcasting and telecommunications regulator, the CRTC, has done nothing to slow the concentration process, save to require companies to make payments for projects it determines will serve the public interest. Some of these have involved payments to Canadian universities that have been happy to supplement their declining budgets and just as eager to return the favour by supporting the companies before the government, through research chairs, and in think tanks. Just as bad has been the performance of the government's Competition Bureau, which has done little to live up to its name and mandate. In Marc Edge, Canada has no better interpreter of how and why this sorry state of affairs transpired. It also has no one better to assess its significance and describe alternatives.

As his 2006 study of the *Castlegar Citizen* strike newspaper put out by journalists walking a picket line showed, Edge is a dialectical thinker. He has recently documented the potential for employee ownership with a review of *CHEK Republic*, by Diane Dakers, a 2014 book on how a television station in BC became an orphan of failed convergence. Rather than fade away into oblivion when the declining media giant Canwest Global shed CHEK, the station's employees bought it and built a coalition that did more than save a vital broadcast outlet. CHEK revived local programming and built a successful business. The best example of Edge's intense commitment to good journalism and the pursuit of alternatives to the failed monopoly model that has dominated the nation's media is his chapter "Can Canada's Media be Fixed?" Here he describes alternative ownership models and new forms of funding for independent journalists that offer genuinely new visions of how journalism can survive and thrive in a digital age. He concludes, in the dialectical spirit of Dallas Smythe, one of Canada's pioneers in the critical political economy of communication, that "there is no shortage of good ideas" for making Canadian media a model for democratic communication in the world today.

The News We Deserve forcefully demonstrates that Marc Edge continues to lead the way in the search for good ideas about how to critically assess Canadian media and how to change it for the better.

Ottawa, 2016

Vincent Mosco is Professor Emeritus and former Canada Research Chair in Communication and Society at Queen's University. He is the author of twenty-one books, including The Political Economy of Communication *and* The Digital Sublime.

Acrimony and Outrage

Canada's news media exploded in acrimony and outrage in late 2015 as many woke up to the possibility that their country's largest news gathering organization had been taken hostage by financial and ideological forces that hardly held public service as their highest ideal. The federal election that October provided the first clue for some as to just how rotten their news media had gotten. For others, it was the last straw. After newspapers owned by Postmedia Network, the country's largest chain, endorsed in unison the decade-old Conservative government of Stephen Harper, *Edmonton Journal* columnist Paula Simons simply had to speak up. "Before you ask, this was a decision made by the owners of the paper," she revealed on Twitter. "As is their traditional prerogative."[1] It wasn't the first time an endorsement order had come from head office, even that year. In May, the *Journal*'s editor admitted that Postmedia had ordered its four Alberta dailies to endorse the Conservatives during the provincial election campaign. "The owners of the *Journal* made that call," Margo Goodhand told Canadaland, the website and podcast that shone an increasingly unflattering light on the country's mainstream media.[2]

Postmedia CEO Paul Godfrey, a former Conservative politician, defended the corporate decision to impose its political will on its journalists and readers. "Since God made babies, I think [endorsement editorials] were always made that way," he told the *Globe and Mail*, "and if anyone thinks otherwise, I think they were dreaming in Technicolor."[3] John Honderich, chairman of the board at Torstar Corporation, which published the competing *Toronto Star*, lashed out at the power broker who was paid $1.76 million* a year to lead Canada's largest news media company, which was owned mostly by US hedge funds. "Really, Mr. Godfrey?" wrote Honderich in a column printed not just in the *Star* but also in several of the chain's other dailies, including its *Metro* commuter tabloids across Canada. "You might want to examine the policies of other newspaper chains that tell an entirely different bedtime story." Postmedia predecessor Southam Inc., noted Honderich, "went to great lengths to emphasize individual publishers in each city were responsible for all editorial content, including election endorsements." So had the erstwhile Thomson chain, which included the *Globe and Mail*, and even the giant Gannett company in the US.

> The reason, of course, was self-evident. What was important or relevant to readers in Vancouver might not be so in Montreal, Ottawa or Windsor. Owning a newspaper, in my view, is a privilege not a right. Nor is it the same as owning a pizzeria or car wash. Newspapers are an essential informing part of the democratic process and their first responsibility must be to the local readers they serve.[4]

Outrage soon grew when, two days before the federal election, Postmedia and Sun Media dailies across the country came wrapped in full-page advertisements. Depending on the location, the aptly yellow ads were headlined "Voting Liberal will cost you" or "Voting NDP or Liberal will cost you" followed by a campaign message and a ballot marked "Conservative."[5] Rancor resounded from coast to coast. "This was crossing the Rubicon," wrote Geoff Olson in the semi-weekly *Vancouver Courier*, mincing no words. "Whoring out front pages across the country just days before an election was a low unworthy even of media mogul Rupert Murdoch and his boss,

---

* All dollar amounts in CDN unless stated otherwise.

Satan. . . . Here was a case of boardroom Judases selling their publications' paper-thin integrity for a few pieces of silver."[6] Godfrey pointed out that advertising was how newspapers made money. "Anybody, the Liberals could have done it, the NDP could have done it, as long as they pay the going rate," he told the *Globe and Mail*. "Newspapers have to seek whatever revenues they can get."[7]

But the capper came on election day, when *National Post* columnist Andrew Coyne resigned as the newspaper's editor of editorials and comments. Coyne's resignation came, he explained on Twitter, after Postmedia decided to drop his column that day because its endorsement of a party other than the Conservatives "would have confused readers and embarrassed the paper."[8] He disagreed. "I don't see public disagreement as confusing," Coyne tweeted. "I see it as honest. Readers, in my view, are adults & understand that adults can disagree."[9] While he resigned his editor position, Coyne continued to write his column, which soon re-appeared. In a series of tweets, he called the editorial interference by his employer "unprecedented" and explained that he "could not allow the precedent to stand."[10] The website Ricochet noted it was the second time in two months that Postmedia management had pulled rank on Coyne. "How can an editor do their job if their decisions are repeatedly overruled by owners who have a clear political agenda and tolerate no dissent?" asked writer Ethan Cox.[11]

A column by author Margaret Atwood that asked some hard questions about Harper, noted Cox, had been pulled from the *National Post* website that August before re-appearing in an edited fashion. "Why is Harper still coyly hiding the two-million-dollar donors to his party leadership race?" asked Atwood in the initial version of her column, a cached version of which was briefly available online. "Don't we have a right to know who put him in there? Who's he working for, them or us?" That passage was reportedly deleted from the final version, along with other criticism of Harper.[12] A Postmedia executive told the *Toronto Star* that Atwood's column had been pulled because it had not been fact-checked. "Senior editorial leadership at Postmedia also had not concluded whether the column was aligned with the values of the National

Post and its readers," *National Post* senior vice-president Gerry Nott explained in an email.[13] Jeet Heer, a senior editor of the *New Republic* magazine, was incredulous. "So every Post column must now align with 'the values of the National Post and its readers'?" he asked on Twitter. "Do these people understand what columns are?"[14] Ricochet's Cox railed against "the ham-fisted meddling of owners with a vested interest in returning the Conservatives to government."

> If a paper no longer tolerates criticism of the government at inopportune (and important) moments, then can it even be said to be a newspaper anymore? In future campaigns it's hard to imagine that newspaper endorsements will be paid any attention by a populace wary that they represent the advancement of corporate interests, rather than the wisdom of editors.[15]

Perhaps the most scathing criticism of the latest disgraceful episode in Canadian journalism history, however, came from beyond the country's borders. "Postmedia achieved its market dominance in step with the rise of Harper's Conservatives," pointed out the website of the *Guardian* in the UK, which had a huge global readership online. When Canada's largest newspaper chain bought 175 of Quebecor Inc.'s 178 Sun Media titles in late 2014—essentially taking over the country's second-largest chain—the federal Competition Bureau meekly approved the deal, noted the *Guardian*. "In seeking permission for the takeover, Postmedia assured the regulator that its newspapers would pursue independent editorial policies. Mere months later they were predictably backing Harper's Conservatives."[16]

Florida-based journalism school and media think tank The Poynter Institute was even more damning in its criticism. "The stain of this shameful moment in Canadian journalism will never wash completely clean," a writer for its popular website concluded. "Not only did they tolerate the ugliest political episode in Canada's post-war era, they signed their names to it."[17] Voters responded by largely rejecting Postmedia's advice on the best political alternatives in 2015, both in Ottawa and in Alberta. The kicker came one month after the federal election, when Godfrey was inducted into the Canadian News Hall of Fame, mainly for helming the Toronto Sun and Sun Media from 1984 to 2000.

Contrast the election-week outrage to the silence that greeted the announcement earlier in 2015 that the Competition Bureau had rubber stamped Postmedia's $316-million acquisition of Sun Media. It evoked "almost no critical commentary or even concern," noted a pair of media scholars. "Godfrey gleefully admitted that ten years ago such a merger would not have been allowed and would likely have provoked a public outcry," wrote Paul Benedetti and James Compton. "This time around, it sparked, well, nothing."[18] Announcement of the deal the previous fall, the *Toronto Star* remarked in an editorial, didn't raise much concern either.

> It should. If the deal is approved by the federal Competition Bureau, one company will own almost all the significant daily papers in English Canada. In most cities, the choice for newspaper readers will be between Postmedia—and Postmedia. Most worrisome, the big decisions that will shape much of English Canada's media landscape will be made south of the border.[19]

The *Globe and Mail* was one of the few media outlets to point out the implications of Postmedia's purchase. The takeover "doesn't just alter Canada's print-media landscape, it takes a bulldozer to it," quipped columnist David Parkinson. "Postmedia's proposed takeover . . . has thrown down the gauntlet to Canadian regulators," he added, "and forced the country to have a conversation that it has long avoided: How much are we willing to compromise the principles of a diverse and competitive press in the name of keeping it alive?"[20] The Competition Bureau, however, rarely stood in the way of corporate consolidation of the country's news media. A 2006 Senate report was sharply critical of both it and the Canadian Radio–television and Telecommunications Commission for what it called their "neglect" of Canada's news industries. "One challenge is the complete absence of a review mechanism to consider the public interest in news media mergers," the report noted. "The result has been extremely high levels of news media concentration in particular cities or regions."[21]

Part of the problem, the Senate report added, was that the Competition Bureau was only empowered to consider the economic impact of a media merger or acquisition on advertisers, not its impact on the news needs of Canadians. "Clearly, a principal public interest about the news media should be the diversity of news and opinion," it pointed out. "For this reason, advertising costs are not always the best indicator of market conditions for the news media."[22] It recommended adding a new section to the Competition Act to deal with news media mergers and suggested automatic review of any that gave an owner an audience share of 35 percent or more. As the Competition Bureau was unlikely to have the expertise to deal with the public interest in media mergers, it recommended that an expert panel review them. "The Competition Bureau's operating procedures may be well suited to analysing most markets for goods and services in Canada," the Senate report concluded, "but not the news media market."[23] Press freedom provisions in the Charter of Rights and Freedoms, on which publishers had traditionally relied in claiming exemption from regulation, should only go so far, the senators reasoned. "The media's right to be free from government interference does not extend . . . to a conclusion that proprietors should be allowed to own an excessive proportion of media holdings in a particular market, let alone the national market."[24] Bad timing doomed the Senate report's recommendations, however, as the Conservatives had been elected earlier in 2006 and would spend almost a decade in power.

The new government wasn't about to place restrictions on ownership of a news media that had helped turn a largely liberal populace into a plurality of Conservative voters, thanks in part to Conrad Black taking over the former Southam dailies and founding the *National Post*. Its stated mission from its first edition in 1998 was to "unite the right" of Canada's fractured right-wing parties. Predictably, the Conservatives looked the other way in 2010 when Postmedia scooped up the country's largest newspaper chain out of bankruptcy. Its majority ownership by US hedge funds was well above Canada's 25 percent limit on foreign ownership of newspapers, but Postmedia circumvented the rules with a two-tiered share structure that kept foreign voting control ostensibly below the limit. Godfrey called the funds "hands-off investors," but the *Globe and Mail* reported in 2014 that he conferred with them frequently.

> In recent months, the fund managers pushed Postmedia's management to strike a deal with Sun Media despite frustrating delays in negotiations. "Paul doesn't make major moves without calling them first," one person close to the company said, referring to the fund managers.[25]

Its 2014 takeover of Sun Media made Postmedia by far the largest newspaper publisher in Canada, with almost three times the paid daily circulation of second-place Torstar. Postmedia owned fifteen of the twenty-one largest English-language dailies and published 37.6 percent of paid daily newspaper circulation in Canada. Even more pronounced was its dominance in Western Canada, where Postmedia enjoyed a 75.4 percent market share and owned eight of the nine largest newspapers in BC, Alberta, and Saskatchewan. In addition to its long-standing duopoly in Vancouver, where Postmedia and its predecessors Canwest, Hollinger, and Southam had owned both dailies since 1980, Postmedia gained similar dominance in three more markets by buying Sun Media, acquiring its main competition in Calgary, Edmonton, and Ottawa.[26]

But according to the Competition Bureau, the sale was "unlikely to substantially lessen or prevent competition" in those cities. After reviewing the acquisition for five months, but without holding hearings, it issued Postmedia a "no action" letter in early 2015, meaning it would not challenge the purchase. A combination of factors played into its decision, according to a press release, including:

- the lack of close rivalry between Postmedia's broadsheet and Sun Media's English-language tabloid newspapers;
- existing competition from free local daily newspapers;
- the incentive for the merged company to retain readership and maintain editorial quality in order to continue to attract readers and advertisers to its newspapers; and
- the increasing competitive pressures from digital alternatives in an evolving media marketplace.[27]

In other words, the Competition Bureau counter-intuitively concluded, the newspapers didn't compete anyway. In a longer statement posted on its website, the Bureau said it found "very little evidence of direct rivalry between the parties' newspapers with respect to advertising." Its economic analysis showed that the newspapers were also "not close rivals from the perspective of readers." Another factor cited by the Competition Bureau was that newspapers competed in "two-sided" markets, a subject on which it said it was "guided by a recent and expanding economic literature." Because they sold a service to both readers and advertisers, newspapers competed in two markets instead of the usual one. "The parties are keenly focused on their circulation and readership figures, and rely on them heavily in marketing to potential advertisers," noted the Competition Bureau, which also pointed to declining readership and advertising. "As a result, market conditions exert downward pressure on the parties' ability to exercise market power."[28]

That's when my old reporter's antennae started twitching. Since leaving the newspaper business after almost twenty years as a journalist, I had been studying media economics for almost two decades, and I had never heard of "two-sided" markets. I had learned the concept as the "dual market" nature of newspapers, and I knew there was an extensive literature on the subject going back decades in the field of communication. The *National Post* article that reported Postmedia's takeover, which was also published in most of Postmedia's dailies across Canada, quoted University of Toronto economist Ambarish Chandra, who had studied two-sided markets in the context of Canadian newspaper mergers during the late 1990s. "Prof. Chandra noted increases in prices for customers are a common concern when companies announce mergers of this scale," the *Post* article pointed out. "However, he said previous news mergers in Canada have not led to significant price increases since newspapers are no longer able to raise prices without losing readers—and, with them, advertising dollars."[29] It was a finding favourable to Postmedia's case for being allowed to take over Sun Media, which is no doubt why the *Post* put it on the record. "There is no relationship between concentration measures and advertising or circulation prices," Chandra's co-authored 2009 study concluded of the mergers that saw 75 percent of Canadian newspapers change hands between 1995 and 1999.[30] Other motives than economic may have instead been behind the studied newspaper mergers, it added. "There is some evidence that media mergers are motivated by reasons unrelated to profits, having more to do with political motives or empire building."[31]

History has shown, however, that newspaper monopolies usually result in sharp price increases for both readers and advertisers. A classic example was in Washington, DC, where the *Star* folded in 1981, giving the *Post* a local monopoly. "Two years after the *Star* folded, the *Post*'s ad rate had risen 58 percent," noted Ben Bagdikian in his classic book *The Media Monopoly*.[32] With the gradual disappearance of newspaper competition in the twentieth century, much research had been done on this subject by media economists. "These price effects are so powerful that they provide ample motivation for the long and steady trend to newspaper mergers and takeovers," noted a 1973 Canadian study.[33] The leading U.S. textbook on newspaper economics concluded in 1993 that the effect of monopoly on advertising rates had been well demonstrated.

> Some studies have found that monopoly power increased the advertising line rate. Other studies have found that competing newspapers tend to have lower advertising prices. . . . Overall, research supports that many monopoly-power newspapers charge monopoly advertising prices.[34]

I began to suspect that the Competition Bureau's economic analysis was based on flawed — or at least incomplete — research. I sent an email to the regulator stating my credentials as a media scholar and requesting a copy of its economic analysis, which I suspected had relied on Chandra's study. This was a matter of public interest and squarely in my area of expertise, after all, so I figured I should be able to get a look at this taxpayer funded research. I waited a couple of weeks and, having heard nothing back, I sent off a more official looking hard copy request on University Canada West letterhead.

I got a letter back a few weeks later denying my request. "The Competition Bureau conducts its merger reviews confidentially," wrote Trevor MacKay, an associate deputy commissioner.[35] Yet after the *Vancouver Sun* and *Province* went into business together in 1957, hearings were held in Ottawa and Vancouver, with a book-length report resulting. Then after the *Winnipeg Tribune* and the *Ottawa Journal* closed in 1980, a Royal Commission was called and it held public hearings across the country, published a report, and released a briefcase full of background studies. After the owner of the *Vancouver Sun* and *Province* bought up most of the area's community newspapers a decade later, the Competition Bureau at least held hearings. But after the country's largest newspaper chain bought the second largest, not only was the acquisition reviewed in secret, but the Competition Bureau wouldn't even release the research on which its approval was based.

Then the other shoe dropped. In January 2016 Postmedia announced that it would combine the newsrooms of its duopoly dailies in Vancouver, Calgary, Edmonton, and Ottawa. Dropping revenues dictated the moves, Postmedia said, which would help it save $50 million a year. Suddenly another ninety journalists were unemployed, with more expected to follow once Postmedia dealt with its unions in Vancouver. "The fallout is about more than adding a small number of people to the list of thousands of unemployed Albertans," wrote a Calgary correspondent for the *Globe and Mail*. "It is, instead, about whether Postmedia's remaining journalists can effectively hold politicians and organizations to account, deliver a diversity of opinions, and produce newspapers that are different enough to retain separate audiences and advertisers, despite containing slews of news stories that are nearly identical."[36]

I knew from researching my book on Pacific Press, the company created by the merger of the *Vancouver Sun* and *Province*, that their owners had promised to keep separate newsrooms indefinitely to gain federal approval for what was otherwise ruled an illegal merger between competitors. I knew that Postmedia had repeatedly promised—publicly and privately—to do the same in Calgary, Edmonton, and Ottawa. In announcing the Sun Media purchase in 2014, Godfrey said the duplicate dailies Postmedia acquired would continue to operate independently with their own newsrooms.[37] Godfrey reiterated when the purchase was approved in 2015 that Postmedia planned to follow in those cities the model that had been used for decades in Vancouver—seeking efficiencies in administration and production, but keeping separate newsrooms.[38] Goodhand, who was axed as *Edmonton Journal* editor in Postmedia's early 2016 bloodletting, revealed on the website of the *Walrus* magazine that Godfrey made similar promises privately to local stakeholders as well. "I attended two of his private dinners in fine Alberta restaurants where he vowed to keep the newsrooms separate," she wrote. "We might even have to reinvest in the Sun newsrooms, he mused aloud in Calgary. . . . They'd be competitive, distinct, and entirely independent, he said."[39]

Postmedia's promises had been spread skillfully through political channels. The *National Post*'s own tick-tock reporting of how the Sun Media deal went down reported that Postmedia chairman Rod Phillips called the mayors of Edmonton and Ottawa, as well as the premiers of Alberta and Ontario. Godfrey reportedly made similar calls to the mayor of Calgary, the federal Heritage Minister, the Prime Minister's Office, and several other cabinet ministers. "Even the leaders of the Opposition parties were brought into the loop," noted the *Post*'s backgrounder to the deal that was published in Postmedia dailies across the country. "Liberal leader Justin Trudeau was reached moments before Postmedia executives took to the microphones to announce the deal."[40]

The *National Post* campaigned hard for the takeover to be approved. "Newspaper owners aren't bluffing this time," warned John Ivison in column headlined "Ottawa likely to see sense in deal."

> They are fighting to survive. Everyone knows this—they see it before their eyes as their papers shrink in size, personnel and ambition. Against this gloomy backdrop, it seems unlikely that the regulator or the federal government will be motivated to intervene and block a deal that offers ballast to an industry buffeted by choppy waters.[41]

Ivison polled three MPs, one from each major party, on whether they would oppose the acquisition. "Provided that there are no mass layoffs, and all titles keep publishing, they said they were relaxed about the union."[42] He then doubled down in an interview with Mark Burgess of the *Hill Times*. "At ground level, there's no trepidation that we're going to see merged newsrooms or anything like that," he said. "The people who are running this company know newspapers. . . . and they know that any attempt to integrate the editorial products would be self-defeating."[43]

But Postmedia backtracked on its promises to keep separate newsrooms as it became increasingly hard pressed to pay the exorbitant interest owing on its more than $600 million in debt, which was largely held by its hedge fund owners. Goodhand expressed the dismay that many Canadians felt. "How could Canada let one media organization buy up virtually all of its newsrooms?"[44] Conrad Black, a minor Postmedia shareholder, had seen it coming. "Management could have spoken more candidly about the cost savings that a merged company could effect," he wrote in his *National Post* column after the deal was approved. "They will be larger than was stated, for public and personnel relations reasons."[45]

But having been a reporter for the *Province* for more than a decade, I knew that I had tried as hard as I could to scoop my competition at the *Vancouver Sun*. Now I saw the same stories published not only in both newspapers, but also often in the *National Post* and the Vancouver commuter tabloid *24 Hours*, which were both also owned by Postmedia.

The worst part, however, was watching some of my fellow journalism educators dismiss or at least excuse Postmedia's increasing stranglehold on Canadian news media. "What we're talking about here is one threatened company . . . buying properties whose future was in doubt," Ivor Shapiro, director of the school of journalism at Ryerson University in Toronto, told the Canadian Press after the takeover was announced. I could scarcely believe what I was reading.

If Calgary has two newspapers with the same owner, so be it, he said. It's been going on in Vancouver for years, with two papers competing editorially with areas of co-operation on the business side, such as advertising sales. "That is way better at the end of the day than seeing both of those news organizations close down," he added.[46]

Shapiro doubled down on his Toronto-centric view of Canada's news media a few days later in an interview with the *Toronto Star*. "Obviously, I would see it as a terrible thing if the *Toronto Star* and the *Globe and Mail* were to be owned by the same owner," he said. "That would be awful. But what we're talking about here is two organizations that were on a death watch. I'd rather have one news organization that is not on death's door than two news organizations that are. Together they are stronger competitors than they were apart."[47] Oxymorons aside, Shapiro confessed ignorance when I informed him that both companies were in fact making double-digit profit margins.

Christopher Waddell, who was Carty Chair in Business and Financial Journalism at Carleton University, echoed Shapiro's sentiment in an interview with CTV when the deal to buy Sun Media was announced. "A year or year and a half from now, how many of those 175 newspapers are still open, and how many does Postmedia own?" he asked. "And I would be very surprised if some of them aren't closed."[48] Eighteen months later, they were all still open, and they were all still owned by Postmedia. But the capper came after the announcement about merging newsrooms. "This is an organization that is losing money and losing a lot of money," Waddell told the CBC in response.[49] He had reviewed *Greatly Exaggerated*, my 2014 book that showed newspapers remained profitable.[50] Had he even read the book? It included data that showed Postmedia made operating profits of 16–17 percent between 2012 and 2014.

They weren't losing money, I reminded Waddell by email — they were losing value. As their revenues went down, the company's value went down. I was hardly about to cry for its mostly American owners, however, if their investment went south. The newspapers were still nicely profitable, and they would continue publishing under new ownership if Postmedia went bankrupt. Part of the problem, however, was that Postmedia had been seemingly designed to fail, saddled with huge debt by the hedge funds, hundreds of millions of which came due in 2017. As its earnings fell, Postmedia was forced by its heavy debt load to cut costs incessantly, but it still seemed doomed to fail.

Bankruptcy court was a prime hunting ground for hedge funds in the US that scooped up newspaper companies out of Chapter 11. Standard operating procedure saw them trade in only enough of the secured debt they held to win the company at auction, then keep the rest on the books. Should the company go bankrupt again because of its debt, the hedge funds would once again be first in line to take it over. It was Financial Engineering 101. Bankruptcy was a recurring theme for some US chains, which declared bankruptcy "strategically." Despite recording enviable profit margins, Journal Register Co. went broke in 2009 and then again in 2012 due to its high debt levels that repeatedly put it under water. Each time it used the courts to shed pesky legal obligations like leases, union contracts, and back taxes.[51]

Ian Gill, a former *Vancouver Sun* and CBC television reporter, perhaps put it best in his 2016 book *No News is Bad News*. "Postmedia [is] essentially now just a debt service agency for an offshore hedge fund," he wrote.[52] The constant cost-cutting required to pay its loans, Gill quipped, had helped reduce the country's newspapers to "a highly concentrated, nutrient-free, quivering intellectual Jell-O."[53] But the worst part according to Gill, who quit journalism in 1994 to become an environmental activist, was Postmedia's close association with energy interests, most notably the Canadian Association of Petroleum Producers.

> Our major newspapers, in particular, are in thrall to big business—energy industries most of all, but also developers, finance industries, and other natural-resource players. . . . I feel like we are being robbed blind, mugged by the oligarchs, and fed a diet of content you wouldn't serve in a hospital during a power outage.[54]

The *Toronto Star* put it more bluntly. "There is a cancer on Canadian journalism," it thundered on its front page in early 2016. Business columnist David Olive performed a biopsy in his fifteen-hundred-word takedown. "Postmedia's 200-plus media outlets, mostly newspapers, including some of the biggest dailies in the country, represent a far greater concentration of news media ownership than exists in any other major economy," he wrote. "And a degree of foreign ownership of the free press that would not be tolerated in the US, France, Japan or Germany."* Postmedia was an "abomination," according to Olive, who echoed what many journalists and increasingly ordinary Canadians felt. "It is a blight on all the communities it underserves." It was controlled by "quick-buck hedge funds in the US," at whose behest it had engaged in "savage non-stop cost-cutting," almost unbelievably laying off more than half its workers in five years.[55] It wasn't the first time Olive savaged Postmedia. He took a deep dive into the company's finances a year earlier. "Canada's free press and the citizens it serves are paying a heavy price to satisfy the short-term profit-seeking of US financiers," he concluded. "The real story is that a Postmedia, leveraged to the hilt, can still generate just enough cash to further enrich Postmedia's mostly US absentee owners."

> The three leading Postmedia investors — GoldenTree [Asset Management], Silver Point Capital LP of Greenwich, Conn. and New York-based FirstMark Capital — have already extracted close to $340 million in interest payments from Postmedia's leading Canadian newspapers. . . . In the looking-glass world of financial engineering, you can profit handsomely from an asset of steadily declining value. That is, from picking the carcass clean.[56]

Believe it or not, Postmedia was probably not even the worst media monopolist in Canada. That dubious distinction had instead long been reserved for the Irving family of New Brunswick, which owned all three of that province's dailies, eighteen of its twenty-five community newspapers, and four radio stations. Its monopoly had been the target of media inquiries dating to the 1970 Senate report

---

* This is incorrect, at least in the US, where foreign ownership of the press is not regulated. This has resulted in some of the largest owners of US newspaper chains being foreigners, including Rupert Murdoch and Canadian companies such as Thomson and Hollinger.

on Mass Media, which described New Brunswick as a "journalistic disaster area."[57] The Irvings were charged with monopoly in 1972 by the Competition Bureau's predecessor, the Restrictive Trade Practices Commission, and were even convicted at trial and ordered to divest one of their dailies, each of which was also fined $150,000. The conviction was overturned on appeal, however, in a case that went all the way to the Supreme Court of Canada.[58] The 1981 report of the Royal Commission on Newspapers recommended breaking up the Irving media monopoly. The 2006 Senate report on news media described it as "an industrial-media complex that dominates the province."[59] The Irvings stifled media competition, according to an exhaustive 2016 investigation by National Observer reporter Bruce Livesey, by using legal intimidation tactics and undercutting upstarts with discounted advertising and subscription rates.[60] Suffice it to say you won't see any critical coverage in their newspapers of the sprawling Irving Oil empire that dominates New Brunswick's economy.[61]

Then there were the media moguls on the country's opposite coast who were playing a real-life game of Monopoly by buying, trading and closing newspapers to eliminate competition, all under the somnambulant nose of the Competition Bureau. Black Press of Victoria, which was owned by David Black, had done numerous deals with Vancouver-based Glacier Media since 2010. Between them, Black and Glacier had closed seventeen of the newspapers they had exchanged, including the *Kamloops Daily News*, the *Alberni Valley Times*, and the *Nanaimo Daily News*.[62] The dailies had been part of a fifteen-newspaper trade between the chains in late 2014, of which more than half were subsequently closed.[63] As a result of their dealings, Black Press owned all of the newspapers on Vancouver Island—which had about the same population as New Brunswick—except for the Glacier-owned *Victoria Times Colonist*.

Peter Steven, who teaches at Sheridan College, has written books on both Canadian and global media. "Canada suffers from one of the least competitive news systems in the Western world," he noted in 2011. "Our media lack a critical backbone. They seem incapable of playing a real watchdog role, independent of the state and the large corporations."[64] I felt I had to do something about the problems afflicting Canada's news media instead of just writing about them. I had been doing that for years without much effect. I had been either a journalist or an academic my entire adult life, however, and both roles supposedly carried a duty of objectivity. But staying neutral, I had learned, was asking too much even of a journalist when something needed to be done and not just written about. What else could I do? I decided it might help to bring my research to the attention of someone who might be able to do something about the problems. It didn't take long to realize who that might be. Hedy Fry was not my MP—I lived in the suburbs on my sailboat—but she was the MP for Vancouver Centre, where University Canada West was located. I made an appointment to see her, and after several postponements I finally got an audience. A medical doctor from Trinidad and Tobago, Fry was the longest-serving MP in the new Liberal government of Justin Trudeau. If anyone could help mend Canada's news media, I figured she could. I gave her a copy of the letter I got from the Competition Bureau. I gave her a copy of *Greatly Exaggerated* and pointed her to its data that showed newspapers were still making healthy profit margins. "I thought they were losing money," she said, echoing the common misconception. I gave her a copy of *Pacific Press* and told her how the *Vancouver Sun* and *Province* had promised to maintain competing newsrooms in return for their illegal monopoly. She seemed as outraged as I was.

A few weeks later, the announcement came that Fry would chair Heritage Ministry hearings into media and local communities. "I know that our government has a strong will to deal with this now," she said. "The thing about politics is that the time comes one day when stuff is facing you so hard that you have to do something about it. That time has come."[65] The committee was tasked to study "how Canadians, and especially local communities, are informed about local and regional experiences through news, broadcasting, digital and print media." It also planned to examine media concentration and its impact on local news reporting, and how digital media had altered local news provision. The committee began holding hearings in Ottawa in February 2016 and planned to hold meetings in communities across Canada in the fall. Since the issues involved will hopefully receive a national airing then, this book is offered as a contribution to the debate. Maybe my research hasn't gone for naught these past fifteen years after all.

ONE

The Press We Deserve

No one who followed the debate over press concentration in the 1970s and '80s should be surprised at the current state of control in the Canadian newspaper industry, ownership of which has been among the most highly concentrated of any major country in the free world since the 1980s. Successive federal government inquiries warned that the inevitable result, absent any measures to slow or reverse the inexorable economics of a business classically subject to the cost-saving advantages of large size, would be ownership of the country's press by a very few powerful corporations. But while the recommendations of inquiries issued in 1970 and 1981 were hotly debated, they were never implemented. Soon the reports languished forgotten by a generation that seemingly grew weary of the debate over press concentration. After that, it was perhaps predictable that the acquisitors who paid increasingly higher prices for publication empires would justify their cost by exerting political influence as a value-added perk. But the new realities of ownership now being visited upon the nation's press crept up quietly, until the overt exercise of accumulated power again raised the question of whether something should, or even could be done about it.

Aside from economic forces, concentration of media ownership in Canada grew as a result of several factors, two of which have been well-recognized, and one which has been under-appreciated. The two familiar complaints have been a lack of political will to enact legislative measures to preserve the independence of the press, and the historic ineffectiveness of anti-trust laws already on the books. A third factor, in hindsight, was increased ownership of newspaper chains by stock market investors, which allowed their eventual acquisition by venture capital firms (also known as hedge funds). By the twenty-first century, following the deregulatory wave of the 1980s brought by the Reagan presidency and the globalization wave of the 1990s brought by technology, neoliberalism was on the ascendancy. Wall Street wizards came to excel at extracting value from almost anything in a phenomenon that came to be called "financialization." Their high-finance gyrations would crash the world economy in 2008, but that hardly deterred the vulture capitalists, who picked up the pieces at bargain prices to begin the cycle again. Included were some of the largest newspaper companies in North America, including the two largest in Canada. This chapter places into historical context the factors that contributed to the situation in Canada, with some comparison to the US. It also identifies a variable that entered the equation at the millennium with perhaps even more disturbing implications.

Political hesitance

In 1965, Winnipeg-based FP Publications merged with the *Toronto Globe and Mail* to overtake the family-owned Southam chain as, briefly, the largest newspaper group in Canada. Observers began to worry that ownership of the nation's press had been accumulated in too few hands. From a Prairie partnership formed in 1958 by *Calgary Albertan* publisher Max Bell and *Winnipeg Free Press* owner Victor Sifton, FP Publications had grown into a national chain with its acquisition of the *Ottawa Journal* in 1959 and the *Vancouver Sun* in 1963.

One of those most concerned about increasing control of the press by large chains that grew by acquiring hitherto independent dailies was Keith Davey. After serving five years as national cam-

paign director for the federal Liberal party, Davey was appointed to
the Senate at his own request in 1966 as a reward for service, especially his fundraising, which earned him the nickname "The Rainmaker." The former advertising executive held a keen interest in the
newspaper business—his father had worked in production at the
Toronto Star for more than fifty years. Davey confessed in his memoirs a fascination with newspapers despite his choice of a career in
radio advertising sales. "Much as I wanted to be in the newspaper
business myself, to my way of thinking I could not work at the Star
because of my father, nor could I work on staff at any other daily
newspaper because of him."[1]

Davey first proposed an investigation into the growing corporate control of Canada's press in 1968, initially considering Parliament the appropriate body to conduct such an inquiry. In the
preface to the report his Special Senate Committee on Mass Media
would issue in 1970, however, Davey noted that he instead decided
appointed senators would be better insulated from pressure
brought by publishers against any measures proposed to counter
press concentration. Davey said his concerns had been borne out
in the interim by easy passage through the elected US Senate of
the Newspaper Preservation Act, which exempted from federal
anti-trust laws dozens of newspapers that had for years been ille-
gally doing business together. President Richard Nixon's flip-flop
on the issue, according to Davey, justified his concern that "politicians looking to re-election must depend substantially upon the
mass media in the very real world of practical politics."[2] Nixon
campaigned in 1968 on a platform opposing an anti-trust exemption for publishers, but he soon reversed field once elected. As a
result, noted Ben Bagdikian in *The Media Monopoly,* Nixon received
the highest modern percentage of endorsements for re-election in
1972 despite a simmering Watergate scandal and his use of prior
restraint against the press in the Pentagon Papers case.[3]

The Davey committee forced Canadian media corporations to
open their books for the first time and not only found their profits
"astonishing," but also declared the secrecy surrounding them hyp-
ocritical. "An industry that is supposed to abhor secrets is sitting

on one of the best-kept, least-discussed secrets, one of the hottest scoops, in the entire field of Canadian business — their own balance sheets."[4] By 1970, "genuine" newspaper competition existed in only five Canadian cities, the Senate report noted. "Of Canada's eleven largest cities, chains enjoy monopolies in seven."[5] The Southam, Thomson and FP Publications chains controlled 44.7 percent of the country's daily newspaper circulation, compared with 25 percent in 1958.

> This tendency could . . . lead to a situation whereby the news (which we must start thinking of as a public resource, like electricity) is controlled and manipulated by a small group of individuals and corporations whose view of What's Fit to Print may closely coincide with . . . What's Good For Business. . . . There is some evidence, in fact, which suggests we are in that boat already.[6]

To remedy the situation, the Senate committee proposed measures that would have slowed press concentration from both the supply and demand sides. Stating that its intention was not to determine whether the tendency toward press monopoly was a good thing or a bad thing — "of course it's a bad thing" — the committee reasoned that the real-world problem was to strike a balance. "How do you reconcile the media's tendency toward monopoly with society's need for diversity?"[7] Its report recommended a Press Ownership Review Board, similar to one in the UK, that would approve — or more likely reject — newspaper sales or mergers. Such a board's basic guideline, according to the report, would be that "all transactions that increase concentration of ownership in the mass media are undesirable and contrary to the public interest — unless shown to be otherwise."[8] Its report also proposed a system of government subsidies, as in several Scandinavian countries, to encourage a "Volkswagen press" of alternative publications.

The Davey report caused a commotion in Canadian political and media circles, but its recommendations for stemming the tide of press ownership concentration were never enacted. "We had to conclude that we have in this country not the press we need, but rather the press we deserve," recalled Davey in his memoirs. "The sad fact is that the media must self-regulate because most Canadians are not prepared to demand the press they need."[9]

The Davey committee marked the first best chance to stem the rising tide of media ownership concentration in Canada. The failure to enact its prescriptions meant that worse would inevitably come. Introduction of a Press Ownership Review Board as proposed by Davey would likely have prevented the events of August 27, 1980, a date that would go down in Canadian newspaper infamy as "Black Wednesday." The Thomson chain, which had earlier that year won a bidding war for FP Publications, closed the *Ottawa Journal* that day, while Southam closed the *Winnipeg Tribune*. The moves gave each chain another local monopoly and resulted in national outrage on a scale that suggested a consensus over the need for limits on the growth of chains.

Prime Minister Pierre Trudeau quickly called a Royal Commission on Newspapers. It was chaired by Tom Kent, who had recently been appointed Dean of Administrative Studies at Dalhousie University. Kent had been editor of the *Winnipeg Free Press* before entering the federal civil service, where he served as chief architect of the modern Canadian welfare state constructed by successive Liberal governments in the 1960s and '70s. He and commission members Borden Spears, a former *Toronto Star* editor, and Laurent Picard, a former CBC president, quickly convened cross-country public hearings into newspaper ownership. Their report pointed out less than a year later what was obvious to everyone. "Newspaper competition, of the kind that used to be, is virtually dead in Canada," it noted. "This ought not to have been allowed to happen."[10]

Even some newspaper owners agreed that something should be done. Southam president Gordon Fisher admitted in an appearance before the commission that his family's chain had grown too large and that an ownership review mechanism, such as suggested by the Davey Committee, would be an appropriate check on the size of newspaper companies. Ken Thomson, on the other hand, insisted that he would know when a reasonable limit had been reached without a government regulator to tell him. "I have the intent, integrity and judgment to know when to stop," said the heir to the Thomson conglomerate, which had also just bought the Hudson's Bay department store chain with its North Sea oil profits. If any oversight of his media holdings was deemed necessary, Thomson added, it should be performed by a non-governmental body.[11]

Noting that the Southam and Thomson chains between them controlled 59 percent of the nation's English-language daily newspaper circulation, the Royal Commission report warned that the situation would only get worse unless limits to ownership were enacted. It proposed to restrict the proportion of any region's press that one chain could control, and called for forced divestiture by the chains to achieve regional ownership diversity. Under Kent's plan, the Thomson chain would have been required to sell a portion of its extensive Ontario holdings, the Sifton family to divest one of its Saskatchewan dailies (the *Regina Leader-Post* or the *Saskatoon StarPhoenix*), and the Irving family to give up part of its press monopoly in New Brunswick.

But the reaction by publishers to the Royal Commission's recommendations was swift and furious. The call for limits on press ownership was portrayed as an attack on freedom of the press. The *Globe and Mail* lambasted the report as a "veritable idiot's delight of interference in the ownership and operation of the nation's press."[12] Kent said it proved the fundamental conundrum of press regulation enunciated by Davey—that its very undertaking was unlikely if left to politicians beholden for their re-election to public opinion molded to a great extent by news coverage. The strident nature of the publishers' campaign against limits on press ownership, Kent observed, "fully confirms the analysis of the state of the problems of the newspaper industry."[13]

A Canada Newspaper Act that was eventually proposed in the wake of the Royal Commission report would have imposed less strict controls, but even those limits never made it onto Parliament's agenda. The Trudeau government, then in its dying days, instead made a priority of repatriating the Constitution from Britain and enacting the Charter of Rights. Thus a second glorious opportunity for media ownership reform was lost.

Legal ineffectualness

The Royal Commission stopped short of recommending divestiture of any dailies by Southam, which owned more of the nation's press than Thomson did but published newspapers the commission considered of higher quality. This despite the fact that Southam now enjoyed a monopoly in Vancouver, where it acquired the afternoon *Vancouver Sun* from Thomson to complement the morning *Province* it had owned since 1923. Southam's $40-million purchase had been overshadowed by the closure of long-publishing dailies in Ottawa and Winnipeg, but it did not escape the attention of investigators for the Restrictive Trade Practices Commission, which policed monopoly business practices. Southam and Thomson were charged by the federal justice department in May 1981 with criminal conspiracy, monopoly and merger as a result of their dealings in Ottawa, Winnipeg, Vancouver, and Montreal, where a 25-percent interest in Southam's *Gazette* had also changed hands.

But federal anti-combines law had been ineffective at preventing newspaper monopolies due to a requirement of proving present detriment to the public, as opposed to the possibility of future detriment. The Restrictive Trade Practices Commission, which had seen its criminal conviction of the Irving family media monopoly overturned in 1976 by the Supreme Court of Canada, was no more effective in deterring the 1980 dealings. Southam and Thomson executives testified at trial in late 1983 that they did not collude and instead acted independently. A lawyer for Thomson argued that monopoly was a valid business goal that was not necessarily detrimental to the public. "In a free enterprise system," argued Lorne Morphy, "it is legitimate for someone to try to put oneself in a monopoly position."[14] Justice William Anderson agreed, dropping the monopoly charges and finding the chains not guilty on the merger and conspiracy charges.[15]

As a result of the difficulty in obtaining criminal convictions on monopoly charges, new civil sanctions were enacted in 1986 by the federal government in the form of the Competition Act. It didn't take long to be tested. Southam countered growing competition in suburban Vancouver by buying up most of the community press there in a series of acquisitions between 1989 and 1991. The new Competition Bureau ordered divestiture of several of the newspapers, but Southam balked, so hearings were held before a Competition Tribunal. It reduced to only one the number of papers to be divested. Southam appealed the order all the way to the Supreme Court of Canada, but the order was upheld.[16]

Financialization of the news

The term "financialization" came to describe the economic shift that began in the 1980s and would see the financial sector of the US economy double as manufacturing output halved. Gerald Epstein defined it in his 2005 book *Financialization and the World Economy* as "the ascendancy of 'shareholder value' as a mode of corporate governance."[17] According to economist Thomas Palley, financialization was a process whereby "markets, financial institutions, and financial elites gain greater influence over economic policy and economic outcomes."[18] Its principal impacts, he noted, were to "(1) elevate the significance of the financial sector relative to the real sector, (2) transfer income from the real sector to the financial sector, and (3) increase income inequality and contribute to wage stagnation."[19]

Along with neoliberalism and globalization, which sent many manufacturing jobs overseas, financialization transformed world economies starting in the 1980s. It especially transformed media industries, which became highly financialized. In her 2010 book *Journalism in Crisis: Corporate Media and Financialization*, Spanish scholar Núria Almiron characterized financialization as "the primacy of financial over industrial logics."[20] In a "truly alarming" development, she noted, "finance capital has become the real owner of the world's top news-media firms."[21] This has come at a cost not just for their journalism but for their very *raison d'être*.

"Media corporatization first and later their financialization have constituted a scenario that turns journalistic autonomy into an illusion," noted Almiron. "Financialized multimedia communication groups are today more of a market power—with multimedia influences and convergent interests with financial groups—than guardians of liberty, creators of consensus, egalitarian democra- . tizers, or subverters of the structures of authority."[22] The journalism of financialized news media companies tended to act not as a check and balance on corporate power, she added, but instead to operate on behalf of the financial elite, loath to report on its financial engineering.

> The economic house of cards built by the financial system based on the culture of greed, as so many times before in history, would have far less chance of progressing in modern societies if journalism hadn't failed in its role. This failure was encouraged by the progressive deregulation of media—that is, by approving rules designed to benefit the consolidation and growth of giant corporate owners rather than public service.[23]

Newspaper chains in North America grew so profitable with the post-World War II advertising bubble that financiers soon began to target them for takeover. In the US, concern over concentration of press ownership and stock market influence over the news grew with the 1983 publication of Bagdikian's book *The Media Monopoly.* He calculated that ownership of most of the US press had become concentrated in only fourteen chains.[24] That seemed a diverse ownership indeed compared to Canada, where 59 percent of English-language dailies were then owned by only two chains. By the 1990s, the chains graduated from buying up increasingly scarce independent newspapers to taking over other chains.

In Canada, concentration of press ownership grew so high by the millenium that cross-media ownership soon offered the most fruitful method of corporate expansion. Newspaper chains thus began to merge—or "converge" in the new parlance—with television networks. In 2000 alone, Southam was bought by

Canwest Global Communications, which owned the Global Tele-
vision network; CTV partnered with the *Globe and Mail*; and the
TVA network in Quebec was taken over by newspaper publisher
Quebecor.

This was enabled by a lack of safeguards against cross-media ownership, unlike in the US, where the Federal Communications Commission banned in 1975 the issuing of television station licences to
owners of newspapers. In Canada, a Royal Commission on Newspapers warning against cross-ownership had briefly led to a similar
prohibition. "Common ownership of different media in one community is clearly a restriction on competition," the commission
noted, "a lessening of the diversity of voices providing information
and expressing opinion."[25] The Liberal government hastily enacted
an Order in Council banning the practice, but it was allowed to
lapse in the mid-1980s by the incoming Progressive Conservative
government.[26]

In the US, increased corporate control of the press resulted in
closer co-operation between newspapers and advertisers, with
the demolition in some newsrooms of the time-honoured wall
separating the "church" of news from the "state" of advertising.[27]
In Canada, the trend instead became one toward increased political advocacy by the former Southam newspapers under their
ownership first by Conrad Black (from 1996 to 2000), then by
the Asper family's Canwest Global Communications (from 2000
to 2009).

Increased corporate funding of journalism schools in the US led
to a muting of criticism from schools that increasingly introduced
courses in corporate communication, marketing, public relations,
and advertising.[28] In Canada, where journalism was taught more
at the two-year college level (as in the UK), university schools of
journalism were much less numerous. Research critical of press
ownership concentration was thus mostly confined to scholars of
communication such as James Winter at the University of Windsor and Robert Hackett at Simon Fraser University. Their criticism
of the growing ownership concentration and commercialization
of news was dismissed by the chains and growing media conglom-

erates with the same ferocity as the Davey and Kent recommendations were.

An increase in the number of university journalism programs in the 1990s, especially in Western Canada, raised hopes for increased scrutiny of corporate media control. The result was the opposite, however, perhaps because of increased corporate funding. As Neil Tudiver noted in his 1999 book *Universities For Sale*, private funding proved problematic by making Canadian universities increasingly subject to financial pressures.[29] A long-planned graduate school of journalism at the University of British Columbia in Vancouver, for example, was founded in 1997 with an endowment from the Hong Kong-based Sing Tao newspaper chain. The corporate support became an embarrassment, however, when UBC agreed to name the school after Sing Tao.[30]

Donna Logan, the founding director of the Sing Tao School of Journalism, proved a vocal advocate of both corporate concentration and media convergence. Far from holding the owners of media corporations to account, Logan turned on its head Davey's dictum that "all transactions that increase concentration of ownership in the mass media are undesirable." With Canwest's purchase of Southam in 2000, Vancouver had the most tightly-controlled news media not just in Canada, but possibly the free world. Canwest owned the dominant BCTV, both the city's dailies, one of the two national dailies, and almost all of the non-daily "community" newspapers in the Vancouver area.

Vancouverites were outraged, but it was all good according to Logan. "What gets me upset is when people automatically say concentration of ownership is bad and divestiture is good," she told the *Vancouver Sun* in 2000 as Conrad Black put the Southam chain up for sale after renouncing his Canadian citizenship to take a seat in the UK's House of Lords. "With a concentration of ownership there is always the possibility for bad things to happen. But some of the major newspapers had improvements in their editorial quality when [Black's company] Hollinger took over. It will really depend on who buys them."[31] When convergence compounded the problem of concentration, Logan emerged as a vocal corporate defender. "If the dangers of media ownership concentration were as dire as some critics would have us believe, the people of Vancouver would be rioting in the streets," she wrote for a special issue of *Media* magazine dealing with the controversy. "The good news is that content really is king as newspapers and TV stations scramble to create live Web sites and cable television stations proliferate at an unprecedented rate."[32]

When Canwest and CTV went before the CRTC in 2001 for renewal of their broadcasting licences and to defend their plans to converge their print and television news operations, Logan went too far for some in her testimony at the week-long hearing.

> One of the things that has always disturbed me about journalism in Canada is that there were too many reporters chasing so few stories. Converged journalism offers an opportunity to break out of that mould by freeing up reporters to do stories that are not being done and are vital to democratic discourse.[33]

Veteran Ottawa journalist Claire Hoy was outraged. "Is she serious?" he asked in the *Hill Times*. "What converged journalism really does is provide an opportunity for the TV-print operation to cover the stories with a single reporter instead of two or more reporters," railed Hoy. "They're not interested in freeing up reporters to chase stories they're not doing now. They're only interested in freeing up their bottom lines by doing the same work with fewer reporters."[34]

Two months after the CRTC's 2001 licence renewal hearings that resulted in convergence being allowed, Canwest announced it was making a $500,000 endowment to UBC's journalism school. "We're going to become the premier news organization in the country," said Leonard Asper on a visit to the Point Grey campus. "We're going to invest in the nuts and bolts of that by starting with journalism. We believe in the principles of journalism and their enhancement."[35] That fall, UBC's journalism school hosted a conference on convergence described as an "invitation-only Summit meeting of journalists, and media and news executives from across the country." Notably lacking in Canadian scholars, the conference was billed as providing "opportunities to get beyond the polarized rhetoric that has dominated the debate about convergence."[36] Putting talk about convergence into action, the proceedings were later broadcast on the Global Television network.

Canwest control

Canwest stirred the long simmering pot of press freedom issues in mid-2002 by sacking *Ottawa Citizen* publisher Russell Mills after his newspaper ran an editorial calling for the resignation of then-prime minister Jean Chrétien, who was an Asper family friend. Logan appeared as part of a panel on Vancouver radio station CKNW's popular *Rafe Mair Show* to debate the issue of media control. "I think it might be going a bit too far to say freedom of the press is in jeopardy," Logan told Mair. "We should really avoid overblown rhetoric." When a caller lamented Canwest's ownership of almost all of the Vancouver-area news media, Logan downplayed the problem.

> I think the situation in Vancouver is one of the things that gets over-blown, because we actually are in a very competitive situation here. Yes, the Aspers control both of the newspapers, but we've got two new television stations that have just come into the market. We've got a third one coming on line. These are not owned by the Aspers, and so the television situation is becoming much more competitive.[37]

When Mair pointed to the company's near-total monopoly in local newspapers, Logan named two giveaway weeklies not owned by Canwest. "There is the *Georgia Straight*," she said. "And there are the *Westender* . . . so there are alternatives. . . . I mean, I don't think the situation is as dire as that."[38] Logan's corporate advocacy signaled a wrong turn for Canadian journalism and, more disturbingly, journalism education. If the corporate model of journalism could succeed in silencing independent voices both in the press and in critical scholarship, Canadians would be left not only with the press they deserved, to quote Davey, but with no inkling they might need more. Concentrated and converged ownership of the press, coupled with corporate funding for schools of journalism, raised serious questions about potential threats to both journalistic and academic integrity. And the warnings of Davey and Kent, even as they grew dimmer with the passage of time, gained resonance to the ear tuned toward their unheeded message.

TWO

Financialization and the Demise of Southam

The Southam name disappeared from newspapers of Canada's oldest and largest chain in 2003, officially ending what one former Southam News correspondent called "a long-lived experiment in quality daily newspapering."[1] The former family-owned newspaper group was renamed Canwest Publications after its latest owner, Canwest Global Communications, a Canadian multimedia company with worldwide holdings, which acquired the Southam chain in 2000. Southam Inc. had been founded in 1895 by printer William Southam, but it was taken over in the 1990s by Hollinger Inc., a Canadian newspaper group that at its peak in 2000 was the third largest in the world and counted among its assets the *London Daily Telegraph*, *Chicago Sun-Times*, and *Jerusalem Post*. Under Hollinger, the Southam dailies underwent a rigorous cost-cutting program. The belt-tightening accelerated in 1998, when Hollinger chairman Conrad Black founded the conservative *National Post* as a national daily distributed across Canada in competition with Thomson's *Globe and Mail*. The expensive new daily drained Southam resources, however, and Hollinger's stewardship of the venerable dailies ended abruptly with the surprise sale to Canwest.

New ownership of the former Southam chain soon saw increased cost-cutting to not only offset *National Post* losses, but also to service

Canwest's high debt load incurred in acquiring the newspapers at the top of an economic boom. It also brought political controversy, as many journalists protested the centralizing of editorial control at Canwest headquarters in Winnipeg, which reversed the long-standing Southam policy of allowing independence for local publishers. Canwest's owners, the Asper family, actively supported the federal Liberals, and patriarch Izzy Asper was once the provincial Liberal party's leader in Manitoba. Their political influence over the newspapers soon became apparent, prompting a Senate commitee to again commence hearings on the Canadian media in mid-2003.

This chapter presents the Southam experience as a case study of the effect of financial markets on newspaper ownership and consequently on management practices. It examines the factors that contributed to the demise of family ownership of the Southam newspaper chain and resulted in radical changes in its operations. In so doing, it chronicles a change from publishing quality newspapers under Southam family ownership to cost- and quality-cutting under the management of Hollinger, to centralization and political partisanship under Canwest.

The impact of financial markets

In the early 1980s, Ben Bagdikian identified financial markets as a major influence on media management that had been overlooked in gauging the impact of increased press ownership concentration. He called stock exchanges a "third market" whose forces newspapers must account for, in addition to their acknowledged markets for readers and advertising.

> The impact of trading newspaper corporate stock on the stock market has meant that news companies must constantly expand in size and rate of profits in order to maintain their position on stock exchanges. . . . Instead of the single master so celebrated in the rhetoric of the industry — the reader — there are in fact three masters.[2]

Bagdikian's 1983 book *The Media Monopoly* brought the debate over media ownership and control into a wider public sphere.[3] The expansion of newspaper chains in the United States during the 1960s and '70s had come largely at the expense of family-owned enterprises whose third-generation owners could only escape heavy inheritance taxes by selling the business. Increasingly these family newspapers became acquired by chains, which also avoided paying tax on their soaring income by re-investing it in acquisitions.

According to Doug Underwood in *When MBAs Rule the Newsroom*, increased corporate ownership of dailies resulted in two trends during the 1970s and '80s—professional management of newspapers, often by executives with little or no background in journalism, and an increasingly bottom-line, market-driven orientation. Underwood argued that both trends were largely the result of stock market influence. "Wall Street, as publishers have learned, can be insatiable in the demand for earnings growth and unmerciful in hammering a stock if earnings drop."[4] Lou Ureneck of Boston University described the effect of stock market trading in newspaper shares as an "uncoupling of newspaper ownership from accountability for community service."[5] The fiduciary responsibility of corporate directors, he pointed out, made them legally responsible for focusing on profit, which created a short-term, bottom-line orientation.

> There is accountability for profit, not for journalism, except as it affects the business plan. It isn't coincidental that two of the nation's leading newspapers, *The New York Times* and *The Washington Post*, have structured their stock so that family members retain control. These families have maintained an interest in their companies that goes beyond making money.[6]

By 2001, many of the ills of journalism were being laid at the feet of chain newspapers owned by publicly-traded corporations. "The chains' desperation to maintain unrealistic profit levels (most of these big companies now being publicly traded) is actually reducing the amount of real news being gathered and disseminated," concluded an investigation by the *American Journalism Review*, "most conspicuously at the local and state levels, where consumers need it most."[7] The authors of *Taking Stock*, a book published the same year, concluded after interviewing fifty editors at publicly-traded newspaper chains in the US that stock market influence had such a negative effect on newspaper quality that federal regulations should be enacted to reverse the trend to share ownership.[8]

The newspaper market in Canada

In his compendious 1988 book *The World Newspaper Industry,* Canadian scholar Peter Dunnett singled out his own country as the most noteworthy example of ownership concentration. "No developed country has so concentrated a newspaper industry," he noted.[9] The high level of press ownership concentration was a result of several factors, including tax provisions designed to limit foreign ownership, a lack of enforcement of competition laws, and widespread share ownership. Buying newspapers from second-generation owners was the main growth strategy of FP Publications. The company's stock became widely held following the deaths of its founders, however, and in early 1980 Thomson beat Conrad Black in a bidding war for it.

Southam stock had been publicly traded since the mid-1940s, when the family's second generation prepared to pass leadership of the chain founded by their father to younger family members. They sought a mechanism for more easily trading shares in company ownership while still preserving control over its operations within the extended Southam clan. Some family members favoured the sale and public trading of only non-voting shares, restricting ownership of voting shares to William Southam's descendants. This strategy preserved family control over some newspaper companies, including the New York Times Co. According to Southam historian Charles Bruce, however, traders on the Toronto Stock Exchange were only interested in voting stock.

> The investment dealers held out for listing of voting common [shares] without restriction. They pointed out that in any event the future of

the company lay in Southam hands; perhaps there was more danger in the possibility of private trading (for instance, in the case of family disagreement) than in open dealings on the market.[10]

When Southam went "public" with its share issue in 1945, about a third of the company's one hundred shareholders were non-family members and together they held about 20 percent of its stock.[11] The shares were offered first to family members at $10 and then to the public at $13. Within days of public trading, noted Bruce, the price hit $15. By 1966, after a 4–1 split, the original shares were worth $160. To allay the concerns of some Southam family members that the issuing of shares might allow outsiders to gain control of the company, directors issued a public statement in 1945. It codified the long-standing company policy of providing its local publishers with decision-making authority "to preserve complete political independence and to present news fairly and accurately."[12]

By the mid-1980s, following the company's "Black Wednesday" dealings with Thomson, widespread ownership of Southam shares had reduced family holdings to below 30 percent, making the company vulnerable to a hostile takeover. Unusual trading in Southam shares in mid-1985 prompted rumors of a takeover bid.[13] As its share price soared amid the speculation, a special meeting of Southam shareholders passed a bylaw requiring a 50 percent quorum to approve transactions involving more than 10 percent of the company's shares.[14] As trading in Southam shares became frantic amid renewed takeover speculation, a "shark repellent" deal was announced with the Torstar Corporation. In exchange for a 30-percent interest in the smaller Torstar, Southam gave up 20 percent of its shares in a "near merger" that made its takeover a practical impossibility.[15] The deal included a ten-year "standstill" agreement, during which Torstar could not increase its holdings in the larger company, but that was later reduced to five years after a legal challenge by minority shareholders.[16]

To bolster its defences against takeover, Southam management decided to rationalize its operations in an attempt to make it a less inviting target for cost-cutting acquisitors. Instead of focusing on quality journalism, improving Southam's financial performance thus became the priority, with a declared target of a 15-percent profit margin.[17] Southam management, then into its fourth generation, also looked in vain to the higher branches of the family tree for future leadership among the hundreds of great-great-grandchildren of William Southam. Unable to find a suitable candidate following the 1991 suicide of heir apparent Harvey Southam, the company named William Ardell, head of its Coles Books subsidiary, CEO in 1992. Profits fell by 95 percent with a recession that year, however, and Southam's share price plunged, again making it a ripe takeover target.

Taking over Southam

After failing to outbid Thomson for FP Publications in 1980, Conrad Black was again an interested buyer when Southam became vulnerable to takeover in 1985, purchasing 5 percent of its stock. Following the share swap with Torstar, however, Black sold his holdings for a profit he used to start an international newspaper empire instead. His company Hollinger International first bought the money-losing *Daily Telegraph* in London for a bargain price and then joined a non-union movement out of Fleet Street. By 1993 he had cut almost three-quarters of the paper's workforce.[18] Soon the *Telegraph*'s annual earnings exceeded its purchase price as it became the profit engine that drove Hollinger's expansion.

In the mid-1980s, Hollinger began buying small newspapers in the US through a regular classified ad in the trade magazine *Editor & Publisher*. By 1997 its subsidiary American Publishing Co. had grown, through one hundred separate deals, into the second-largest newspaper chain in the US as measured by number of titles, although it never did place in the top ten by circulation. By then, however, Hollinger International ranked as the third-largest newspaper company in the world.[19] Its 340 US newspapers were mostly smaller dailies and weeklies, but they also included the *Chicago Sun-Times*, which had a circulation of five hundred thousand. In 1989, Hollinger bought the ailing *Jerusalem Post* and not only imposed a cost-cutting regime in its newsroom, installing a clock on which journalists were required to punch in and out, but also a radical change to its once-liberal politics.[20] Hollinger gained a reputation for both cost-cutting and imposing a conservative editorial stance on its newspapers.

But despite its growing international empire, Hollinger had been shut out of the newspaper market in its Canadian home base, except for minor purchases by its Sterling chain. According to biographer Richard Siklos, Black set his sights on Southam after the "standstill" agreement expired in 1990, making repeated offers to Torstar for its stake in the chain, which it had increased to 22.5 percent.[21] Frustrated by rising Southam losses of $153 million in 1991 and $263 million in 1992, Torstar also faced capital expenditures of $400 million for new presses. Finally in November 1992 it sold its holdings in Southam to Black for $18.10 a share, or a 15-percent premium over market value. Horrified Southam family members quickly sought a counterbalance to the takeover artist they dreaded.

One of the few Canadian businessmen with the resources to match Black was Montreal businessman Paul Desmarais, whose Power Corporation held an estimated $27 billion in assets, including the Gesca chain of forty-one newspapers in Quebec. Southam directors approached Desmarais to sound him out on maintaining their company's traditional values of quality newspapering, according to Siklos, and they found him amenable. Falling Southam share prices had created a problem for the company with its bankers due to its increased debt-to-equity ratio, and raising cash by issuing shares from its treasury to Desmarais would solve that problem, dilute Black's ownership, and create a shareholder with equal or greater power.[22]

When Black learned of Southam's plan to sell Desmarais $200 million in stock at $13.50 a share, he protested to its board that the price was too low and he lobbied directors to vote the deal down. According to Siklos, this backroom dealing sowed the seed of Southam's demise and allowed Black to eventually take the company over. Black and Desmarais owned neighbouring vacation homes in Palm Beach, Florida, noted Siklos, and the two men "shared a fascination with Southam and had discussed their respective ambitions to own it over the years."[23] It was in Palm Beach that Black and Desmarais agreed to their equal ownership of Southam, including voting and board parity and the first right of refusal should the other decide to sell his shares. Although between them they would still own less than a majority of Southam shares, their combined stakes gave them effective control of the company. After the deal to issue Desmarais thirteen million shares for $14 each was announced in March 1993, Black told reporters that with more than 40 percent of the stock between them, "if you can't control a company you should join a monastery or something."[24]

The effect on management

Even before Black bought into Southam, company management had instituted a cost-cutting program aimed at tightening up operations and boosting its share price as a defensive measure against takeover. In late 1991 Southam sold off its printing and graphics division and in July of 1992 it sold its shares in Torstar. In October of that year the company moved out of its long-time suburban Toronto headquarters into less expensive premises. A three-year job cutting program was instituted in 1991 with the aim of trimming $75 million from the payroll by 1994, and it saw 679 employees leave the company in 1992.* With Black and Desmarais on the Southam board in time for the company's annual meeting, the *Globe and Mail* remarked that shareholders might be excused for "wondering whether they've walked into the wrong room" given the changes.

> A whole new cast of characters has taken control of the company . . . and they have stacked the board of directors with their own kind. The gentlemen's club . . . has been overthrown by financiers determined to extract the highest possible return even if it means hacking off a limb or two.[25]

---

* Including the author in early 1993 after fifteen years with the *Calgary Herald* and *Vancouver Province*.

But despite their combined holdings, according to Siklos, Black and Desmarais grew increasingly frustrated over the next few years at the slow pace of change at Southam. The sale of Coles Books in 1995 brought some improvement to the bottom line, but in early 1996 another 750 jobs were cut. The payroll by then stood at 6,400 following the departure of more than a thousand workers since 1993, plus more who departed with discontinued or divested divisions. A move to cut the second largest newspaper cost (after labour) saw the narrowing of page sizes by two-and-a-half inches at Southam papers with the aim of saving $10 million annually on newsprint. But when Southam announced a loss of $53.4 million for 1995, largely as a result of the $120 million cost of severing 750 more employees, Hollinger president David Radler labeled the results "totally inadequate" and noted that his company could have done better by investing in bonds.[26]

According to Siklos, Southam executives refused to provide Hollinger and Power Corporation board members with detailed financial reports because they were considered industry competitors.[27] Animosities on the Southam board built, and they soon brought long-time neighbours Black and Desmarais into conflict. Black offered to buy out Desmarais, who countered with a proposal to break up the Southam chain, with Black taking ten of its smaller dailies in exchange for his minority ownership. When independent directors on the Southam board blocked that move, citing a forecast that the sell-off would drop Southam's share price from $16 to $11, Desmarais agreed in frustration to sell his shares to Black for $18 apiece and a total of $294 million in May 1996, giving Black 41 percent of Southam.

Black's effective control of Southam came on the eve of Hollinger's 1996 annual meeting, at which he made comments that alarmed many Canadians who again became concerned about the increased level of concentration of ownership of the country's press. In his speech to shareholders, Black noted both the demise of family control and his opposition to the company's traditional operating philosophy. "Southam management long accepted inadequate returns for the shareholders, published generally undistinguished products for the readers and received exaggerated laudations from the working press for the resulting lack of financial and editorial rigour." He disparaged Southam for panicking in 1985 at the takeover rumors that prompted the share swap with Torstar, which ultimately proved its undoing. "If Southam management had been a little more courageous," he crowed, "it might still be a family-controlled company."[28]

Taking Southam private

Black quickly bid to gain majority ownership of Southam, first offering $18.75 a share for more stock, then increasing the offer to $20 when that proved insufficient. The acquisition of 8.5 million shares as a result gave Hollinger 50.7 percent of the company in November 1996.[29] Black then ingeniously moved to buy up all remaining stock, first using his majority control in April 1997 to distribute the firm's accumulated cash reserves in a $2.50 per share special dividend.[30] This enriched his Hollinger most of all, by $47 million, and helped it make a $923-million bid one week later to buy out Southam's remaining shareholders. It was not accepted by enough shareholders to enable Black to take Southam private again by having it de-listed from stock exchanges, however, as only 15.6 percent of Southam's minority shareholders accepted it, giving Hollinger 58.6 percent ownership.[31]

The following year, Black bought a block of more than 8 million Southam shares from the Franklin mutual fund for $31.68 each, a premium of 22 percent above market value, raising his ownership of Southam to 69.2 percent.[32] That set the stage for his second bid for the remainder of Southam shares in December 1998, which was again made with the benefit of creative financing. First, Hollinger used its majority control of Southam to declare a special dividend of $7 a share, which was financed by borrowing $532 million. Then it offered $22 a share for the remaining Southam stock in a bid that was largely financed by the special dividend.[33] That offer was rejected by independent members of the Southam board, but when Hollinger increased it to $25.25 early in 1999, they voted to recommend it.[34] When the offer expired two weeks later, more than 90 percent of the twenty-two million remaining Southam shares had been tendered, raising Hollinger's ownership of the company to 97 percent.[35] Under Ontario securities law, that allowed Black to force out the remaining shareholders and delist the company that Southam family members had taken public fifty-four years earlier.

The emergence of Canwest

Black soon turned his attention to starting up a second national newspaper in Canada, in competition with the *Globe and Mail*, which he considered dangerously liberal. The launch of his *National Post* in October 1998 exceeded expectations for circulation, quickly soaring to sales of 272,000 daily, although critics pointed to the large number of heavily-discounted sales that inflated its figures. More significantly, advertising lagged below projections, resulting in editions often including only 20 percent advertising content.[36] An all-out "newspaper war" resulted in Toronto, where Black hoped to establish a beachhead in a market dominated by the *Star*, Canada's largest daily with a circulation of 458,000 on weekdays and more than 700,000 on Saturdays. The *Globe and Mail* circulated 330,000 copies nationally from its Toronto base, where it also published a Metro edition with local news. The downscale end of the market was dominated by the tabloid *Sun*, which sold 240,000 copies daily and more than 400,000 on Sundays.

The *Post's* operating losses of $44 million in its first year proved a drain on Hollinger, and its share price fell almost 20 percent during the period. In a bid to ease the company's $2.4 billion in debt, Black announced he would sell up to half of his accumulated Canadian publishing empire, offering the smaller publications for sale. In response, Hollinger share prices immediately jumped 26 percent.[37] Black's actions were prompted by a dispute with Prime Minister Jean Chrétien, who in mid-1999 blocked the *Daily Telegraph* owner's appointment to the House of Lords. He cited an obscure rule prohibiting Canadians from accepting foreign titles without federal permission.[38] Black, a dual Canadian and British citizen but resident of London, could only accept his seat in the House of Lords by renouncing his Canadian citizenship. That would make him a foreign owner of press holdings in his native land, and under Canadian tax law advertisers would no longer be allowed to claim as an income-tax deduction the expense of buying space on Hollinger's pages.[39] Black countered with a lawsuit against Chrétien for "abuse of process," claiming $25,000 in damages for "public embarrassment," but it was dismissed in March 2000.[40]

Black's preference for being a British lord over a Canadian press baron resulted at the end of July 2000 in the sale, not of Hollinger's smaller Canadian newspapers, but of all its thirteen largest and 130 smaller titles to Canwest Global Communications for $3.5 billion.[41] Announcement of the deal sent Hollinger stock, which had languished near $10 in April, soaring to $16.25. The deal put the bulk of the former Southam newspaper chain in the hands of Israel "Izzy" Asper, who had founded Canada's third television network in 1977 and expanded into Australia, New Zealand, Chile, and Ireland. In a column published in the *National Post* and other Southam dailies, Black attributed his selloff to the "contramathematical disparity" between the worth of Hollinger shares "and the value attributed to them on the stock markets."[42] Siklos agreed, noting that due to its high debt load Hollinger stock had risen an average of only 6.9 percent annually since its 1994 IPO on Wall Street. "The real story behind Mr. Black's 'retreat' from Canada is that he missed out on the biggest bull market in history," wrote Siklos in *Shades of Black*. "Despite all the improvements Hollinger has made, and several Wall Street analysts decrying its low valuation, Hollinger stock has been what they call 'dead money.'"[43] Black then renounced his Canadian citizenship and assumed his peerage as Lord Black of Crossharbour.

Convergence and partisanship

Canwest soon faced debt problems of its own, first in raising sufficient funds to even complete its purchase of the former Southam empire. In November 2000, amidst a declining economy, it canceled a planned $800-million bond issue. It was unwilling to pay the estimated 12 percent interest rate required to attract the needed capital after failing to entice investors at rates of 10 to 10.5 percent. Of more immediate concern to its bottom line, however, were the growing losses of the *National Post*, of which Canwest had initially acquired only half, with Black retaining half and assuming the publisher's chair. *Post* losses in the first nine months of 2000 came in at $36 million, however, bringing the two-year total to $133 million.[44] With its share price at $16, Canwest announced to stock analysts at the end of November a plan to reduce costs by $60 million through company-wide synergies and cutbacks.[45] By mid-2001, as the economy declined, Canwest shares dropped to $12.50 and third-quarter earnings came in 73 percent lower than the previous year, due largely to a 13.7-percent drop in earnings at its new Southam Publications division.[46]

In August, as *National Post* losses reached an estimated $190 million, Canwest bought Black's remaining half-interest in the newspaper.[47] With its stock trading at $11.35 in mid-September, the company announced it would suspend payment of its annual dividend to shareholders to save $53 million. It also announced the layoff of 120 employees from the *National Post*, or 20 percent of its workforce, news of which boosted Canwest's share price by 85 cents.[48] Lower advertising revenue in a slumping economy and rising debt servicing costs more than doubled Canwest's fourth-quarter loss for fiscal 2001 to $37 million.[49] In a bid to trim more costs, it announced in November cancellation of the long-running Southam Fellowships, which since 1962 had provided mid-career education for journalists from all media across Canada.[50]

Canwest's financial problems seemed tame, however, compared to the firestorm of criticism from journalists that erupted as a result of new editorial policies it imposed on the former Southam dailies. Canwest ordered chain-wide publication of editorials written at its head office in Winnipeg in December 2001, prompting reporters at its *Montreal Gazette* to withdraw their bylines for two days in protest.[51] In early 2002, long-time *Halifax Daily News* columnist Stephen

Kimber quit because he said his columns had been changed "to match the owner's point of view." The editor of the *Daily News* then resigned after claiming Canwest headquarters in Winnipeg had interfered in the newspaper's content.[52] The *Columbia Journalism Review* reported that one mandatory Canwest column, which argued that Canada should back Israel no matter how it responded to Palestinian suicide bombings "without the usual handwringing criticism about 'excessive force,'" even came with a no-rebuttal order. "Papers in the Southam chain were told to carry neither columns nor letters to the editor taking issue with that editorial, according to journalists at two Southam papers, who said the order came via a conference call."[53]

In March, reporters at the *Regina Leader-Post* went on byline strike after they claimed a story quoting a speech at the University of Regina journalism school about Canwest's national editorial policy was rewritten to remove a reference to censorship.[54] In April, Canwest's second-quarter results showed a loss of $21.7 million due to flagging ad revenue, which sent its share price down to $11.20.[55] In June, forty former Southam executives took out a full-page advertisement in newspapers not owned by Canwest, criticizing the company's national editorial policy and calling on the federal government to enact measures to ensure local editorial independence.[56] The controversy heightened later that month when Russell Mills, the long-time publisher of the *Ottawa Citizen*, was fired after his newspaper called for Chrétien's resignation amidst a growing patronage scandal. After politicians across Canada renewed their calls for an inquiry into the press and more than five hundred *Citizen* subscribers cancelled home delivery, Canwest shares slipped to a six-year low of $8.50.[57] The Vienna-based International Press Institute called the firing "an attack on press freedom by an unholy coalition between politics and big business."[58] Televised debates in Parliament were dominated for days by Opposition accusations that the prime minister had ordered the firing over dinner the previous evening with Izzy Asper.[59] On July 2, workers at Canwest's *Vancouver Sun* and *Province* went on strike, dropping its shares to $6.98.[60]

Canwest began dumping assets in a desperate attempt to pare down its debt and boost its share price, selling its dailies in Atlantic Canada for $255 million.[61] In September, it quietly abandoned its policy of imposing national editorials on its newspapers.[62] The moves could not stem the slide of Canwest shares on the Toronto Stock Exchange, however, where they closed on October 4 at a low of $3.32.[63] By month's end, however, Canwest stock had rebounded to $6 a share when it reported a fourth-quarter loss of $104 million.[64] In January 2003, the *Globe and Mail* reported what it described as "this country's most aggressive attempt to centralize editorial operations across a newspaper chain" when it revealed an internal Canwest memo detailing plans for a centralized news desk in Winnipeg to co-ordinate coverage at the former Southam dailies across Canada.[65] Senator Joan Fraser, who had been editor of the *Montreal Gazette* when Conrad Black first bought into Southam almost a decade earlier, announced the following month that the Committee on Transport and Communications she chaired would hold public hearings on news media starting later in 2003.[66]

The most notable feature of the Southam case was the marked change in its management practices following the firm's takeover by Hollinger in 1996 and its subsequent sale to Canwest in 2000. Deep cuts to staffing resulted from a new focus on the financial bottom line at the expense of quality journalism as had been traditionally emphasized under Southam family ownership. This change of direction was both caused by and exacerbated by stock market forces. The widespread distribution of Southam shares allowed its gradual takeover by Hollinger, which was well known for operating its newspapers on a very tight budget. But the debt burden incurred in acquiring the Southam empire in turn put pressure on Hollinger's stock. This made further cost-cutting necessary to reduce its losses in order to keep share prices from falling further, and it finally led to its sale to Canwest. The television network's acquisition of the former Southam dailies at the top of a stock market boom in 2000 proved bad timing, as the scenario of increased debt reducing share values repeated itself, with the result again being increased cost cutting.

The effects of stock market influence on the Southam newspapers can be traced back to the 1980s, however, when the threat of a hostile takeover first influenced management practices. Even under family control, emphasis had to be shifted from quality journalism to quarterly earnings in order to keep Southam's stock price from falling and prevent it from being bought up by takeover artists looking to acquire the historic firm below its true value. To those who prize quality journalism, the situation went from good to bad as a result, but it did not get truly ugly until the long-publishing newspapers became acquired by owners with overt political motives. The sale to the public of voting stock, as the Southams had agreed to in 1945, had the perhaps inevitable consequence of eventually locating company ownership and control increasingly outside their family, thus making its management practices ever more subject to market forces. The radical change in operating philosophy that resulted was of such significance that the Senate again began inquiring into the operations of the press.

THREE

Journalism Education Goes Corporate

Journalism education at the university level in Canada has had a comparatively brief history marked by antagonism from working journalists and disdain from faculty members in more established academic disciplines. The field is not as mature as it is in the US, where journalism education progressed through several stages of development over almost a century.[1] The same pattern of development was seen in Canada, according to one study, but when compared with the US "each stage seems to have come roughly a half-century later."[2] As a result of a shift in emphasis from the teaching of skills to more conceptual coursework in US journalism schools, some scholars have seen journalism itself moving from craft status to profession there, unlike in other countries where teaching of the subject is "still in the stage of transition from trade school to academic institution."[3] Journalism education in Canada lagged in its development, obviously fitting the latter pattern.

There were 480 four-year US journalism schools in 2013, some of which have been operating since the early years of the twentieth century.[4] Journalism schools at the university level in Canada were a post-WWII phenomenon, and until the mid-1970s there were only three programs in the subject, all in Ontario. An upsurge in four-year journalism programs was seen in the late 1990s in British Columbia, however, with the conversion there of several former two-year colleges into universities granting bachelor's degrees.[5] Even into the new millennium, while journalism education had finally spread from coast to coast in Canada, the number of university programs could still be counted on the fingers of two hands.[6]

At the latest count in 2013, universities and colleges in the US enrolled almost two hundred thousand undergraduates and more than fourteen thousand graduate students in journalism and mass communication, annually awarding more than fifty thousand Bachelor's and almost six thousand graduate degrees.[7] In Canada, journalism has traditionally eschewed the university tradition in favour of on-the-job training or, at most, the British craft-school approach to education at two-year colleges. As a result, Canadian schools of journalism at the university level are relatively few, although a 2013 study found twenty-five schools that offered a certificate, bachelor's, or master's degree in the subject.[8] The most recent comprehensive survey of degrees granted was in 2001, however, and it found that only 339 undergraduate degrees and another 66 Master's degrees had been awarded that year.[9]

The underdevelopment of journalism education in Canada has led to a relative paucity of media scholarship, resulting in a disparity in media criticism, with academics often outnumbered by industry advocates and marginalized to a significant degree. "The academic tradition in the United States . . . produces a relatively abundant flow of writing about news media," noted Peter Desbarats in 1989 while he was dean of the graduate school of journalism at the University of Western Ontario. "By contrast, public debate about journalism in Canada suffers from a constant shortage of historical perspective and reliable data."[10] This chapter examines the state of university journalism education in Canada, looks at how it has affected the development of media criticism and journalism, and ponders implications for the future of the subject in Canadian higher education.

Practitioner resistance

Until recently, most working journalists entered the business through an informal apprenticeship system, and many were opposed to the very concept of journalism education. Some of the most prominent pundits do not hesitate to make their contempt for journalism schools known, as former *National Post* editor Ken Whyte did after hiring 135 journalists for the start-up daily in 1998. "Given a choice of two people with more or less equal experience, we would choose the person who hasn't gone to journalism school," declared Whyte. "Journalism schools leave people with a narrow appreciation of the craft and a hard-and-fast idea of what it takes to be a journalist."[11] Former *Saturday Night* magazine editor John Fraser was even more damning in his criticism in 1994 when he blamed most of the ills of Canadian journalism on J-schools that "foster institutional rancour and disbelieving zealotry" in students.

> I can sniff journalism grads a hundred miles away, and increasingly at *Saturday Night* I tried to avoid them, unless they could prove to me that they had repented of nearly everything they had been taught. . . . What I would really like to do is take the budding journalists by their collars and pants, and force-march them into literature courses, philosophy courses, psychology courses, political-science courses, law courses, theology courses, even basket-weaving courses—anything that would keep them away from Journalism 100.[12]

The academic voice was sometimes heard in response, but only from the margins, while "journalism professor" was used as an epithet by industry advocates who played on rampant anti-intellectualism in countering scholarly calls for media reform. The academic view of journalism education as a valid, even vital, field of study was overshadowed by the more prominent opinions of some of the country's most popular columnists.

• Robert Fulford, *National Post*: "A highly dubious enterprise. . . . an embarrassment to many who teach it and some who study it."[13]

- Barbara Amiel, Southam Newspapers: "I suspect the good people are good 'in spite of' not 'because of' their journalism studies."[14]
- Allan Fotheringham, *Maclean's*: "You can't teach journalism, any more than you can teach sex. You're either good at it or you're not."[15]

Columbia of the north

The professional voice has dominated the skills-vs.-theory debate in Canada largely because the journalism school tradition here has had much less to sustain it than in the US. There the first university journalism programs, at Missouri and Columbia, were founded in the early 1900s. The first university journalism schools in Canada didn't open their doors until after WWII. The model that was followed at all three of the original post-war journalism schools—Ryerson, Western Ontario, and Carleton—came from the prototype program at Columbia, according to Desbarats.[16] Western Ontario's journalism school even followed Columbia's move from an undergraduate offering to a master's program in 1974, although requiring three semesters to complete instead of only two.

UWO was also the first to depart from the Columbia model, supplementing skills training with courses in ethics, history, law, and theory, according to Desbarats, a former Global television news anchor who was dean of the journalism school there from 1981 until 1997.[17] But the Western Ontario program almost fell victim to cost cutting in 1993 and was only saved by a last-minute appeal, after which the university's board of governors narrowly overturned a decision by the university senate to close the journalism school.[18] The UWO graduate program in journalism, however, suffered a significant loss of identity in 1994 when it was merged with a much larger program in library sciences into a new Faculty of Information and Media Studies. This led alumnus Larry Cornies to complain that "the soul of the journalistic enterprise had taken a beating. The art of storytelling had taken a back seat to info-crunching and a preoccupation with 'technoculture,' in which undergraduates may now obtain a degree."[19]

The journalism program at Carleton University in Ottawa was not only regarded by many as the leading J-school in Canada, but perhaps not coincidentally it was also the one that moved furthest from the Columbia ideal, according to Desbarats. Carleton's journalism school was also unique in Canada for including a considerable mass communication component. An undergraduate program in communication studies was added in 1977 to supplement the journalism stream, a master's program commenced in 1991, and since 1997 Carleton has also offered a PhD program in the subject.[20] According to Desbarats, the comprehensive scope made Carleton's journalism school "closer than any other Canadian school to the type of institution now prevalent in the United States."[21] But through this scholarly expansion, Carleton's journalism program thrived despite the increasingly academic approach, according to Desbarats, because it also stayed true to its professional roots. "At Carleton, under a succession of directors with journalistic as well as academic qualifications, journalism has remained the dominant element."[22]

The only one of the original three post-war Canadian journalism schools that stuck doggedly to the Columbia ideal was the one at Ryerson, which emulated its model program in many ways, not least for its position in the center of the country's media capital. From its origins in 1948 as the Ryerson Institute of Technology and an orientation toward printing instruction in graphic arts, within a decade the program had re-oriented itself almost exclusively toward journalism, according to long-time Carleton professor Wilfred Kesterton in his classic 1967 book *A History of Journalism in Canada*.[23] Since Ryerson became a degree-granting institution in 1972, the report of the Royal Commission on Newspapers observed in 1981, a prejudice against its graduates as "merely uncultured technicians" had been dispelled.[24] But even after Ryerson graduated in 2001 from polytechnic to full research university status, its journalism school retained a mostly vocational approach. A two-year master's in journalism program was launched in 2007, but its courses were also mostly

54 • CHAPTER THREE

practical. This points up Ryerson's position, when it comes to university journalism education, as Columbia of the North, immune from the 1981 plea of the Royal Commission on Newspapers.

> Instead of turning out narrowly trained journalists, sealed off in their shells producing journalistic pearls, with no concern for the outside world, could not the schools develop a critical look at the news media? To be sure, it would be necessary to combine this with teaching the practical aspects of the craft. There are some important questions that bear on the future which can be studied in depth only at university. [25]

The Royal Commission saw Canadians as particularly well-positioned to deal with the era of new media technology then emerging due to the "solid foundation of theoretical studies" built in the 1950s and '60s by Harold Innis and Marshall McLuhan of the University of Toronto. Their contributions to understanding media, according to the Royal Commission, "altered mankind's appreciation of the influence of media."[26] Medium Theory, as the "technological determinism" of Innis and McLuhan became better known in its second generation of development, was instead advanced mostly by American scholars, notably Neil Postman and Joshua Meyrowitz. Incorporating this area of study as a staple of the Canadian J-schools to examine how "the medium is the message" might be an ideal way to integrate theory with practice, combining as it does aspects of history, political economy, culture, epistemology, and sociology.

The school of corporate journalism

The growth of university journalism schools in English Canada did not extend beyond Ontario until the mid-1970s, when Concordia University in Montreal began offering a degree in the subject. By the end of that decade, two more four-year programs commenced in both the Maritimes, at the University of King's College in Halifax, and Western Canada, at the University of Regina. But despite a promise dating from 1980 of a graduate school of journalism at the University of British Columbia, higher education in the subject did not reach the West Coast until 1998. The reason for the delay demonstrates the major problem that has beset journalism schools in Canada—a lack of funding—and subsequent events illustrated the perils of seeking that funding from corporate sources.

For many years the only journalism courses offered in BC were in two-year diploma programs, in print journalism at Vancouver City College (now Langara College), and in broadcast journalism at the BC Institute of Technology in suburban Burnaby. The 1990 report of an industry task force that studied the situation joked that "if BC's system of post-secondary journalism education was a baseball team, it would be playing in the minor leagues, occasionally sending a player up to swing a bat in the majors."[27] Task force co-chair Ron Robbins, founding director of the University of Regina J-school and a former head of CBC's national television news, was more blunt in his assessment of BC's system of journalism education, or lack thereof, calling it "something more than a horror story."[28] Part of the reason for the lack of university journalism education in BC was perhaps the success of not only the two-year programs but also of university student newspapers in graduating apprentice journalists with practical experience. The long-publishing *Ubyssey* student newspaper at UBC in Vancouver was noted for producing some of Canada's best journalists, and the cross-town *Peak* at suburban Simon Fraser University, which opened its doors in 1965, also proved a productive training ground for many young journalists.*

But the lack of a university-level school of journalism in Canada's westernmost province became a source of some embarrassment by the 1980s, especially after such schools had spread, at least thinly, across the rest of country. The Royal Commission on Newspapers was premature by fifteen years when its report mentioned that journalism education in Canada would soon be enhanced with the opening of a school at UBC in 1983.[29] When a journalism school still hadn't materialized there by 1988, *Vancouver Sun* columnist Jamie Lamb observed that UBC's embracing in principle of

---

* Including the author.

journalism as a scholarly subject eight years earlier had come with one important caveat.

> The UBC senate agreed to a journalism department if somebody would finance it. UBC made this decision just as the economic recession arrived. . . . There were a lot of jokes about who would finance the school—The Mac-Blo School of Journalism and Stumpage Fees; The Keg "Hi, I'm Ken And I'll Be Your Journalist Tonight" Program; Labatt's Blue School of Journalism—but nobody seemed willing or able to kick in the required funds.[30]

Lamb's column was a spoof in the best tradition of columnist Allan Fotheringham, a UBC and *Vancouver Sun* alumnus. His analysis of the state of limbo in which the prematurely-conceived school of journalism at UBC existed—and of the dilemma facing university administrators—was closer to the truth than most realized at the time, however. Although the recession of the early 1980s had caused severe cutbacks in higher education and sent public universities in search of private money with which to make up the shortfall, in exchange often naming buildings and even courses after donors, UBC had not gone so far as to name a school or academic department after a corporate sponsor.

It took almost another decade to come up with the money needed to get a school of journalism off the ground at UBC. When the identity of the mysterious donor was finally announced, some were shocked that it was not even a Canadian, but instead *Hong Kong Standard* publisher Sally Aw. Outrage followed when it was revealed that in exchange for a $3-million initial donation and a promise of continued financial support, the university agreed to name the new school after her Sing Tao newspaper chain that published an edition daily in Vancouver. "Aren't there limits?" asked UBC political science professor Philip Resnick after a vote in the university's senate failed to prevent the unprecedented corporate christening of the Sing Tao School of Journalism. "Isn't there a point at which one has to say that certain things are for sale and certain things are not?"[31] Fotheringham was even more pointed in his criticism shortly after the school opened in 1998. "What does [Sing Tao] have to do with

British Columbia?" he asked in a campus speech that year to a reunion marking the eightieth anniversary of the *Ubyssey*, on which he apprenticed in the early 1950s. "It is goddam ridiculous."[32] Fotheringham followed up from his long-running back-page column in the next issue of Canada's weekly newsmagazine, *Maclean's*.

> Why does my alma mater have to go offshore for this loot? . . . If anyone wants a journalism school, or needs one, what's with the locals? Especially since the timber barons made much of their richness by selling newsprint to the sheets that supposedly educate the masses.[33]

The furore flared up again in early 1999 when several Sing Tao executives were jailed for fraud in Hong Kong after an investigation into inflated circulation figures there found advertisers had been overcharged.[34] Aw escaped prosecution despite being named as a co-conspirator, but financial problems forced her to sell a controlling interest in Sing Tao's Canadian newspapers to the Torstar Corporation. Sing Tao's legal and financial difficulties also prevented it from keeping up its promised funding commitment to UBC. University administrators managed to keep that quiet until word leaked out just before the first seventeen graduates of the Sing Tao School of Journalism were set to receive their master's degrees in 2000. To make up the resulting shortfall in the journalism school's budget, the UBC Board of Governors moved money from its special purposes funds before approving an annual allocation of $420,000 from its general operating revenues.[35] The university also stripped the name Sing Tao from the school's title, rendering it the generic Graduate School of Journalism. Many UBC journalism students learned of the name change from reading about it in the *Ubyssey* In response they formed a student union with the stated aim of gaining greater transparency from administrators.[36]

Increased corporate funding

One alternative source of funding for Canadian journalism schools has been corporate money from the Canadian Radio-television and Telecommunications Commission (CRTC) and its "public benefits" program, which was conceived in the late 1970s to ensure that payments required from corporate takeovers of broadcasting companies go toward worthwhile media projects. One 2001 study found that some of the corporate takeover money found its way into schools of journalism.

> These packages usually emphasize direct programming initiatives, but nevertheless a number of endowed professorships have resulted. Examples of this so-called "greenmail" are chairs at Ryerson, King's College, and Regina that were funded by Maclean Hunter in 1988; one at Western [Ontario] established by Rogers Communications in 1995; and chairs endowed in 2000 by the largest private television network, CTV, at Laval and Carleton.[37]

The "greenmail" endowments served several purposes for media companies—satisfying the demands of the CRTC that they give something back for the public's benefit, ensuring perpetual brand recognition in the named chairs and professorships they created, adding some scholarly lustre to the corporate name, and making media scholars who should be their closest critics beholden to them for millions of dollars. The latter point was made uncomfortably clear to Desbarats while he was dean of the journalism school at Western Ontario, which benefited from a $1 million donation from cable television giant Rogers Communication in 1995. "When journalists subsequently asked me to comment on the Rogers takeover of [magazine publisher] Maclean Hunter, all I could do was draw their attention to the donation," noted Desbarats after leaving UWO. "They understood right away that I had been, to express it crudely, bought."[38]

The takeover of the CTV television network in the spring of 2000 by telecommunications giant Bell Canada Enterprises (BCE) provided an even greater windfall for Canadian journalism schools, as the public benefits package that came along with the $2.3-billion deal amounted to $230 million. Of that, $2.5 million was earmarked for an endowed chair in convergence at Ryerson.[39] Another $3.5 million went to fund a Canadian Media Research Consortium (CMRC) set up between several universities, including Ryerson,

York, Laval, and UBC, with a mandate to "focus on the development of Canadian data for use in media planning."[40] By 2001, however, convergence would be a hot topic at CRTC licence renewal hearings. Concern over convergence grew after the Bell–CTV alliance announced a partnership with Thomson's *Globe and Mail* and Canwest Global Communications, owner of the Global Television network, bought the Southam newspapers from Conrad Black's Hollinger Inc. The resulting fallout led one journalism advocacy group to wash its hands of public benefits money and cut ties with the CMRC.

The moves came after *National Post* columnist Terence Corcoran described the CMRC as "a hitherto unknown group founded for the sole purpose of skimming a graft off the CTV takeover."[41] The funding, Corcoran pointed out in May 2001, effectively recycled the Public Benefits money paid by the acquiring corporation back toward its own private interests. "If the major corporations . . . want research into the media, then surely they can spend their own money up front rather than cash extorted . . . via a regulator."[42] A series of revelations by *Post* media reporter Matthew Fraser earlier that month about a letter-writing campaign to the CRTC by academics supporting the media mega-merger led the Canadian Journalism Foundation to sever its association with the CMRC over allegations of conflict of interest. Corcoran urged the CJF to "leave the academics to wallow in their own petty corruptions" and outlined the conflicts otherwise involved.

> That leaves the foundation, set up by major corporations to raise ethical standards in the media, in the position of having participated in the extortion of money from BCE in return for providing a fawning defense of its takeover of CTV. Lining up for part of the payoff are some of Canada's leading journalism academics. All of this should make good fodder for the next foundation educational session to help raise the standards of journalistic ethics and reporting.[43]

Just before the CJF scandal broke, however, the question of convergence had been the subject of CRTC hearings following the takeover of the former Southam dailies by Canwest and the *Globe and Mail*'s merger with BCE. Canwest in particular gained a multimedia advantage in many Canadian cities, including Vancouver, where it suddenly owned both daily newspapers, most of the community press, and the two largest television stations.[44] The CRTC was able to pay close scrutiny to the arrangement, however, as the seven-year broadcast licenses of Canwest and CTV were due for renewal less than a year after the moves. Consumer advocates urged the CRTC to require an editorial "firewall" between CTV and Canwest's Global Television news operations and those of their newly-acquired newspapers in order to protect what diversity remained in Canadian news media. Some academics, however, argued against any such safeguard being placed on the broadcasters' news operations, instead testifying that news media convergence would be in the public's best interest. The BCE and Global broadcasting licenses were then extended without restriction.

Fred Fletcher, a professor at York University, which was a founding member of the CMRC in a graduate collaboration with Ryerson's school of journalism, told the CRTC hearings that rather than decreasing the diversity of voices, media convergence provided the "potential for greater journalistic competition in the Canadian media system as a whole through collaboration in investigative reporting and foreign coverage."[45] UBC's Donna Logan went even further in singing the praises of convergence to the CRTC, as noted above, claiming that convergence offered an opportunity "to do stories that are not being done."[46]

Appearing before the CRTC as part of Global's delegation in 2001 was Peter Desbarats, who was dean emeritus of journalism at Western Ontario and had been named Maclean Hunter Chair of Communications Ethics at Ryerson the year before. "There is no way, short of placing secret agents in newsrooms, that any system can effectively monitor all forms of communication between journalists working for the same organization," he later wrote in the *Globe and Mail*. Desbarats called Quebecor's proposed "code of conduct," in which it promised that its newspaper and TV journalists would not communicate with each other, a "Big Brother" mechanism. He claimed it would create "a degree of cross-media state intervention that may well be unprecedented in modern democracies."[47] While such a code might save the jobs of a few journalists in the short term, he warned, it could not prevent the manipulation of news.

> As every journalist knows, the primary means of influencing the character of the news produced by a media organization is through recruitment and promotion of key personnel. This can be done as effectively within a split as within a unified organization. Trying to build a "firewall" between print and TV newsrooms is an exercise in futility.[48]

A question of balance

The development of journalism education at Canadian universities has been the subject of little research and, as a result, perhaps inadequate discussion. While Canada was the first country outside the US to adopt university-level journalism education on a significant scale, its development lagged behind that in the US significantly in terms of both scale and scope, although arguably not in terms of quality.[49] As a result, media criticism in Canada suffered from a lack of academic credibility, along with the "constant shortage of historical perspective and reliable data" noted by Desbarats.[50] While many journalism issues here are similar to those in the US, there are also significant differences between the countries in terms of politics and culture, not to mention media. As a result, the expansion of university-level journalism education here was badly needed, although perhaps not as much as some consideration of the cost at which it has been gained.

The question of balance in J-school curricula, in Canada, as in the US and other countries, will likely never be resolved to the satisfaction of all those with a stake in journalism education. The nature of journalism as a quasi-professional endeavour requires that students be acquainted with the fundamentals of its practice, yet in order to earn a place alongside established university disciplines, journalism schools must go well beyond vocational training and ensure their graduates are familiar with the accumulated knowledge in their field. In determining an appropriate balance between skills training and more conceptual coursework, however, schools of journalism must first decide for whose benefit they exist—the student's in gaining entry into a career, the media's in recruiting employees, or society's in ensuring that journalism's higher ideals of providing public service are met. The aims of industry are in some ways antithetical to those of higher education, as Robert Blanchard and William Christ point out.

> Despite substantial occupational, organizational, and societal pressures, the liberally educated professional has the ability to reason independently and possesses a capacity for "moral imagination" to get around major constraints and act on principle, rather than to rely unthinkingly on occupational or company conventions, policies and rules of procedure.[51]

A question of influence

The limiting of journalism education to providing training for media industries became increasingly unacceptable for many universities, as witnessed by the movement toward reform that was manifested most publicly at Columbia in 2002. As a result, it was expected that many journalism schools in Canada would follow that influential example by offering a more academically rigorous curriculum. But a larger question of influence emerges from the corporate funding of journalism schools, raising the issue of in whose interest university educators should be expected not only to operate, but also to advocate. As Desbarats noted from experience, the independence granted to faculty by universities through tenure can become "rapidly eroded" by a different kind of dependence—on industry through the need for fundraising. "Unavoidably I gave up something in return," he concluded after accepting a corporate endowment. "No one should pretend, least of all university presidents, that this experience, multiplied many times and repeated over the years, doesn't damage universities in the long run."[52]

The public benefits program set up by the CRTC seemed an ideal source of needed funding for higher education in journalism, but as long as media companies could decide which university programs got the money, the question of corporate influence remained of concern. Similarly, the "data for use in media planning" obtained by bodies established with this funding, such as the Canadian Media Research Consortium, likewise tended to serve private interests rather than advancing understanding of the political and journalistic implications of increased corporate control of media. Ensuring that the public benefits program operated to the benefit of the public and not toward private ends would require an arm's-length relationship from funding corporations to ensure the money is allocated in an impartial way. Only through an independent body administering the funding could the appearance of influence over journalism education in Canada be dispelled and any possibility of conflict of interest avoided. Insulation from corporate influence would also help to better decide the question of balance in curricula at university journalism schools in Canada.

FOUR

Convergence and the "Black News Hole"

In mid-2003, after two years of study and public hearings across Canada, the standing Heritage committee issued an 872-page report that one scholar described as "the most comprehensive review of Canadian broadcasting in 20 years."[1] Titled *Our Cultural Sovereignty: The Second Century of Canadian Broadcasting*, the report made ninety-seven recommendations for addressing concerns that had been widely voiced in Canada since a spate of media mergers and acquisitions in 2000 saw television networks join with some of the country's largest newspaper companies. The Davey and Kent reports in the 1970s and '80s had fruitlessly urged limits on the growing concentration of newspaper ownership. Now corporate consolidation had gone to another level. The phenomenon of newspapers merging with television and other media even came with a fancy new twenty-first century name—convergence.

The 2003 report of the Heritage committee chaired by MP Clifford Lincoln called for measures to halt convergence and reconsider its wisdom. It recommended an immediate moratorium on new broadcast licenses issued to companies that also own newspapers pending a government review of convergence. "The danger is that too much power can fall into too few hands and it is power without accountability," it warned.[2] A firm federal policy on convergence was badly needed, the report added, recommending that one should be put in place by mid-2004. "The potential problems with cross-media ownership are sufficiently severe that the time has come for the federal government to issue a clear and unequivocal policy on this matter."[3] Restrictions on foreign ownership, which some industry advocates had argued should be lifted, should instead be retained in order to better preserve Canada's cultural sovereignty, the report concluded. It also urged increased funding for the CBC for the same reason.

But despite the obvious amount of government resources that went into producing the report, not to mention the importance of the issues it addressed, media coverage of the Lincoln report and its recommendations was sparse, noted media critics. *Toronto Star* columnist Antonia Zerbisias concluded from the paucity of press coverage that it "virtually fell into a black news hole."

> You'd think that, when five pounds of government reportage about broadcasting in this corporately merged and converged Canada hit all the desks in Media Land, the thud would be deafening. Instead, the mediaocracy has been strangely silent. Or, maybe not so strangely. . . . These are not proposals that some media barons wanted to see. To them the CBC is competition, unfairly aided and abetted by a billion bucks or so of government funding every year. Some media chiefs would like to sell out to foreigners in order to boost their stock value. And none wants to see limits placed on their growth, even if that growth is against the public interest in a democracy that depends on a diverse marketplace of ideas.[4]

The federal government's response to the report, which was required within six months, saw little more coverage when it came in November 2003. The response cautioned the industry not to expect much action. The statement issued by the new minister responsible for broadcasting, Bev Oda, deemed convergence "an essential business strategy for media organizations to stay competitive in a highly competitive and diverse marketplace." Oda was a former executive of CTV, Canwest, and Rogers. "Many of the issues addressed by the Standing Committee are complex and interrelated," noted her statement. "Accordingly, many of its 97 recommendations call for further analysis, examination and policy development before any decisions are taken."[5]

The lack of government support for the Lincoln committee's recommendations was "appalling," said a spokesman for the advocacy group Our Public Airwaves. "They're not prepared to commit even in principle," complained executive director Arthur Lewis.[6] The industry journal *Playback* labeled it the "under-reported" report. "Sank like a cinder block. Gone the way of the dodo. Fell off the radar. These are the phrases that spring to mind when one thinks of the Lincoln report."[7] Public broadcasting advocates complained that the report was "unfairly buried" and "shouted down by big media," according to *Playback*.

> The report made no splash, eliciting only a lukewarm formal response from Ottawa and little mainstream media attention, leading some to suggest that maybe—just maybe—the whole thing had been willfully ignored by this country's biggest congloms, Canwest Global and BCE, which would prefer to see ownership laws relaxed and the CBC cut down.[8]

The scant press coverage the Lincoln report received was evidence to some Canadians of a conspiracy of silence in their highly-concentrated and now converged media. Others pointed to alternative, less Machiavellian explanations. This chapter examines coverage of the Lincoln report in major Canadian daily newspapers, compares it with an analogous scenario being played out in the US, and analyzes media conspiracy theories and alternative explanations for plausibility.

Merging and converging

Canada caught the convergence wave more than most countries because there were no safeguards here against newspapers merging with TV or other media. The US wisely maintains a ban to this day in the form of a FCC prohibition on issuing television licences to owners of newspapers. Despite decades of pressure on regulators by media owners worldwide to drop restrictions on convergence, the US prohibition has been regularly renewed (although not without controversy), as recently as August 2016.[9] Cross-ownership of media, as convergence was officially called, had been similarly banned in Canada by an Order in Council following the 1981 report of the Royal Commission on Newspapers. The prohibition had been allowed to lapse in 1985, however, after control of the federal government passed from the Liberal Party to the Progressive Conservatives of Brian Mulroney.[10] The Kent commission's proposed Canada Newspaper Act would have addressed the cross-ownership issue, along with limiting the size of newspaper chains, but it died on the order paper with the change of government.

The convergence wave crested with the marriage in early 2000 of America Online (AOL) and Time Warner in the US. Ironically, however, that merger included no newspapers. The first in a series of transactions in Canada that raised concern and led to the creation of the Lincoln inquiry came that March, when Bell Canada Enterprises (BCE) bought CTV, the country's largest privately-owned television network, for $2.3 billion.[11] Canwest Global Communications, which owned Canada's other major private TV network, Global Television, trumped that in July with a $3.2-billion deal to buy the Southam newspaper chain. Adding major dailies in many cities where Canwest already owned television stations gave it considerable multimedia clout. In Vancouver, for example, it suddenly owned both daily newspapers, most of the community press, and the dominant television station, BCTV. By combining newsgathering operations between its television outlets and the Southam newspapers across the country, Canwest estimated it could save $100 million annually.[12]

In September, BCE went Canwest one better by partnering with Thomson's *Globe and Mail* national newspaper to create a new a $4-billion entity called Bell Globemedia. The partnership was announced shortly before the CRTC was to hold licence renewal hearings for both CTV and Global, so convergence became a key issue at the hearings. Thomson took just 29.9 percent ownership in the new Bell Globemedia, however, preventing the need for CRTC approval, which was only required for transactions exceeding 30 percent ownership of broadcasting companies.[13]

The prize for the largest Canadian media transaction in 2000, however, went neither to BCE nor Canwest but instead to Quebecor, which published about half the daily newspapers in Quebec. It had expanded nationwide in 1998 by taking over the Sun Media chain of fifteen English-language dailies and more than one hundred community newspapers across Canada. In a seven-month takeover battle throughout 2000, Quebecor outbid Rogers Communications, which until then was the country's largest media company, for Quebec cable giant Groupe Vidéotron.[14] The $5.4-billion takeover included TVA, the province's largest private television network. The tectonic shifts in the Canadian media landscape in 2000 left Bell Globemedia as by far the largest media firm in the country. Canwest Global ranked a solid second, followed by Quebecor. Rogers was suddenly fifth (see Table 1).

TABLE 1: LARGEST MEDIA FIRMS IN CANADA[15]

| | Revenue (millions) | | |
	2003	2002	Operations
Bell Globemedia	2,734	2,176	telecoms, CTV, *Globe and Mail*
Canwest Global	1,897	1,821	Global TV, Southam newspapers
Quebecor	1,217	1,173	TVA television, Sun newspapers
Torstar	894	832	*Toronto Star*, CityMedia newspapers
Rogers	845	785	cable TV, radio, magazines

Licence renewal hearings

The CRTC had jurisdiction over broadcasting in Canada, but none over print media, which were subject to no regulation other than what governed any business in Canada. It was the job of the Competition Bureau to scrutinize consolidation in the print media and prevent monopolies, just like in other industries. Convergence between newspapers and television, however, was something new. It prompted concern at the CRTC, as it did with many Canadians fearful their news media were becoming controlled by fewer and fewer large owners. The biggest concern was the business plan that came with convergence. By combining their newspaper and television newsrooms, converged media companies could theoretically eliminate half their journalists by having them cover the news for two media instead of just one. The vision this offered for the future of journalism was outlined most starkly in 2001 by Leonard Asper, the youthful CEO of Canwest Global.

> In the future, journalists will wake up, write a story for the Web, write a column, take their cameras, cover an event and do a report for TV and file a video clip for the Web. What we have really acquired is a quantum leap in the product we offer advertisers and a massive, creative, content-generation machine.[16]

But while this might have been a great corporate cost-cutting plan, it would only come with a loss of diversity in newsgathering, which is what gave the CRTC and others pause. Responding to concerns from consumer groups, it insisted on a "firewall" of separation between print and television newsgathering. TVA's hearings were held first, and its new owner Quebecor offered to implement a detailed six-page code of conduct that prevented its print and broadcast journalists from even communicating with each other. Hearings into the renewal of the CTV and Global Television licences were then held in April 2001. They did not go as well. Network owners Bell Globemedia and Canwest Global balked at keeping their print and broadcast news operations separate, offering only to maintain separate management structures. They also stopped short of accepting a binding code of separation as Quebecor had, and proposed only a one-page "Statement of Principles and Practices" as a voluntary commitment. They insisted they should be allowed to police their own operations without CRTC scrutiny, yet the *Toronto Star* noted that in pledging to keep separate management structures, "they did that . . . in concert with one another."[17] The networks were supported by several academics in their refusal to agree to keep their print and broadcast news operations separate. Even before their licence renewal hearings began,

Donna Logan (director of UBC's journalism grad school) deemed any required code of conduct "draconian and excessive."[18] Canwest Global executives also threatened to launch a constitutional challenge if the CRTC imposed a binding code of conduct separating its print and broadcast news operations.

In July 2001, the CRTC renewed Quebecor's licence for the TVA network. The only condition was adherence to the code of conduct that Quebecor had proposed. Quebecor was also ordered to increase from $35 million to $48.9 million the public benefits payments it had pledged in order to gain approval of its TVA acquisition. In August, the CRTC renewed the licences of CTV and Global for the usual seven-year term without requiring any code of conduct such as the one Quebecor had offered to follow. The CRTC required nothing beyond the separation of management structures that Canwest and CTV had volunteered.[19] CTV president Trina McQueen called it "one of the best things that has ever happened to Canadian journalism."[20] She predicted that international reporting and investigative journalism would be strengthened with the combined newsgathering resources of her television network and the *Globe and Mail*, as there would thus soon be a "bigger pot of information."[21] But the Brussels-based International Federation of Journalists said it was "very, very worried" that the moves toward convergence of media would lead to a lower quality of news.[22]

Aspers exercise influence

By late 2001, dark clouds gathered over Canadian journalism after Canwest's owning Asper family began to meddle in Southam newspaper content, ordering "national" editorials written at head office in Winnipeg and insisting columnists and local editorial writers not disagree with them. Suddenly convergence didn't seem like such a good idea. Journalists at the *Montreal Gazette* withdrew their bylines in protest of interference in favour of the Liberal party and of Israel, both of which the family strongly supported.[23] David Asper ridiculed what he called "the bleeding hearts of the journalist community" in a speech that was reprinted in Canwest newspapers. "It's the end of the world as they know it," he said, paraphrasing a song by the rock band R.E.M., "and I feel fine."[24] The controversy grew in 2002 after several columnists and editors at Southam newspaper quit in protest of editorial interference. Canwest chairman Izzy Asper wrote a column that criticized the CBC as "an anachronism and a waste of public funds," and a "huge bureaucracy" of "overpaid, underworked CBC head office executives who are living well off the taxpayers of Canada."[25]

While Asper had long opposed the very concept of a public broadcaster, which competed with Canwest's Global Television network, observers noted that his campaign had been stepped up since Canwest's acquisition of the Southam dailies.[26] Criticism of the CBC became a regular feature in Canwest's newly acquired newspapers, including charges of pro-Palestinian bias in news coverage.[27] Soon the Aspers began demanding that the CBC drop revenue-generating programming such as sports and local news that could just as well be covered by private broadcasters and focus instead on money-losing cultural and dramatic productions.[28] The controversy crested in June 2002 after the long-time publisher of the *Ottawa Citizen* was fired by Canwest for calling for the Liberal prime minister to resign. Opposition politicians renewed calls for an inquiry into the press in Canada.

The Lincoln Committee

Heritage Minister Sheila Copps asked MP Clifford Lincoln, as chair of the standing Heritage committee, to investigate concentration of press ownership. The Heritage committee's investigation began to take shape in February 2001. It was tasked to hold hearings into the future of the broadcasting system in Canada and to issue a report by the end of 2001.[29] The following month, however, opposition MPs began demanding an inquiry into press ownership as well because of concerns about Asper family influence over the news. All three opposition parties combined to demand an inquiry into concentration of media ownership in Canada.[30] Copps responded by first promising a "blue-ribbon" panel of experts to study the impact of increased media ownership concentration in Canada.[31] Within days, however, she reversed herself and announced that media ownership would instead also be studied by the Lincoln committee, along with broadcasting policy, with a report to issue in 2002.[32] "Ours is not a race against convergence," Lincoln said the following week in unveiling the expanded terms of reference of his non-binding review. "We're going to lose that race. . . . We've got to find out what the impact is."[33] Televised hearings were held across Canada in the spring of 2002, with a report promised by mid-December.[34]

The Lincoln Committee did not issue its report until mid-2003, however, more than two years after its inception. Rumours began to leak out that spring of a split between committee members from the New Democratic Party, the Canadian Alliance, and government MPs. The *National Post* reported on June 6 that the committee had been unable to achieve a consensus, "with even the Liberal vice-chairman of the committee saying yesterday he will provide his own recommendations separately from the report."[35] The *Post* also scooped the report's conclusions by reporting not only the recommendations it would make, but also that Alliance party members of the committee would issue their own dissenting report calling for "greater openness to foreign ownership and less stringent Canadian content regulations."[36] The *Post* enjoyed two days of leaked coverage of the recommendations and the Heritage committee's rift before the report's official release on June 11.

> The Canadian Alliance, Bloc Quebecois and even the Liberal vice-chairman of the committee are filing separate opinions disagreeing with or amplifying parts of the report, which includes in its title the words "Cultural Sovereignty." The fact that Wendy Lill, the nationalist NDP member of the committee, is not filing a dissent is as telling about the report's philosophical direction as the title.[37]

Coverage of the report's official release, its conclusions and recommendations, as well as the subsequent reaction to it, must be considered in light of the circumstances surrounding it, from its halting inception to its leaked release.

Newspaper coverage

Press critics were correct in pointing to the paucity of daily news-paper coverage the Lincoln report attracted. In some dailies, cover-age of the report and its recommendations was comprehensive. In at least one major daily, however, it was non-existent. In newspapers on opposite ends of the political spectrum, there were significant differences in how the recommendations of the Lincoln report were framed. Database searches of Canadian newspaper coverage of the report's release reveal the extent of coverage. By combining use of the databases Factiva and Canadian Newsstand, the coverage of most of the largest-circulation daily newspapers in Canada can be captured. Table 2 lists the English-language daily newspapers with a circulation of greater than fifty thousand in 2003.

No stories appeared in either the *Edmonton Journal* or the *Mont-real Gazette* that were archived in those databases. On querying or examining microfilm of those dailies, however, it was discovered that the *Edmonton Journal* did carry a news item, but that page was found not to have been archived. Newspapers of the Sun Media chain were not archived in either of the databases, nor was the inde-pendent *Halifax Chronicle-Herald*. As a result, coverage of the Lincoln report's release could only be obtained for sixteen of the twenty-two dailies listed. These included ten of the twelve largest news-papers, however, as measured by circulation. Table 3 shows results of the database searches, listed in order of circulation, including the number of words devoted to the story, its page placement, headline, and source.

The missing news

The most striking feature of the results, apart from the total lack of coverage in the *Montreal Gazette*, is the way that news of the Lincoln report was "buried" in the *Vancouver Sun*. The reduction of the news of such a major government report to a mere seventy-one-word "business brief" can perhaps be explained in part by the headline atop the story: "More cash for CBC recommended." Rather than focus on the issues of cross-media ownership or foreign ownership, which would admittedly be difficult to do in seventy-one words, the thrust of the story was the increased funding urged for public broadcasting. Given the antipathy exhibited toward the CBC by the Asper family, however, it is hard to escape the conclusion that the influence of ownership on the *Vancouver Sun*'s coverage of this story was considerable, directly or indirectly.

TABLE 2: CANADIAN ENGLISH–LANGUAGE DAILY NEWSPAPERS

Title	Market	Owner	Circulation
1. *Toronto Star*	ON	Torstar	440,654
2. *Globe and Mail*	Nat'l	Bell Globemedia	314,178
3. *National Post*	Nat'l	Canwest Global	246,504
4. *Vancouver Sun*	BC	Canwest Global	212,724
5. *Toronto Sun**	ON	Quebecor	208,429
6. *The Province**	BC	Canwest Global	159,963
7. *Edmonton Journal*	AB	Canwest Global	151,718
8. *Montreal Gazette*	QC	Canwest Global	143,595
9. *Calgary Herald*	AB	Canwest Global	143,210
10. *Ottawa Citizen*	ON	Canwest Global	137,474
11. *Winnipeg Free Press*	MB	Canadian Newsp.	119,117
12. *Hamilton Spectator*	ON	Torstar	105,765
13. *Halifax Chronicle-Herald*	NS	Independent	93,015
14 *London Free Press*	ON	Quebecor	92,213
15. *Victoria Times Colonist*	BC	Canwest Global	78,110
16. *Windsor Star*	ON	Canwest Global	74,686
17. *Edmonton Sun**	AB	Quebecor	70,984
18. *Calgary Sun**	AB	Quebecor	65,988
19. *Kitchener-Waterloo Record*	ON	Torstar	65,879
20. *Saskatoon StarPhoenix*	SK	Canwest Global	62,915
21. *Regina Leader-Post*	SK	Canwest Global	57,578
22. *Ottawa Sun**	ON	Quebecor	50,883

* tabloid

Source: Canadian Newspaper Association, 2003

Other explanations were advanced for the paucity of press coverage the Lincoln report received upon its release. As *Toronto Star* media critic Antonia Zerbisias noted, the report's length and complexity saw even public broadcasting advocates digesting its recommendations for weeks after it was released.

TABLE 3: NEWSPAPER COVERAGE OF THE LINCOLN REPORT

Rank	Newspaper	Words	Page	Headline	Source
1	Toronto Star	966	A4	Cross-ownership under attack	Staff
2	Globe and Mail	630	A4	Broadcast review proposes overhaul	Staff
3	National Post	629	FP1	Freeze new cross-media licenses, report says	Canwest
4	Vancouver Sun	71	D8	More cash for CBC recommended	none
6	The Province	263	A37	Keep lid on foreign ownership of our media, says report	CP
7	Edmonton Journal	318	A9	Report attacks media convergence	Canwest
8	Montreal Gazette	0			
9	Calgary Herald	413	A12	Moratorium urged to control cross-media ownership	Canwesr
10	Ottawa Citizen	543	D1	Cross media ownership slammed	Canwest
11	Winnipeg Free Press	552	A9	Broadcast blueprint urges more for CBC	CP
12	Hamilton Spectator	834	E1	Increase CBC funding: study	CP
15	Victoria Times Colonist	882	C1	Ottawa outlines media rules	CP
16	Windsor Star	312	A13	Freeze cross-media ownership: Report	Canwest
19	Kitchener-Waterloo Record	587	D9	Limit foreign ownership, media convergence: report	CP
20	Saskatoon Star-Phoenix	156	C4	Put media convergence on hold, report suggests	CP
21	Regina Leader-Post	572	D12	Committee concerned about media ownership	Canwest

Was it just too big? Too complex? Too ambitious? Should it have been pre-masticated into corporate PR-style, bite-sized bits for overworked journalists with other stories and other deadlines? . . . Perhaps it's simply bad timing; the report came just as Parliament was heading for the cottage hills, while journalists had Olympic bids and other matters on the news schedule.[38]

The timing of the report's release also came within weeks of several other reports on the broadcasting industry. These included one prepared for the CRTC on television drama by former CTV president Trina McQueen, one written for the Heritage committee on Canadian content by former National Film Board chairman François Macerola, and one on Canadian drama by the Coalition of Canadian Audio–Visual Unions.[39] One Alliance party member of the Lincoln committee even predicted three weeks before its report was released that it would "likely be ignored because it's too long and will be released during the Liberal leadership campaign."[40]

Another explanation for the lack of press coverage that takes the trade's own practices into account is the leaking of the report's contents to the *National Post* almost a week prior to its release. As most of the report's major recommendations were thus already "old news" by the time it was officially released, editors might have considered that the news value of timeliness was somewhat reduced as a result. Whether this would explain why the story got the treatment it received on the pages of the *Vancouver Sun* is questionable, however. The peculiar relationship the *National Post* had with the monopoly dailies there must also be taken into consideration. In an attempt to sell more copies of the *National Post* in Vancouver, it regularly appropriated *Sun* and *Province* stories, which the local dailies were then prohibited from carrying. This reportedly led journalists at the Vancouver dailies to consider themselves as playing "second fiddle" to the *Post*.[41] Also illustrative are the headlines the leaked news of the report's contents garnered earlier in the *National Post*. They were framed in such terms as "TV protectionists score win" and "Give Canadian TV more cash." This might have been taken by *Sun* editors, not to mention those at other Canwest-owned dailies across the country, as a signal from ownership as to how they should treat the story.

The American parallel

Just as the Lincoln report was being released in Canada, public awareness of almost identical issues in the US was beginning to crest in grassroots outrage despite news media coverage that was also sparse. The similarity between the scenarios on opposite sides of the border may provide some clues to help explain the paucity of Canadian coverage. The FCC began hearings in late 2002 into proposed rule changes on media ownership, including lifting a 1975 prohibition on cross-media ownership in local markets. By the height of the debate in February 2003, however, the *American Journalism Review* noted that a survey by the Pew Research Center found 72 percent of Americans had heard "nothing at all" about the proposed relaxation of media ownership rules.

> As the FCC moved toward final action on a plan that would greatly benefit a handful of large companies, most newspapers and broadcast outlets owned by those companies barely mentioned the issue. . . . The survey also found that the more people did know, the more they tended to oppose what the FCC was doing. In other words, Big Media had an interest in keeping people uninformed.[42]

The *American Journalism Review* did a content analysis of coverage of the FCC hearings in major media outlets for the first five months of 2003, prior to its June vote to lift the cross-ownership ban. "While some newspapers produced a respectable flurry of stories in the weeks prior to the FCC's action, the major networks — where most people get their news — acknowledged the issue only after protests in Washington had grown impossible to ignore."[43]

The *Columbia Journalism Review* concluded that the coalition between politicians and activists on both the left and right to oppose the FCC changes surprised even industry insiders. "It is not every day that the ideological lines get redrawn over an issue. . . . Media had become a political issue, as deeply felt as the economy, health care, or education."[44] The question of censorship and self-censorship had been taken up by the *Columbia Journalism Review* several years earlier with a survey of journalists by the Pew Research Center. While direct censorship of the news by media owners was not found to be a widespread problem, the more insidious forces of self-censorship were found to be "pervasive" among media gatekeepers. "Pressure from local power brokers may be less pernicious than the self-censorship of editors, producers, or reporters who simply choose a service story or an easier topic and shortchange their public."[45] While the line between overt censorship and self-censorship often blurs, interviews with journalists found that "subtle and not-so-subtle signals" define the boundaries of news.[46]

Concern in the US over the influence of press owners in shaping news content dates to at least the 1947 report of the Commission on Freedom of the Press. It proposed self-regulation of the press in the form of "social responsibility" to forestall government regulation, which it concluded might otherwise have been imposed. The Hutchins Commission, as it was known, concluded that the news published in US newspapers was "twisted" by numerous influences, including the personal interests of owners.[47] The "exaggerated drives for power and profit which have tended to restrict competition and promote monopoly" had worked against the public interest, the commission concluded, and should be addressed by government action if needed. "If the freedom of the press is to achieve reality, government must set limits on its capacity to interfere with, regulate, or suppress the voices of the press or to manipulate the data on which public judgment is formed."[48]

Sociological studies of influences on journalists dating to the 1950s have shown a considerable impact of ownership on shaping the news. Warren Breed's classic 1955 study of newsroom socialization revealed the mechanism of social control used by publishers to enforce adherence to a newspaper's editorial policy through the "slanting" of news stories. The enforcement of a newspaper's policy on certain issues, Breed concluded, was not achieved through the use of formal guidelines, but instead informally through a publisher's use of power over "mobility aspirations" of journalists.[49]

> "Slanting" almost never means prevarication. Rather, it involves omission, differential selection, and preferential placement, such as "featuring" a pro-policy item, "burying" an anti-policy item in an inside page, etc. . . . Policy is covert, due to the existence of ethical norms of journalism; policy often contravenes these norms. No executive is willing to risk embarrassment by being accused of open commands to slant a news story.[50]

A study conducted in the 1960s and '70s of major several US news media outlets by Herbert Gans showed that while executives of media corporations have "virtually unlimited power" over news content, they are not able to exercise it continuously due to time constraints and their location outside the newsroom. According to Gans, however, this made the occasional intervention of ownership in news content all the more influential. "Their role in story selection and production is intermittent. . . . They do not exercise their power on a day-to-day basis. Perhaps because they do not do so, the journalists pay close attention to their periodic suggestions, and at times, they overreact."[51] The same phenomenon was seen by Pamela Shoemaker and Stephen Reese in *Mediating the Message*, their 1996 compendium of influences on news content. "The absence of visible attempts at control does not mean that none are being made," it noted. "Whenever media workers deduce what their supervisors want and give it to them, de facto control has been exercised."[52]

The limits of laissez-faire

One of the strongest arguments against the Kent commission's proposed reforms in 1981 was that, while the commission had chronicled the potential for the abuse of political power accumulated through increased concentration of press ownership, it had not proven that such power had actually been abused. The commission's report itself admitted as much. "The effect," it noted, "is to create a power structure of which the best defence, on the evidence of the principal corporate proprietors themselves, is that they do not exercise that power."[53] Two decades later, however, the obvious exercise of ownership influence over the news published in Canadian dailies changed all that. Whether exercised directly or, more likely, indirectly through the more insidious mechanisms of socialization and self-censorship, the end result was the tailoring of news content to suit the political preferences of ownership. Given that the owners of the largest newspaper company in Canada were not only overtly political but also owned one of its television networks, it was understandable why Canadians began to question the lack of press regulation. The scarcity of news coverage of matters not favorable to newspaper owners, such as the Lincoln report, added credence to calls for reform.

FIVE

How the Camel Got In the Tent

One cold night, as an Arab sat in his tent, a camel gently thrust his nose under the flap and looked in. "Master," he said, "let me put my nose in your tent. It's cold and stormy out here." "By all means," said the Arab, "and welcome" as he turned over and went to sleep.[1]

The parable of the camel and the tent, of course, ends badly for the accommodating Arab man. The next time he is awoken, the animal has its neck inside, then its entire body. Soon there is no room for the host. The illustrated principle of incrementalism also applies in such metaphors as the "domino effect," the "thin edge of the wedge," and "getting a foot in the door." In law and public policy, arguments against adopting an action due to its inevitable future effects are known as "slippery slope" arguments. More worrisome in public policy are slippery slope "events," which commence an unstoppable descent toward an undesired result.[2]

A few large multinational media owners have challenged the foreign ownership restrictions of national regulatory systems worldwide over the past two decades in order to expand their corporate reach. Rupert Murdoch's battles with regulators in the US, the UK, and China have been well documented. A pair of Canadian entrepreneurs who also challenged foreign ownership rules in the mid-1990s, however, gained less global attention. Conrad Black and Izzy Asper were perhaps less visible internationally than Murdoch in their assault on foreign media ownership limits because the nation they infiltrated was not a world power but, instead, Murdoch's native Australia. This chapter chronicles the Canadian challenge to Australia's foreign ownership limits and argues that it was a slippery slope episode—equivalent to the metaphoric camel's nose—because it was influential in the country lifting its restrictions on foreign media ownership in 2006.

Foreign media ownership

Academic research on regulation of foreign media ownership has been limited because the topic falls in a gray area between several fields. Communication historians and policy researchers tend to ignore the international context, while scholars of international communication often fail to address domestic legislation. As a result, noted Rita Zajacz, most of the research into the genesis of and justification for foreign media ownership limits has fallen to legal scholars.[3] Most countries have prohibited or limited foreign media ownership, according to Ann Hollifield, "at least partly out of fear that foreign owners would use those outlets to manipulate public opinion in times of national crisis."[4] As a result, multinational media ownership was not widespread outside of magazines before the late 1980s, and there is thus little research on the impact of foreign ownership. Literature on media ownership deregulation more generally, on the other hand, has been plentiful since the late 1980s. According to Robert Horwitz in his 1989 book *The Irony of Regulatory Reform*, the libertarian rhetoric of the Reagan era was underlain by a commercial ethic that promised to unleash entrepreneurship by "getting the government off the backs of the people." Deregulation of media industries, noted Horwitz, unfortunately resulted in a vast reduction in diversity of viewpoints. Technical advances in communication that allow the transmission of information digitally across borders have been predicted by globalization proponents to render national regulatory agencies obsolete.[5] Others, however, see an important role for the state in shaping global media markets, including in setting the citizenship requirements of national media owners.[6]

Australia began enforcing limits on foreign ownership of broadcasting starting in the 1920s, when licenses for radio transmitters were denied to non-British subjects.[7] The 1951 acquisition of Broadcasting Associates, which held several commercial radio licences, by UK-based MPA Productions prompted parliamentary debate on foreign media ownership. A resulting resolution declared it "undesirable that any person not an Australian should have any substantial measure of ownership or control of any Australian commercial broadcasting station."[8] A 1955 report on television licensing by the Australian Broadcast Control Board suggested a 15-percent limit on foreign ownership in that medium, which was incorporated in amendments to the Broadcasting Act the following year. The limit was imposed, according to legal scholar Lesley Hitchens, to "protect national sovereignty by preventing foreigners being able to influence domestic opinion."[9] Foreign ownership of newspapers, along with other industries, was governed by the Foreign Investment Review Board (FIRB).

In late 1986, two major changes to media ownership laws were announced by the Labor government that had profound effects on the newspaper and television industries. One restricted cross-media ownership of newspapers and television stations in any market by placing a limit of 15 percent on ownership of outlets in one of those media. That meant media owners were forced to choose, in the words of then-treasurer Paul Keating, between being "princes of print" or "queens of the screen." The resulting ownership scramble saw much of the country's press bought, sold, traded, or shut down over the next few months.[10] Rupert Murdoch chose print, selling his stations of Channel 10, but he soon became the king of newspapers in Australia by acquiring the Herald and Weekly Times Limited. Adding the country's largest newspaper chain by far to his second-place News Corporation gave Murdoch more than 58 percent of the country's newspaper circulation. It also brought Australia's concentration of press ownership to among the highest in the world, alongside Canada's.[11] The Labor government also lifted the two-station rule that had prevented television broadcasters from expanding into national networks, and a similar ownership upheaval visited that medium as a result. Combined with a sharp economic downturn, the increased competition resulted in what media historian Bridget Griffen-Foley described as a "shakeout," with both the Nine Network and Network TEN going into receivership.[12] The disarray in Australian media ownership opened the door for two opportunistic Canadians who offered their expertise in operating newspaper and television firms profitably.

Black and Asper

Black and Asper had both sold off investments in other industries to focus on their Canadian media holdings. Both expanded into international markets in part due to a resistance in their native country to their ownership of domestic media. Black owned a chain of small newspapers in Canada that he hoped to expand, but he was thwarted in takeover bids for the country's two largest chains in the early 1980s. Instead he expanded overseas, buying the money-losing *Telegraph* in London for a bargain price in 1985. After moving to non-union operations at new premises, almost three quarters of the 3,900 *Telegraph* staff were cut from the payroll and its finances quickly improved. From a loss of £8.9 million in 1986, the *Telegraph* recorded a profit of £41.5 million in 1989.[13] Black's company Hollinger International also expanded into the US and Israel, buying the *Jerusalem Post*, Israel's oldest and largest-circulation English-language daily, for US$20 million in 1989.

Black's next newspaper investment would result in him becoming what one biographer described as "the central character in one of the most vicious and highly-politicized takeover battles that Australia has ever seen."[14] His *Telegraph* headed a 1991 consortium which bid to buy John Fairfax Ltd., Australia's second-largest newspaper chain. Fairfax had gone into receivership after a highly leveraged privatization bid by heir Warwick Fairfax went awry with an economic downturn. What was left of Fairfax equity was claimed by its creditors. The *Telegraph* and US investment bank Hellman and Friedman together subscribed for 35 percent of one rescue bid, code named Tourang, which was a level of foreign ownership beyond what the FIRB had approved previously. Irish newspaper owner Tony O'Reilly was part of another consortium vying for Fairfax that included 26 percent foreign ownership. The Tourang bid was better capitalized, however, and had gained the approval and participation of Fairfax's American debt holders.

In addition to its level of foreign ownership, what made Australians nervous about Tourang was the presence in its consortium of the country's richest man, Nine Network owner Kerry Packer. While Packer stayed within the overall 15-percent limit of cross-ownership, Nine Network owned television stations in several markets where Fairfax published newspapers. His former lawyer Malcolm Turnbull, who was elected Liberal Party leader in 2015 and thus prime minister, also represented the American bondholders and his former CEO Trevor Kennedy was proposed as Fairfax head. The Australian Journalists Association protested that the appointment of Kennedy as Fairfax CEO meant Packer could control the newspaper chain. Former prime ministers Gough Whitlam and Malcolm Fraser also went public with their concerns.[15] Almost five hundred journalists protested in Sydney, handing out leaflets headlined "A Black Day for Australia." The group Friends of Fairfax demonstrated in Melbourne, asking people to close their accounts with ANZ bank, the company's main creditor, if the Tourang bid was accepted.[16] Tourang dropped Turnbull and Kennedy, while Packer withdrew after the Australian Broadcasting Tribunal (ABT) threatened to investigate the cross-media ramifications of his participation. Despite these concessions, Tourang was disqualified by Treasurer John Kerin due to its level of foreign ownership.

The remaining Tourang principals reformulated their stakes in a structure devised by lawyers from the Sydney law firm Freehills. Two types of ownership were proposed—voting common shares and non-voting debentures, a long-term debt instrument similar to a bond. The proposed 15-percent investment in Fairfax by Hellman and Friedman would be held as non-voting debentures, which under the innovative proposal would have been considered a foreign "interest" but not foreign "ownership." Kerin again rejected the Tourang bid and approved that of the O'Reilly consortium, but the Treasurer was coincidentally fired the same day by Prime Minister Bob Hawke. The change allowed Tourang a reprieve prior to the bid deadline. In a last-minute re-arrangement, Black reduced the *Telegraph*'s proposed ownership of voting shares in Fairfax to 15 percent and Hellman and Friedman slashed its participation to 5 percent. The debt holders would own 6 percent of Fairfax if their bid was accepted. That 26-percent level of foreign voting ownership was the same as proposed by the O'Reilly group.[17] The Tourang bid was also favoured by creditor banks, which would be fully reimbursed under its terms. New treasurer Ralph Willis approved its reformulated offer in late 1991. Black took management control and set about reducing the chain's workforce by 10 percent, which boosted Fairfax profits. A public offering of stock in May 1992 saw Fairfax's share price double, earning Black a paper profit of $39 million within five months.[18]

Black claimed he had initially been told by Hawke and Kerin that 35 percent foreign ownership of Fairfax would be acceptable, and he subsequently pressed the issue with Keating, who succeeded Hawke as prime minister in 1993.[19] Prior to the election, Black met with Keating about raising his ownership in Fairfax. The prime minister, according to Black, urged him to apply to the FIRB to raise his stake to 25 per cent, and he promised to personally "champion" the bid. "If he was re-elected and Fairfax political coverage was 'balanced,'" Black wrote in his 1993 autobiography, *A Life in Progress*, "he would entertain an application to go higher." Black added that Opposition leader John Hewson had "already promised that if he was elected he would remove restraints on our ownership."[20] The Canadian edition of Black's memoirs made no mention of exercising influence in foreign political affairs, recalling only that Keating "was entirely encouraging of our long-term presence in Australia."[21]

Senate inquiry

The publication of Black's autobiography caused an uproar in Australia, as he had been allowed to increase his stake in Fairfax to 25 percent only weeks after Keating was re-elected. A Senate inquiry was called to investigate Black's account of political back-room dealing and the Fairfax takeover. Witnesses painted Black in unflattering terms during proceedings that foreshadowed the legal circus that would surround him thirteen years later in the US. Turnbull described Black as an "extraordinary egoist," which came as no news in Canada or England. "He [has] almost no regard for telling the truth," testified Turnbull. "Black consistently overstates his role in things. . . . I don't believe his word can be trusted on matters where his own involvement is concerned."[22] Hawke concurred. "The simple fact is that Conrad Black does not tell the truth," he testified. "He has the habit of distorting events through the prism of his own perceived self-interest."[23] When Black took the witness stand, he claimed the entire affair had been a misunderstanding. "There was no nudge, there was no wink, there was no undertaking," he told the inquiry.

> We are not lapdogs of any regime. Mr. Keating was certainly not using the word balance as a euphemism for support or favouritism . . . or as hostile to his enemies. . . . I do not know what else I can do to bury this putrid corpse, short of driving a silver stake through a copy of this committee's terms of reference.[24]

Black called Turnbull "notoriously unstable" and claimed Hawke had offered to spy on Keating for US$50,000.[25] Hawke went on television to deny the allegation and to speculate about Black's own "mental instability."[26] The Senate inquiry report concluded Keating had indeed "attempted to exert pressure at Fairfax for favourable election coverage by making a linkage between 'balance' in election coverage and an increased ownership limit for Mr. Black."[27] If a political disaster, Black's efforts at raising Australia's media ownership limits proved a financial windfall, as he sold his shares two years later to a New Zealand-based group for a reported profit of $300 million.[28] On exiting Australia, Black had some harsh words for what he saw as the country's fluid foreign ownership policies.

> It's not a politically mature jurisdiction and foreigners should understand what they're getting into there. I'm not one who has an exaggeratedly lofty view of politicians, in general, but politicians in Australia as a group are at another level altogether.[29]

It was against this acrimonious backdrop that Asper began his own battle with Australian media regulators a few months later.

Canwest rising

The business model of Canwest Global Communications, which Asper founded in 1974, was described by Paul Taylor, a former Global Television journalist, as a "carefully constructed and fiercely defended regulatory freedom."[30] It became Canada's most profitable TV company in the 1980s by exploiting provisions in the country's broadcasting regulations that provided revenue, and by avoiding others that required expenditure. Taylor concluded Canwest Global was "invisible to researchers" because it did not fit the dominant network form. It changed television in Canada nonetheless by the "unique and carefully crafted regulatory position devised by its owners."[31] Canwest Global exploited its junior status to the national networks CBC and CTV, noted Taylor, in order to reduce costs. Because it lacked outlets in several Canadian provinces, Canwest was exempt from some obligations endured by the national networks, such as transmitting into remote locations. By confining itself to the more lucrative urban markets, Canwest could skim the cream of advertising dollars because, as far as the CRTC was concerned, it was not a network but instead a "system." Canwest Global was also required by the CRTC to invest only $44 million in Canadian content for the 1990–91 programming season, which was half of CTV's required expenditure.[32]

Airing more popular American content, which could often be purchased for 10 percent of its production cost, made Canwest more profitable than the larger CTV, but its programming strategy resulted in Canwest being derided as the "Love Boat Network."[33]

Canwest took its template for financial success in the television business onto the international stage in the 1990s, first taking advantage of New Zealand's near-complete deregulation of broadcasting. According to New Zealand scholars Margie Comrie and Susan Fountaine, the government there removed foreign ownership restrictions expressly to allow Canwest to "rescue" bankrupt network TV3 in late 1991.[34] The media shakeout that followed the dropping of the two-station rule cast doubt on whether Australia could support three television networks. TEN was losing $2 million a week in 1991, but Asper was anxious to apply the turnaround strategy he had pioneered in Canada and exported to New Zealand. As a foreigner, however, he was restricted by the Broadcasting Act to owning 15 percent. He sought Australian investors for 85 percent of the $240 million asking price for Network TEN, but he was able to get commitments for only half that amount. Consultations with Freehills modified the short-lived non-voting equity model it had devised for Tourang. That provided the loophole in Australia's foreign ownership rules which allowed Canwest to take equity in TEN as debt instead of as shares of ownership. The modified design, according to Australian journalist Mark Westfield in his 2000 book *The Gatekeepers*, was an "even more aggressive version" of the model it had devised for Fairfax.[35]

As a result, Canwest contributed 57.5 per cent of the purchase price but took only 15 per cent of the voting shares. It held the other 42.5 per cent interest as non-voting debentures that would pay dividends equivalent to TEN's rate of profit.[36] The Australian Broadcasting Authority, which had recently replaced the ABT, approved the arrangement in 1992. According to Westfield, the structure allowed Canwest to "pull the wool over the eyes of the ABA," with the result that the regulator was seen as an "easy touch" from then on.

> In any other industry a shareholding of this magnitude, whether it be voting or economic, would constitute clear control, but the fledgling Australian Broadcasting Authority later cleared Canwest of allegations that it controlled Ten, much to the amazement of the industry.[37]

Battling the ABA

While conforming to the letter of the law, Canwest Global's ownership arrangement for Network TEN stretched the limits of credulity. Australian media regulations also prohibited foreigners from exercising control over television broadcasters, yet the manager of Canwest's Global Television station CKVU in Vancouver moved to Sydney in 1993 as CEO of Network TEN. A complaint by the network's former director of programming that Canadians were running TEN's operations soon came to the attention of the ABA. It began an investigation that went on for more than a year, generated 950 pages of testimony, and subpoenaed 15,000 pages of documents.[38] Network TEN profits soared to $103 million in 1995 due to Canwest management's cost cutting and programming changes, which saw the injection of cheap American programming. As a result, Canwest more than recouped its Network TEN investment through stock dividends and debenture payments in three years.

As the ABA inquiry dragged on through most of 1995, Asper expressed defiance of the broadcasting regulator. He appeared on a Nine Network business program to complain that Australia's media ownership laws lacked consistency due to the removal of restrictions on foreign ownership of radio stations in 1992. "I can leave here as a non-Australian and buy a radio station in Sydney as a foreigner," he said. "Why can't I buy a television station?"[39] If the ABA forced it to sell its TEN debentures, Asper promised Canwest would expand into media sectors that were not as tightly regulated, mentioning cable television as a possibility. He also threatened to broadcast into Australia from the South Pacific.

> From 1997 I can put a satellite up from Fiji. Whatever technology will permit, the laws can't stop. It will be done. If I can reach every home in this country from Fiji, there's no sense passing any laws about foreign ownership.[40]

Canwest was eventually absolved by the ABA, whose report cleared the Canadians of exercising control over Network TEN.[41]

Despite the vindication, Asper threatened to pull out of the country after changes proposed to Australia's media ownership laws by Liberal leader John Howard would have allowed no increase in foreign ownership. "It may well be if the government of Australia doesn't want, for whatever reason, foreign ownership or foreign investment, or Canwest in particular," Asper told ABC Radio. "Well obviously there are lots of places in the world where one can invest. . . . And reluctantly but certainly we would divest our interests in Network Ten and employ our resources where they are welcome."[42]

Not only did Canwest remain in Australia, however, it quietly increased its stake in Network TEN. ABA officials noted in late 1996 that four of the network's six minority shareholders had sold their Network TEN holdings to numbered companies based in Australia. Asper denied Canwest had increased its ownership of TEN. "Canwest has not bought any shares in Network Ten whatsoever," he told reporters.[43] ABA investigators, however, found that the holding companies had bought the shares with money borrowed from a subsidiary of Canwest located in the Netherlands. As a result, Canwest was in a position to control 76 percent of TEN. After a four-month investigation, the ABA ruled Canwest in breach of the law and gave the Canadians six months to sell the excess shares or face a $2 million fine.[44] A separate investigation by the FIRB also demanded divestiture "irrespective of price."[45]

A 1996 change in government from Labor to a Liberal coalition led by Howard brought proposed changes to Australia's cross-media ownership laws, but not on foreign ownership, changes to which the new prime minister opposed. Non-voting shares were also banned, meaning Canwest should have had to reduce its ownership of TEN to the 15 percent limit allowed of foreigners. Asper flew to Canberra to lobby for an exemption from the new regulations. "You don't change the ground rules retrospectively," he told reporters. "That is something that we civilised countries do not do."[46] As recounted by Asper, his message to Treasurer Peter Costello was more succinct: "Let commerce rule, not the law."[47] The dispute threatened to turn into an international incident when the Canadian government intervened on Asper's behalf, warning Australia it would consider the demand for divestiture a breach of international treaty obligations.[48] Asper took the dispute to Federal Court, where his lawsuit was dismissed. He won a small victory, however, when the judge overruled the FIRB requirement that Canwest sell at any price.[49] Still Asper pressed his case, appealing the ruling. "The man simply does not give up," marveled *The Australian* of Asper's "interminable game of snakes and ladders."[50]

Finally a deal was struck in which, as part of a public listing of Network TEN shares for sale, Canwest's debentures were exempted from the prohibition on non-voting shares. Broadcasting, foreign investment, and stock market regulators, noted the *Australian Financial Review,* had all "appeared powerless against Asper flouting the Australian law."[51] TEN's share price soared, boosting Canwest's five-year investment twenty-seven times over to AUS$1.4 billion.[52] "With the benefit of hindsight," noted Westfield, "this was the bargain of the decade."[53] By the time of Asper's death in 2003, the ingenuity of his Network TEN acquisition had come clear, according to the *Australian.*

> It was a brilliant design, and many potential foreign buyers of media assets pleaded to be able to "do a Canwest" to get around pesky foreign ownership limits. After two inquiries, the federal government put a stop to any further "Canwests." It remains a unique structure.[54]

Ownership rule changes

A decade-long revisiting of Australia's media ownership regulations agreed on eliminating limits to cross-media ownership. Many predicted that would bring even higher ownership concentration, however, if foreign ownership limits were not lifted as well.[55] Rupert Murdoch had already boosted his ownership of the country's newspaper industry to about two-thirds despite being forced to take out US citizenship in order to start the Fox Network there. Canwest's ability to circumvent Australia's foreign ownership limits, noted media scholar Jock Given, was another reason advanced for abolishing them.[56] Canwest made a submission in 1999 to the Productivity Commission, which the Australian government created the previous year to review economic and regulatory policy. It criticized the limits as "outdated and unnecessary," arguing that "foreigners have less reason to interfere in local domestic affairs because they are less likely to have a substantial range of other investments which could lead to the risk of conflicts of interest."[57] Noting a consensus among the commercial networks, the Productivity Commission's report the following year urged the lifting of both cross-media and foreign ownership restrictions.

> Restrictions on foreign investment and control restrict the options open to Australian media businesses. Australia is a small market within which to attract the sorts of interests who have the capital, skills and content rights to operate a large scale media business. Removing the foreign investment constraints opens up the capital market for television, and improves access to technology and managerial know how.[58]

The debate over cross ownership of media in Australia was finally resolved in 2006 with the dropping of limits on cross-ownership, subject to a "diversity" test. The political *quid pro quo*, however, was lifting of the country's restrictions on foreign ownership of media as well. After the changes were quickly "rubber-stamped," noted journalist Eric Beecher, a series of multi-billion-dollar transactions transformed Australia's media.[59] Unexpectedly, one of them did not include Canwest selling its majority ownership in Network TEN to a newspaper company because it couldn't get the AUS$1-billion price it wanted. The failure to sell its Australian holdings when it could have would soon prove disastrous for Canwest.

After Australia

In the mid-1990s, Black and Asper turned their attention back to Canada, where their experiences would be similar to those in Australia. Black at first appeared to succeed, but in the end failed spectacularly. Asper steadily worked media ownership regulations to his advantage, and in the end much of Canadian media, including Black's former holdings, belonged to Canwest.[60] Black used the proceeds from his sale of Fairfax shares in 1996 to aid in finally taking over Southam Inc., which he had long coveted. After only a few years, however, he sold it to Asper after renouncing his Canadian citizenship to take a seat in the UK House of Lords. Hollinger, which by the late 1990s ranked as the world's third-largest newspaper chain (after Murdoch's News Corp. and the US chain Gannett), began to implode in 2003. Minority shareholders complained that asset sales, such as that of Southam to Canwest Global, unfairly enriched company insiders like Black because they included lucrative "non-compete" agreements with the executives personally instead of with the company. Black resigned under pressure and an investigation counted more than US$400 million that he and others allegedly appropriated between 1997 and 2003. That amounted to more than 95 percent of Hollinger International's adjusted net income during the period.[61] Black was convicted in Chicago on four counts of fraud and obstruction of justice in 2007, for which he was sentenced to six-and-a-half years in a Florida prison.[62] After an appeal resulted in three of the fraud counts being dropped, he ended up serving three years and six months.

Asper left Canwest Global Communications to his three adult children, who were all trained as lawyers at his insistence. They saw its future in international markets and thus decided against selling their majority ownership of Network TEN in 2007 despite an earnings downgrade due to growing concern over the economy.[63] They also launched a challenge to Canada's foreign media ownership laws that year, partnering with US investment bank Goldman Sachs to buy thirteen cable television channels. The Americans put up 64 percent of the $2.3-billion purchase price, which was well in excess of Canada's foreign ownership limits in television. These two decisions may have contained the seeds of Canwest Global's demise, however, as the 2008 financial crash dropped advertising revenues sharply and the heavily indebted company was forced to declare bankruptcy.

Black and Asper experienced markedly different outcomes from their respective challenges to Australia's media ownership regulations, perhaps as a result of their different methods. Black engaged in political manipulation, while Asper instead challenged the country's ownership regulations legally. Their interventions were key to the media deregulation that soon visited the country. According to Australian media scholar Terry Flew, a neoliberal phase in the country's policy discourse began in 1992, which resulted in an opening up of the broadcasting market at the expense of the public interest.[64] Due to its short-term economic problems, Australia was perhaps ripe for the deregulation the Canadians urged, which was ultimately enshrined in the country's 2006 dropping of its media ownership limits. The activism of Black and Asper was undoubtedly instrumental in this change, as their strategy proved a "slippery slope" episode in the history of Australian public policy. Irony is to be found, however, in Black's 2008 incarceration and in Canwest Global's 2009 bankruptcy, which were due in large part to their dealings in other countries that ran afoul of the law and economic forces, respectively.

SIX

Convergence After the Collapse

Convergence proved a controversial concept after it was advanced in the 1990s as the inevitable future form of mass media. It sparked debate not least because many were unclear on its very meaning. To some, convergence simply meant the introduction of digital media. It was much more than that, however, entailing the displacement of old media by new. "One of the challenges of studying media convergence is that the concept is so broad that it has multiple meanings," noted media economist Michael Wirth. "As a result, the academic literature in this area is diverse and underdeveloped from both a theoretical and an empirical perspective."[1] Convergence as a metaphor was used in numerous fields, including mathematics, biology, economics, education, and political science. Even in media, the term had multiple meanings. It was used to refer to device convergence between computers, television, and telephones; to service convergence between telephone, telecommunications, and cable television; to journalistic convergence; and to ownership convergence.[2]

The notion that traditional media — print and broadcast — would in the future be delivered only online led media companies to scramble at the turn of the millenium to get in on the expected digital gold rush by diversifying into as many media as possible.

The theory was that by delivering content across multiple media, companies could increase profits by sharing content across media, by selling advertising across multiple platforms, and through the "synergy" of having one journalist cover a story for multiple outlets. If they had instead paid attention to the lessons of history, media owners would have realized that multimedia ownership had been tried before in the 1920s, when newspapers were among the first licence holders for radio. That multimedia marriage proved unworkable, as would this one.

The literature on media convergence is abundant, but most deals with organizational, managerial, and journalistic aspects while little deals with financial aspects.[3] Some scholars found evidence early on that questioned the economic viability of convergence as a business model. Scottish media researcher Gillian Doyle interviewed newspaper and television executives in the UK and found strong skepticism of the supposed cost-saving synergies of convergence. Due to fundamental differences between television and newspapers, Doyle concluded that there were no economies to be achieved and that the only special advantages of convergence were the cross-promotion of content and increased corporate size and influence.[4] Interviews with Canadian media executives found similar skepticism over the business advantages of convergence and also expressed concern over the increased conglomeration of Canada's news media.[5]

Owners of media firms worldwide, however, pushed for the reduction or even removal of national restrictions on the cross-ownership of newspapers and television stations as unnecessary and outmoded. These efforts were successful in countries such as the UK and Australia, which nonetheless put limits on consolidation by requiring diversity levels to be examined before a merger or acquisition could be approved. Critics of ownership concentration argued that allowing unrestrained cross-media ownership would further reduce the dwindling diversity of viewpoints, which would allow too much power in the hands of a shrinking number of large media corporations. Two attempts by the Bush administration in the 2000s to lift a 1975 FCC prohibition on cross-ownership in the US were thwarted after a grassroots political protest.

The financial expectations for convergence went unrealized after the bursting of the stock market "bubble" in technology stocks in the early 2000s, but that hardly slowed the push by media owners for deregulation of cross-media ownership. An even deeper recession at decade's end, however, left many multimedia companies in dire straits financially, and in a few notable cases even in bankruptcy. That cast even more serious doubt on the long-term viability of convergence as a business model for media. In Canada, a lack of restrictions on cross-media ownership made it simple for the country's media giants to embrace convergence. The unregulated convergence of Canadian media, however, resulted within a decade in small-market station closures, political intervention, and public campaigning for regulatory relief by media corporations claiming financial hardship.

The computer revolution

Convergence gained popularity as a business strategy in the 1990s as media companies sought to exploit the computer revolution that had transformed the newspaper industry in the 1970s with word processing and electronic typesetting. As radio and television companies prepared to convert their signals from analogue to digital, computerization promised to revolutionize communication once again on the internet.[6] The January 2000 merger of Time Warner and America Online seemed to show the way of the future just as the new millennium dawned. Within a few years, however, differences in corporate culture, accounting irregularities, and the bursting of the stock market bubble in technology stocks combined to make AOL–Time Warner perhaps the most disastrous merger in business history.[7] Convergence quickly fell from favour among investors as a result, and given the slow pace of device convergence (i.e., between computers, telephones, and television), some wondered if convergence was "nothing more than an over hyped illusion."[8] This led to a re-appraisal of convergence, with some media economists arguing that a viable business model would first have to be developed before expectations could be turned into profits.[9] It became obvious, however, that some of the touted financial benefits of convergence, such as cost savings from sharing staff and increased advertising revenues, had been unrealistic.[10]

Part of the problem with convergence in Canada was that many media companies had taken on high levels of debt in acquiring outlets in multiple media. With the downturn in advertising revenues that attended the early 2000s recession, some of the newly converged companies became hard pressed to pay the interest on their loans. As they grew larger, their debt ironically made these companies weaker and more vulnerable.[11]

Much of the problem with monetizing convergence was the inability of media companies to sell advertising across multiple media. Because advertisers expected a lower price for a multi-platform ad package than for advertising purchased in separate media, joint ad sales produced less revenue, not more. Due to greater competition online, advertising rates on the internet were much lower than for newspapers or TV and consequently brought in much less revenue. Multimedia sales staff thus tended not to push online ads.[12]

Publishing their content online for free also created a conundrum for media owners because it had a negative impact on sales of their legacy media products.[13] According to Gordon Pitts, another motive behind convergence in Canada was a US initiative before the World Trade Organization for removal of restrictions on foreign media ownership. The expectation was that prices for Canadian media companies would jump on a wide open market. The "kings of convergence," as Pitts called them, thus bet on political factors to increase the value of their companies and help make their wager on convergence pay off. The strategy failed when limits on foreign ownership of Canadian media were not lifted and media stock prices fell instead.[14]

The 2001 crash and recession

The disastrous AOL–Time Warner merger exemplified the plight of multimedia companies, which worsened with the bursting in

2001 of the stock market "bubble" in technology stocks. Its share price fell from a high of US$55 in mid-2001 to a low of US$8.70 in one year as the company posted a world record year-end loss of US$98.7 billion. AOL was removed from the company's name in 2003 and 5 percent of the online division was sold to Google in 2005 for US$1 billion.

In Canada, the financial fortunes of converged media giants followed a similar downward trend. Before 2001 ended, Canwest Global, which had taken on close to $4 billion in debt in acquiring the Southam newspapers, posted a quarterly loss of $37 million. Advertising sales slowed down with the recession and Canwest struggled with the cost of servicing its debt. From a high of twenty-two dollars in 2000, its share price fell below seven dollars in mid-2002. Canwest sold three of its daily newspapers in Atlantic Canada, which cut their ties with Global Television's stations in those markets. The sale suggested to some that Canwest was abandoning its convergence strategy, but CEO Leonard Asper claimed the newspapers were "not central to the company's over-all media integration strategy."[15] In October 2002, the price of Canwest shares fell to $3.32 and the company cut costs and moved to further lower its debt. In early 2003, it sold four more minor dailies and twenty-one weeklies for $193.5 million.

Quebecor encountered similar problems after its takeover of Groupe Vidéotron. It was financed in partnership with the Quebec provincial pension plan, which acquired a 45-percent interest in a new company called Quebecor Media. Quebecor took on massive short-term debt to finance its share of the all-cash acquisition, but it had been counting on the sale of non-core assets, such as Vidéotron's home telephone division and its Microcell mobile phone company, to lessen that burden. The faltering economy prevented their sale, however, and Quebecor was forced to enter the US junk bond market to raise $1.3 billion. By the end of 2000, it was an estimated $6.7 billion in debt. It sold its 11-percent holding in forestry firm Abitibi-Consolidated Inc. for $600 million to pay down that amount, and about one quarter of its subsidiary Quebecor World, the world's largest printing company, for another $500 million.[16] In September 2002, after four consecutive quarters of losses, Quebecor's debt still stood at $4 billion, however, which prompted bond rating agency Standard & Poor's to lower its rating and to place it on credit watch.[17] From a high of $61.50 before its Vidéotron purchase, Quebecor stock price bottomed out in 2002 at $12.25. By early 2003, however, Quebecor had sold more assets, paid off most of its high-interest debt, restructured other debt, and was taken off credit watch.[18] With the improving economy, it began turning a modest profit by mid-2003 and was able to pay down more debt, which stood at $1.4 billion by that fall.[19]

Unlike Canwest and Quebecor, Bell Globemedia was a privately-owned partnership that did not trade shares on the stock market. It also did not carry high levels of debt. It thus weathered the recession of the early 2000s better than its debt-laden, publicly-traded counterparts. Bell Globemedia even managed to finance a modest expansion during the downturn, paying $74 million in 2001 for Quebec television network TQS.[20] It also paid $100 million in early 2003 for a 15-percent interest in Maple Leaf Sports & Entertainment, which owned the Toronto Maple Leafs and the Toronto Raptors, as well as the cable networks that broadcast their games and the Air Canada Centre where they played.[21]

Mid-2000s: The outlook improves

With the economic recovery, the financial fortunes of all three Canadian media giants improved. Canwest recovered to the point where it began making acquisitions again. In early 2006, it bought 30 percent of the US magazine *The New Republic* for US$2.3 million and a year later bought the rest for a reported US$5 million. It bought radio stations in New Zealand and Turkey in 2006 and bid for the English-language *Jerusalem Post* newspaper in Israel. In early 2007, despite still being deeply in debt, Canwest made another major acquisition, buying thirteen Canadian cable television channels from Alliance Atlantis for $2.3 billion. The purchase was made in partnership with US investment bank Goldman Sachs, which contributed almost two-thirds of the purchase price despite Canada's foreign ownership limits, which amounted to 46.7 percent directly and indirectly through a holding company. Cultural and industry groups protested that majority American involvement in the purchase would open the door to more foreign ownership of Canadian media. The CRTC held hearings into the arrangement, under which Canwest held two-thirds of the company's voting shares, and accepted the argument that Canadians were in control.[22]

Quebecor Media's financial fortunes also turned around in the mid-2000s, and through its cable television and cellular divisions it began to expand into such areas as broadband internet and 3G wireless telephony. Its TVA network helped demonstrate the cross-promotional potential of convergence in 2003 with the hit program *Star Académie*, which was described as a cross between *American Idol* and *Big Brother*. It was heavily cross-promoted in Quebecor's French-language newspapers and its online and cable divisions. Analysts began rethinking the possibilities of convergence, at least in the unique Quebec market. "If convergence can work anywhere," noted *Toronto Star* business writer David Olive, "it should work in Quebec, a homogenous island of French-speakers in the New World where Quebecor is Number 1 in most media categories."

> *Star Académie* boosted TVA's audience share, was the launch vehicle for Vidéotron's video-on-demand service, pulled thousands of new subscribers to Vidéotron's high-speed Internet service, and yielded Quebecor-produced CDs, DVDs and books that were peddled in the company's music, books and video-rental shops.[23]

Its improved fortunes enabled Quebecor to embark on another expansion program. In 2004, it bought TV station Toronto 1 for $46 million.[24] In 2007, it won a takeover battle with Torstar for Ontario publisher Osprey Media, which owned fifty-four newspapers, including twenty dailies. When added to its Sun Media chain, the $414-million purchase made Quebecor the country's largest newspaper owner, slightly ahead of Canwest.[25]

Bell Globemedia transformed its corporate ownership during

the mid-decade economic upturn, then engineered a major media acquisition that brought renewed concern over concentration of media ownership in Canada. In late 2005, Bell Canada sold most of its majority interest in Bell Globemedia to three buyers: Thomson, the Ontario Teachers Pension Plan, and Torstar. Because Bell's ownership was reduced to 20 percent, the corporate name was changed to CTVglobemedia. In mid-2006, the company announced the acquisition for $1.4 billion of Toronto-based CHUM Ltd., which included thirty-three radio stations, a dozen television stations of the minor CITY-TV and A Channel networks, and twenty-one cable television channels.[26] That brought the number of television stations owned by CTVglobemedia to thirty-three, including multiple outlets in several major Canadian cities, and its cable television channels to thirty-eight.

The CHUM purchase came three weeks after the Senate report on news media urged limits on media ownership, and it resulted in three companies receiving more than half of the advertising revenues in Canada. Concentration of press ownership had risen to 87.4 percent by the five largest newspaper chains, while three-quarters of Canadian television stations had become concentrated in the hands of only five owners.[27] That was "too much power in too few hands in too small a country," according to *Toronto Star* media critic Antonia Zerbisias.

> It will not only create a media behemoth. . . . it will dominate the advertising, cultural, music and sports landscapes as well as the news agenda. Consider advertising. With one fewer competitor, media costs will rise and will undoubtedly be passed on to consumers.[28]

The CRTC forced CTVglobemedia to divest the five-station CITY network it had acquired from CHUM, which it sold to cable company Rogers Communication for $375 million.[29] The CRTC also held "media diversity" hearings, but the policy announcement it made in early 2008 disappointed critics of convergence and advocates of ownership reform. In limiting cross-ownership of Canadian media, the CRTC prohibited only ownership of outlets in three media—television, radio, and newspapers—in any market. Critics pointed out that because no Canadian company owned outlets in all three media, the effect of the policy was only to endorse the status quo.

The late 2000s recession

Where Canada's broadcasting regulator failed to limit media concentration in any meaningful way, the marketplace stepped in as the ultimate regulator and forced a diversification of ownership. In mid-2007, Canwest followed its contentious acquisition of Alliance Atlantis with two more moves that stock market analysts questioned. First, it paid $495 million to buy back 26 percent of its newspaper division, which it had sold just two years earlier. Analysts expected Canwest to pay for the purchase by selling its majority interest in Australia's Network TEN. Despite again being almost $4 billion in debt, however, Canwest decided not to sell when it could not get its price. CEO Leonard Asper explained the decision by claiming Canwest had no immediate need for the money. "I don't think there's any point just having it sit there in a bank in Canada," he said as Canwest announced a 36-percent drop in its third quarter earnings due to slumping ad markets. According to the *Globe and Mail*, shareholders "headed for the door" as a result, and Canwest's share price fell 10 percent in a month to below ten dollars.[30]

The recession that began in late 2007 caused advertising revenues to plummet worldwide, dropping television network profits in Canada from $113 million in 2007 to only $8 million in 2008.[31] In mid-2009, Canwest missed a number of interest payments to bond holders and its stock price sank to as low as six cents. To raise cash to meet its debt payments, Canwest put its five-station E! network up for sale.[32] It sold only two stations—CHCH in Hamilton, Ontario, and CJNT in Montreal—and only for nominal sums totaling twelve dollars, just to avoid having to close them.[33] It converted its E! network station in Kelowna, BC, to an affiliate of its main Global Television network, but it threatened to close its stations in Red Deer, Alberta, and Victoria, BC, if buyers could not be found. Only the Alberta station CHCA was closed, however, after employees of Victoria's CHEK paid Canwest a token two dollars for the station.[34] Canwest eased its debt crisis somewhat in late 2009 by finally selling its majority interest in Network TEN for only CDN$634 million.[35] The sale also erased CDN$582 million of Network TEN's debt from Canwest's books, lowering its total debt to an estimated $2.5 billion.[36] Just when it appeared that Canwest might escape bankruptcy, however, it was forced to file for court-ordered protection from its creditors, who had begun to slap it with lawsuits.[37] In early 2010, control of Canwest's television division was sold to cable company Shaw Communications of Calgary, while its newspaper division was put up for sale separately.[38] In mid-2010, it was bought by a consortium of its creditors with backing from several US hedge funds led by GoldenTree Asset Management. The former Southam newspaper chain, now on its fourth corporate owner in fifteen years, was renamed Postmedia Network Inc. after its flagship *National Post*.

CTVglobemedia also suffered financially during the downturn despite its private ownership. To lower costs to match its falling ad revenues, it eliminated 105 jobs at its broadcasting operations in 2008, including its all-news network CTV Newsnet.[39] CTVglobemedia reported a loss of $13.3 million for 2008 and forecast that its loss in 2009 would be $90-100 million. It also took a $1.7-billion accounting writedown on the book value of its television assets, which represented three-quarters of their worth.[40] In early 2009, the network announced the elimination of 118 jobs at its A Channel network, or 28 per cent of its staff, and announced the cancellation of morning shows at several of its local stations.[41] It also laid off more than two dozen employees at its national morning show Canada AM and dropped its last remaining early morning local newscast.[42] CTVglobemedia sold half of its share in Maple Leaf Sports & Entertainment to help pay down the debt it had taken on in its CHUM purchase, and it sold the other half six months later. It also sold its cable channels Drive-In Classics and SexTV to radio company Corus Entertainment for $40 million.[43] In late 2009, it was revealed that regulatory filings by publicly-traded Torstar showed CTVglobemedia had been forced to renegotiate loan agreements for its more than $1.9 billion in debt to avoid defaulting.[44]

Like Canwest Global, CTVglobemedia also threatened to close several of its money-losing television stations in smaller markets if it could not find a buyer for them or gain regulatory relief from the CRTC. In early 2009, it offered to sell stations in Brandon, Manitoba; Windsor, Ontario; and Wingham, Ontario, for one dollar each. Shaw Communications offered to meet the asking price, but it backed off after researching station finances. Brandon station CKX was tentatively sold for one dollar to another buyer, which also reneged after failing to secure carriage on Canadian satellite television systems.[45] CTV closed CKX, converted its Wingham station into a rebroadcaster of its London, Ontario A Channel station, and announced it would close its Windsor station. It granted the Windsor station a one-year reprieve, however, after the CRTC boosted annual subsidies for local programming by 50 per cent to more than $100 million.[46]

Quebecor Media, which experienced the most severe financial problems of the Canadian multimedia giants during the recession of the early 2000s, emerged from it the healthiest. Due to the company's inadvertent diversification into cable television and wireless telephony, its timely divestitures and debt reduction, it weathered the recession the best of Canada's three major converged media companies. While the CTV network reportedly lost more than $13 million and Canwest Global lost $1.8 million in 2008, Quebecor's television operations recorded earnings before interest and taxes of $33.2 million.[47] The advertising slump affected its television and newspaper properties, but Quebecor Media's telephone, broadband, and cable television divisions more than made up the shortfall with increased profitability. The company was also helped by the fact that media in Quebec did not suffer the steep advertising decline seen in other parts of Canada due to the recession.[48]

Like Canada's other converged media companies, however, Quebecor used the recession as an opportunity to trim costs. In late 2008, despite posting a $45 million quarterly profit, it laid off six hundred staff across its Sun Media division, or 10 percent of its workforce.[49] In early 2009, it locked out more than 250 workers at its *Journal de Montréal* newspaper and continued to publish with management personnel while demanding contract concessions. They included lengthening the workweek by 25 percent without additional pay, reducing benefits by 20 percent, laying off seventy-five staff, and introducing an "unlimited convergence plan." The plan would have required newsroom staff to produce content for all Quebecor media, including its Canoe (Canadian Online Explorer) websites and its television outlets.[50] The lockout lasted more than two years and only ended with capitulation by workers, more than 75 percent of whom lost their jobs.[51]

Fee for carriage

The apparent disintegration of Canadian broadcast television was played out against the backdrop of a dispute between the networks and cable companies that may in part explain the tumult of lay-offs, station sales, and closures. As CTV and Canwest Global profits fell, the networks pointed to Canada's cable companies, which were making record profits, and claimed the country's television system was "broken."[52] To fix it, the networks asked the CRTC to order the cable companies to pay them fifty cents per subscriber in a "fee for carriage" to transmit their over-the-air signals, which the cable companies had always carried for free. The regulator had turned down the request twice before, in 2007 and 2008. As the recession deepened, however, the networks applied political pressure by threatening station closures, which prompted hearings in Ottawa.[53] The cable companies claimed the networks were taking advantage of the economic downturn to exaggerate their financial problems.[54] CTV launched a "Save Local TV" advertising campaign and launched a website (savelocal.ctv.ca) to lobby for carriage fees, focusing on the threat of local station closures.[55] The cable companies responded with newspaper and television ads and a website of their own describing the proposed fee for carriage as a "TV tax" (stopthetvtax.ca) and promising to pass along to consumers any fee for carriage, which they estimated at five to ten dollars per subscriber monthly.[56]

The CRTC, however, pointed to data that showed much of the financial hardship suffered by the networks was self-inflicted. Not only had they taken on enormous debt to make acquisitions, they had spent a record $775 million on foreign (mostly US) programming in 2008, compared with $619 million on Canadian programming. Due to increased bidding between the networks, expenditures on foreign programs had increased 43 percent in five years, from $541 million in 2003. The CRTC threatened to impose a spending limit, suggesting that the networks be restricted to spending only as much on foreign content as they did on Canadian content.[57] The networks claimed they were losing viewers to cable channels and the internet, but a study showed that conventional television viewership aged 18–34 fell just 2.4 per cent between 1998 and 2007. *Globe and Mail* television critic John Doyle saw the job cuts and station closures as "part of a strategy to force a radical redrawing of the Canadian TV landscape."

> It's a matter of scaring the local and national power structure. Members of Parliament are among the first to panic when their local TV stations shrink or disappear. They are being sent a blunt message about the economics of television. And, as TV is regulated in Canada, Parliament and government have the power to do something about it. The television industry is not in crisis. The economy is in crisis.[58]

The parliamentary committee that heard arguments on fee for carriage ordered the CRTC to reconsider the matter again, and the regulator held hearings at the end of 2009. Meanwhile, the networks joined forces to launch a newspaper, radio, and television advertising campaign of their own around the theme "Local TV Matters," along with a website (localtvmatters.ca) that hosted a "viral" video.[59] CTVglobemedia threatened to close ten of its eleven stations in Ontario if the CRTC did not order fee for carriage. The networks also reframed what they were seeking to the more neutral "negotiation for value."[60] In March 2010, the CRTC ruled the networks had the right to negotiate carriage fees with common carriers.[61] By then, however, most of the networks were owned by cable and satellite companies following the purchase of Global Television by Shaw Communications.

Financial outcomes

Because they rely on advertising, which is a discretionary expense for most businesses, media companies tend to be more vulnerable to a recession than other businesses.[62] Diversification can be used as a strategy to weather the boom-bust economic cycle. It can be accomplished through expansion into businesses that are either related or unrelated. Firms that diversify into related fields tend to be more profitable, while those that diversify into unrelated areas tend to be more stable.[63] Research on the diversification strategies of media companies has found that while the search for content-sharing synergies has been largely unsuccessful, diversification into unrelated fields can help ameliorate the effects of economic downturns.[64] The *Washington Post*, for example, acquired the Kaplan educational preparation company in 1984, and it became one of the major drivers of its profits.[65] Torstar bought the Harlequin romance novel publisher in 1981.[66] Most media companies, however, tend to diversify into related enterprises, hoping to find the elusive synergies. By the end of the 2000s, however, enthusiasm for convergence had waned.[67] In late 2010, Thomson asked out of its marriage with CTV due to the irreconcilable differences that convergence brought. CTVglobemedia was renamed Bell Media to reflect its new majority ownership.

In their quest for convergence, Canada's largest private broadcasters overextended their empires, took on enormous debt, then sought government assistance when the recession dropped their revenues. More prudent debt management by Quebecor Media left it in a better position to weather the recession of the late 2000s. Its accidental diversification into the high-growth areas of cable television and wireless telephony, while intended to be short-lived, was another key to its relative health. When those assets could not be divested quickly due to the recession of the early 2000s, they ironically contributed to the firm's recovery.[68]

The perceived threat to conventional television in Canada, however, may not have been as severe as portrayed by the networks. While their profits were not as high as they had been, and in the case of Canwest were not enough to cover its loan payments, accounting methods may explain much of the apparent red ink. CTVglobemedia did suffer a loss from its conventional television operations in 2008, but according to public filings by its business partner Torstar the company turned an overall profit of 9.7 percent that year when its newspaper and cable television revenues were included. CTVglobemedia's reported $13.3 million loss for that year was mostly the result of the large accounting writedown it incurred on the book value of its conventional television assets, and the company actually recorded an operating profit of $214 million on revenues of $2.2 billion.[69]

A study by Carleton University media economist Dwayne Winseck examined the financial statements of the eight largest media companies in Canada from 1995 to 2009 and found that all were consistently profitable until the 2008 recession, when only one suffered a yearly loss. "In the end," noted Winseck, "we can conclude that there are no clear cases in which specific media sectors are 'in crisis.'"[70] Any financial problems experienced by large media companies in Canada have been transitory and related to economic downturns, he added, and as a whole the country's media sector had expanded and enjoyed above-average profits.

> Even Canwest has been profitable, sometimes extremely so, every year since 1991 in terms of operating profits and all but two years (2004 and 2008) in terms of return on equity. . . . Its profits were in the low- to mid-20% range for the last decade before falling to 16% on the eve of its demise in 2009. How is it possible for highly profitable firms to be in such disarray? The answer is debt.[71]

Annual reports for publicly-traded Canwest Global and Quebecor, as well as financial data for CTVglobemedia contained in Torstar's annual reports, show that the multimedia conglomerates weathered the recession of the late 2000s without significant financial hardship. Quebecor, in fact, saw its return on revenue (earnings as a percentage of revenue) increase steadily from 26.7 percent in 2006 to 33.7 percent in 2009 (see Table 4).

Globe and Mail business reporter Derek DeCloet noted the penchant of network executives for telling investors one story and the CRTC another. He compared Leonard Asper's forecast to investors of 10-20 percent profitability with the doom and gloom he conveyed to the regulator. "It must be so confusing to have to talk out of both sides of your mouth," quipped DeCloet, who wondered if the double talk had more to do with the fee-for-carriage fight than with the falling economy. "The broadcasters won't take no for an answer. You want proof, they say? We'll give you proof."[72] As the financial facts emerged, the conflicting versions of reality made the networks' bid for regulatory relief problematic. They cast doubt on whether the financial distress CTV and Canwest Global claimed was as serious as their public pleadings portrayed. Instead, the episode may serve to demonstrate that convergence in Canada has indeed, as its critics warned, allowed too much power over public perceptions to accumulate in the hands of too few owners, who will use it to their advantage.

TABLE 4: RETURN ON REVENUE FOR CANADIAN MULTIMEDIA CONGLOMERATES, 2006–2009

	Canwest*			CTVgm†			Quebecor		
	Rev.	Earn.	Return	Rev.	Earn.	Return	Rev.	Earn.	Return
2006	2.7b	459m	17.0%	n/a	n/a	n/a	3.0b	800m	26.7%
2007	2.8b	487m	17.1%	1.9b	286m	14.8%	3.4b	949m	28.2%
2008	3.2b	616m	19.05%	2.2b	214m	9.7%	3.7b	1.12b	30.0%
2009	2.8b	462m	16.1%	2.1b	214m	10.2%	3.8b	1.27b	33.7%

* Year ending August 31.
† Year ending November 30.

Source: Company annual reports

SEVEN

Public Benefits or Private?

One of the most well-documented and seemingly inevitable phenomena that economists have observed in government regulation is "regulatory capture."[1] According to media scholar Robert Horwitz, this occurs when a regulatory agency "*systematically* favors the private interests of regulated parties and *systematically* ignores the public interest."[2] The public interest thus becomes "perverted" as a regulator matures through several phases. "As the agency hits old age, it becomes a bureaucratic morass which, because of precedent, serves to protect its industry."[3] *National Post* media columnist Matthew Fraser used the same analogy of life stages in 2000 to explain the evolutionary process of regulatory capture. "In their infancy, regulators show youthful activism. By middle age, they have succumbed to subtle co-option by industry interests. In their final stages of bureaucratic senility, they degenerate into passive instruments of the corporate interest under their purview." By that description, Fraser added, the Canadian Radio-television and Telecommunications Commission (CRTC) provides an excellent example of regulatory capture.

It would take formidable powers of self-delusion to deny that the CRTC's evolution has followed the capture theory with alarming fidelity. Created in 1968, the commission was already slipping into complicity with industry interests by the late 1970s. A decade later, it was totally captured.[4]

The CRTC has long been criticized for failing to prevent increased concentration of media ownership in Canada, which has risen to among the world's highest levels.[5] According to the regulator, however, preventing ownership concentration was not part of its mandate. "Concentration of ownership within the broadcasting system is not itself necessarily of concern to the Commission," it explained in a landmark 1986 ruling, "provided that there continues to be an effective degree of diversity of ownership and of programming sources."[6] The ruling denied the application of Montreal-based Power Corporation to take control of Télé-Métropole, owner of the largest private French-language television station in Quebec and controlling shareholder of the TVA Network. In it, the CRTC observed that Canadian broadcasting could benefit from "larger entities with larger pools of resources."[7]

The CRTC had since the late 1970s accepted proposals from corporations looking for regulatory approval for acquisitions that included payments devoted to worthwhile projects, mostly programming initiatives aimed at boosting Canadian content. These "public benefits" payments often persuaded the CRTC to allow a transaction, despite the increased ownership concentration it brought, because the payments offset the effects of the concentration, as outlined in its 1986 ruling. "The Commission will . . . have to be satisfied that the purchaser demonstrates that the advantages of any such concentration clearly outweigh the disadvantages, and that the transaction is in the public interest."[8]

The CRTC in that case noted public concern over the fact that Power Corporation and its majority shareholder, Paul Desmarais, controlled numerous other media outlets in Quebec, including radio stations and newspapers such as Montreal's daily La Presse. In seeking approval of its $97.8-million purchase, however, Power Corporation proposed a package of benefits totaling only about 4 percent of the price. For the CRTC, that was too low, and it denied Power Corporation's application to assume Télé-Métropole's licence.

In an attempt to give its members guidance in the mysterious benefits requirement, the Canadian Association of Broadcasters (CAB) commissioned a lengthy study in 1987 that analyzed CRTC transfer decisions and reviewed its rationale for the benefits test.[9] For years, however, the CRTC never quantified the extent of payments required to gain approval of a licence transfer, leaving media owners to estimate how large a package would be sufficient. A 2007 study commissioned by the CRTC noted that in the early days of the benefits program there was a wide range of payments, depending on the applicant's perceived chances of success.

> Often if an applicant had a significant policy obstacle to overcome, such as concentration or cross-media ownership that would result from the proposed transfer, the applicant would propose a very large benefits package, hoping that the benefits package would be too attractive for the Commission to deny the application.[10]

The public benefits requirement, also known as "tangible benefits," was estimated in 2007 to have provided more than a billion dollars in payments to Canadian artists and other beneficiaries.[11] Despite that, the CRTC considered canceling the requirement due to criticism from media owners and others, but in 2008 it decided to continue the program. Since then, some of the largest takeovers in Canadian broadcasting history have resulted in the payment of hundreds of millions more in public benefits. For some, however, the system is an obvious symptom of regulatory capture and a means for media companies to "pay off" the CRTC to allow excessive levels of ownership concentration. This chapter reviews the history of CRTC benefits payments and examines one of its progeny, the Canadian Media Research Consortium, for evidence of regulatory capture.

Public Benefits

The public benefits program evolved on a case-by-case basis from its inception in the late 1970s, with only an occasional policy statement issued by the CRTC to illuminate the requirement. Its next major application after the Télé-Métropole case came in 1988 when magazine publisher Maclean Hunter paid $600 million for Selkirk Communications, a media conglomerate that owned cable systems, radio stations, and television stations. It was the largest broadcasting acquisition in Canadian history at the time, so to boost its chances of gaining CRTC approval, Maclean Hunter proposed a package of $74 million in public benefits, or 12.3 percent of the purchase price. The CRTC disallowed some of the proposed benefits payments as part of the regular cost of doing business, but it allowed the transaction to proceed.[12] It clarified matters somewhat by issuing a policy statement outlining some of the items it was prepared to accept as benefits payments, and some it wasn't. Included in the latter category were normal capital expenditures and such items as "marketing surveys and similar studies."[13]

In 1992, the CRTC commissioned an outside study of its benefits program, after which it conducted an internal review. It calculated that $317 million in benefits payments had been made since 1985, which it deemed a "reasonable" 14.8 percent of transactions worth $2.135 billion. Payments in radio totaled $58.3 million, ranged from none to 23.3 percent of purchase price, and averaged 14 percent, enough to lower the industry's operating profit margins in 1991 from 6.45 percent to 5.88 percent. In television, they had totaled $162 million, ranged from 7.3–49.9 percent of transaction value, averaged 18.4 percent, and had lowered operating margins in 1991 from 12.51 percent to 11.03 percent. In cable, the corresponding figures were $97 million, an average of 11.6 percent, a range of 2.4–37.1 percent, and a reduction in 1991 profits from 39.01 percent to 38.62 percent. In television, more than 70 percent of benefits were programming related, mainly in news and drama, while about two-thirds of benefits in cable involved capital expenditures to upgrade or consolidate systems. In radio, the CRTC's review found that benefits were more evenly distributed between improved technical facilities, enhanced programming, and talent development.[14]

The following year, the CRTC responded to complaints about falling profits in the radio industry during a recent recession by deciding to forego benefits payments for unprofitable stations. In the same public notice, the commission stated that it would "generally consider research and development initiatives as acceptable tangible benefits," but reiterated that it would not accept marketing and audience surveys.[15] In 1994, the *Globe and Mail* obtained under the Access to Information Act the confidential multi-volume study done for the CRTC in its review of the benefits system. While heavily edited, the newspaper reported that the study contained some interesting findings.

> The largest payouts have generally come from the big players in the industry and "this is true even when the properties they were acquiring were small," the document said. "Evidently, ability to pay is a key consideration."[16]

Increased concentration

The Maclean Hunter takeover of Selkirk Communications was dwarfed in 1994 when Rogers took over Maclean Hunter at a cost of $3.1 billion, or more than five times what it had paid for Selkirk. Most of Maclean Hunter's assets were in publishing and thus not subject to CRTC regulation, but it also owned $933 million in broadcasting and cable assets. These included thirty-five Ontario cable companies serving 9 percent of the national market, twenty-one radio stations in Ontario and the Maritimes, two television stations in Alberta, and 14.3 percent of CTV shares. Rogers proposed a benefits package of $94 million, but journalists pointed out that $54 million of it was earmarked for upgrading its cable infrastructure, which was an expenditure that would likely have been made anyway.[17]

Critics pointed to the degree of cross-media ownership the deal would give Rogers, including *Maclean's* magazine, the Sun newspaper chain, and the *Financial Post*, on top of its radio, television, and cable holdings. Adding Maclean Hunter's national market share in cable to the 24 percent Rogers already controlled would give it one in every three Canadian cable subscribers, noted Ian Morrison of the advocacy group Friends of Canadian Broadcasting. "In effect, Rogers would be in a position to privatize public policy and to play the role the public expects the CRTC to play of determining which channels get on the air waves."[18] Morrison had an even harsher assessment of the CRTC's benefits process, under which such media concentration could be achieved.

> It's a very bad way to conduct public policy — to set up a system where applicants are encouraged to bribe the CRTC so they can make more money, especially when they are using cable subscribers' money to make the bribe.[19]

The CRTC approved the takeover but required Rogers to sell the two Alberta television stations and the CTV shares, which together were valued at $72 million, or 7.7 percent of the regulated assets. It also required a strict separation of management and newsgathering between its newspapers and broadcast outlets, and banned Rogers executives from sitting on the editorial boards of its newly-acquired newspapers. It ruled, however, that the benefits pledged by Rogers "outweigh the concerns of interveners regarding the increased concentration of ownership and media cross-ownership." Also included in the public benefits package proposed by Rogers was $3 million in grants "directed primarily to educational institutions," which the CRTC pointed out "have been generally rejected" under the guidelines contained in its public notice earlier that year. It nonetheless allowed Rogers to make the payments.[20]

The CRTC made two major changes to the benefits system in the late 1990s. In 1996, it exempted cable companies from making benefits payments in response to competition the industry was beginning to face from direct-to-home (DTH) satellite broadcasters.[21] Then in 1998, after having long resisted placing a percentage value on required benefits payments, insisting that it considered each case individually, the CRTC finally did just that. It noted that the payments had "generally represented approximately 10% of the value of a transaction," which established that as a benchmark. The remark came in a ruling that lowered the level of payments in radio, which it set at 6 percent, due to reduced profits and the expected cost of digital upgrades.[22]

Media Research

In 2010, Ira Wagman of Carleton University succinctly articulated a common complaint of Canadian media scholars as "the problem of data." Researchers seeking hard facts must turn to Statistics Canada, he noted, but find there only undifferentiated figures lacking specifics. This dearth of facts, he argued, had led to "a state of malaise Canadian academics and their students feel working in a research terrain with so many potholes."[23] In seeking data on ownership, Monica Auer of the Forum for Research and Policy in Communications similarly lamented the lack of facts and figures and found fault with the CRTC specifically for not making more of its information available.

> The CRTC's failure to publish complete information about its ownership policies and their effects leaves the general public at a clear disadvantage relative to . . . Canada's privately owned broadcast media, whose long-established lobbyist, the Canadian Association of Broadcasters (CAB), likely has ample empirical information through its members.[24]

The convergence deals at millennium provided a fresh infusion of benefits payments, and Canadian journalism schools were among the first in line for a share of the bounty. Its takeover of CTV in 2000 cost Bell Canada Enterprises (BCE) $2.3 billion and thus required a payments package of $230 million. Of that, $2.5 million went to fund an endowed chair in convergence at Ryerson University.[25] BCE pledged another $3.5 million to fund a Canadian Media Research Consortium (CMRC) that had been established by a group of journalism schools, including those at the University of British Columbia, Ryerson University, and Université Laval. The CMRC's stated mandate was to "focus on the development of Canadian data for use in media planning."[26]

The Canadian Journalism Foundation (CJF), an industry group that hosted an annual awards banquet, was another planned affiliate of the CMRC. In May 2001, however, the *National Post* revealed that when Bell's acquisition of CTV had been before the CRTC for approval the previous year, CJF executives had written letters to the commission in support of the deal. One letter by CJF executive director Bill Wilton pointed to the "lamentable" lack of media research in Canada in endorsing the takeover.

> This benefits package is providing a long-overdue opportunity to conduct ground-breaking research into media issues in a Canadian context. The CJF is convinced that findings disseminated from this collaboration will provide not only invaluable information and material for use by the media elites and decision makers to provide improved news and public affairs programming, but will also foster an unprecedented constructive debate among the general public as to the media's role, now and in the future.[27]

That letter and one written by Peter Desbarats, in his dual capacities as the CJF's research director and the Maclean Hunter Chair of Communications Ethics at Ryerson University, were reprinted in the *National Post*. "It was partly at my insistence that the Canadian Journalism Foundation included media research in its mandate when it was formed 10 years ago," wrote Desbarats. "The Canadian Media Research Consortium would add significantly to the resources available in Canada for media research."[28] One letter to the CRTC in support of the BCE takeover of CTV that was not reprinted by the *National Post* was written on behalf of the CMRC by Fred Fletcher, who was chair of York's joint graduate program with Ryerson in Communication and Culture. Fletcher wrote to support BCE's "proposal to fund its media research and related activities as part of the benefits package in the above [licence transfer] application." The CMRC, he promised, would "put Canada on the global map in the leading-edge field of media research," would "focus on important economic, social and cultural issues," and would "produce stimulating and socially important research for public debate."[29] (See Appendix 1 on page 131.) The CJF responded quickly to the *National Post*'s reports, quitting the CMRC "to make sure that everything is on the up and up and to make sure that there is not even a possibility of a perception of conflict of interest."[30]

Convergence had been the subject of CRTC hearings in April 2001, a month before the *National Post* exposé, into the licence renewal applications of CTV and Global Television. Some consumer advocates suggested the network licences be renewed for shorter than the usual seven-year period in order to monitor the effects of convergence. The CRTC demanded that the networks erect an editorial "firewall" of separation between their television and newspaper newsrooms. Several academics, however, argued against any mandated separation between news operations and testified that convergence would be in the public interest. They included Fletcher, who was then chair of the CMRC, and Donna Logan, who was director of the School of Journalism at UBC, where the CMRC was headquartered. Desbarats appeared as part of a Canwest Global delegation but did not testify, instead publishing his thoughts on the matter in a *Globe and Mail* column that was headlined "Get out of our newsrooms"[31] (see pp. 60–61).

Two months after the hearings concluded, Canwest announced a $500,000 endowment to the School of Journalism at UBC to fund a visiting professorship and thus "assist media studies in Canada."[32] It was part of an $82-million public benefits package Canwest had promised the previous year following its acquisition of television stations owned by Vancouver-based Western International Communications, including the provincial superstation BCTV.[33] By then the CMRC was already up and running with $3.5 million in funding after the CRTC approved BCE's takeover of CTV in December 2000.[34]

CMRC research

The first major study conducted by the CMRC was titled "A report card on the Canadian media," and was released in 2004. More than 3,000 Canadians were surveyed in late 2003 by professional pollsters (not by students) on their news consumption habits and on the credibility of news. In releasing the study's findings at the Banff Film Festival, Logan attributed the study's "disturbing" findings on news media credibility to groups other than media owners, whose editorial interventions had recently prompted a Senate inquiry into Canada's news media. "I think the media has to do a much better job of demonstrating its independence," said Logan. "Canadians . . . feel that reporters are influenced by government officials, by bureaucrats, by powerful groups and people with money."[35] She told the Senate news media hearings the following year, when they took a field trip to her school, that the study showed Canadians were "quite cynical" about the news. "A surprising number of Canadians do not think the news is impartial," she said. "Almost 80 per cent of Canadians think that reporter's bias influences news often or sometimes. The finding of reporter bias is very similar to results in the United States."[36]

The international comparison, however, was a case of apples and oranges. The US survey had asked whether "news organizations" were politically biased in their reporting. The CMRC survey question instead attributed any possible bias to individual journalists, asking: "How often do you think reporters let their own political preferences influence the way they report the news?"[37] When I queried him on this, CMRC chair Fred Fletcher explained that "identical or functionally equivalent questions would have been preferable for some purposes but when you are working with two surveys you must take what you can get." Another question in the report card survey focused on the behaviour of news organizations and asked: "In general, do you think news organizations are mostly independent, or are they often influenced by powerful people and organizations?" Answers to that question showed that 76 percent of Canadians felt their news media were not independent, compared to 70 percent of Americans.[38] A follow-up question asked: "Apart from journalists and editors, what outside groups, if any, do you think influence the news?" The wording of the question was open-ended, so as to not suggest any answers. "It is noteworthy that here only 12 per cent mentioned media ownership," UBC faculty member Mary Lynn Young pointed out to the visiting senators.[39] The way the question was phrased, however, inquiring about "outside groups," may have influenced the low percentage naming media ownership, which might more reasonably be considered an "inside" influence.

The CMRC's report card was criticized by this author as a survey that "would be valuable most of all to media outlets, their owners, and marketers." I characterized the CMRC in my 2007 book *Asper Nation* as a corporate creation designed to advocate for private interests over those of the public. "The study . . . fulfilled the CMRC's stated mandate to 'focus on the development of Canadian data for use in media planning,'" I noted. "It did not, however, ease the shortage of 'historical perspective and reliable data' from which Desbarats noted debate about media in Canada had long suffered."[40]

The Credibility Gap

The CMRC then conducted several studies of internet usage among Canadians. "Canada online!" was a comparative analysis of internet users and non-users in Canada and other countries that was based on telephone interviews with 3,014 adults (age 18+) conducted in 2004. The research was replicated three years later for "Canada online revisited," which was based on telephone interviews of 3,037 youth (age 12–17) and adults.[41] Another internet study, "Online Canadians and News," was based on an online survey of one thousand respondents. It found that the average "online Canadian" adult spent 2.3 hours per day consuming news and information and got 24 percent of it from television. Another 22 percent came from each of the Internet and newspapers. The internet was found to be the most important source for younger Canadians (age 18–29), accounting for 32 percent of their total time spent consuming news and information.[42] In 2008, the *Canadian Journal of Communication* published a literature review the CMRC had commissioned in an attempt to "place CMRC reports in the context of published Canadian and international media research." It found that Canadian scholarly references comprised only 2–3 percent of peer-reviewed published sources in three key areas of media research. The study also interviewed thirty-four subjects for their perceptions of Canadian media research. Interviewees fell into four categories: media executives and consultants (fourteen), public opinion researchers (eight), academics (seven), and government appointees (five). They identified five areas of research need: 1) changing media usage in a digital era; 2) media ownership and consolidation; 3) new media forms; 4) media and diversity; and 5) media policy.[43]

Four years after issuing its controversial report card, the CMRC conducted a replication of the research that found "significant, largely negative" changes in the relationship between Canadians and their news media. "The Credibility Gap" was based on telephone interviews with 2,011 adults (age 19+) conducted in February 2008. It found two main problems for media outlets—declining interest and increasing cynicism among audience members, whom it described as "very sophisticated and fussy." On the other hand, it found among young Canadians "increasing engagement and novel news habits," which it concluded offered "perhaps the greatest hope for conventional media in the future of news." On the subject of political bias, the controversial 2004 question was rephrased from inquiring about reporters to ask: "Would you say that news organizations are politically biased in their reporting?" A majority (53 percent) answered in the affirmative, compared to 60 percent of Americans asked the same question three years earlier. Another new question asked respondents if they agreed that journalists were able to report the news "freely, without interference from owners," to which only 37 percent answered in the affirmative. That compared to 45 percent of Britons, 38 percent of Americans, and 33 percent of Germans asked the same question in 2006.[44]

The CMRC's 2008 internet studies were combined into a report that was released at an invitation-only "Future of News Summit" held in Toronto in 2009. Also included in the report was research into the quality of journalism in Quebec and some economic data gathered by a Winnipeg media consultant. Missing, however, was any mention of the "credibility gap" research.[45] By the time the "summit" of media executives, bureaucrats, and academics was held, after all, the picture had changed considerably both for Canadian media and for the CMRC. An economic downturn the previous year had dropped advertising revenues sharply and Canwest, which was highly-leveraged with debt, neared bankruptcy after missing several loan payments. Both Canwest and CTV threatened to close several of their television stations in smaller markets if the CRTC did not provide regulatory relief.[46]

The outlook was also uncertain for the CMRC because its seven-year benefits grant had lapsed a year earlier. The CMRC sought a continuation of its funding from the benefits flowing from CTVglobemedia's $1.4-billion purchase of CHUM Ltd. in 2007. Instead of going through the acquiring corporation to seek inclusion in its public benefits proposal, however, the CMRC approached the CRTC directly. It asked the regulator to earmark a minimum level of funding for its research from future public benefits payments "so that researchers would not have to seek corporate support on a case-by-case basis, as is now standard procedure."

> Under the current policy, funding for research depends on the goodwill of corporations [and] creates doubts in the minds of some about the independence of researchers whose funding is associated with a particular transaction. . . . Some could see our involvement in the matter as support for the transaction and a favourable stance on media concentration.[47]

The CRTC denied the request.[48] The CMRC continued to operate, according to its 2008-09 annual report, "using the remaining funds from the original grant, and seeking new resources from the original donor and other sources."[49] In 2011, it released the results of two final surveys of internet usage by Canadians. One found that the vast majority were unwilling to pay for online news.[50] The other found that of all available media, Canadians would be least prepared to give up home internet service.[51]

The fate of public benefits

The CRTC's benefits program came in for considerable criticism over its first few decades. Broadcasters questioned its fairness and relevance and characterized it as a tax. Catherine Murray of Simon Fraser University criticized the program as "unwieldy, secret, and subject to the whim of the private broadcasters' largesse," and pointed out that "there are no systems to monitor the performance of the public benefits."[52] University of Windsor economist Peter Townley studied the program and found it "anti-competitive" and "costly to the Canadian economy" because broadcasters were able to pass along the cost of benefits payments to advertisers through the market power they acquired. Advertisers in turn passed the cost along to consumers in the form of higher prices for their goods and services. "As Canadians ultimately bear the burden of this levy in a variety of markets," concluded Townley, "an obvious alternative to the CRTC's arrangement would be to use general tax revenues to fund the same objectives and not to allow the acquisition of market power." Greater economic efficiency would be created, he added, through the increased competition allowed by preventing ownership concentration. "A better policy prescription would be to remove the reason for the CRTC to levy its tax and to leave competition matters to the Competition Bureau."[53] A pair of communication lawyers retained to review the CRTC's regulatory framework in 2007 found that the benefits program was "uneven in its scope and application, and produces somewhat quixotic results."[54]

As a result of falling profits in small markets, the CRTC decided in 2007 to eliminate benefits payments for the transfer of television licences for stations with less than $10 million in annual revenues.[55] However, it decided as part of its "Diversity of voices" review the following year to continue the benefits program in the public interest. "The benefits policy makes it possible for the market to govern changes in effective control of broadcasting licences while simultaneously ensuring that the public interest is still served."[56] In its annual monitoring report for 2010, the CRTC calculated the value of benefits payments in radio at $205.3 million from 1998 to 2009, and in television at $860 million from 1999 to 2009, for a total of $1.065 billion.[57]

Canwest was forced to declare bankruptcy in 2009 due to its high debt load, which remained from its 2000 acquisition of Southam and was increased by its controversial 2007 acquisition, in partnership with US investment bank Goldman Sachs, of cable channels owned by Alliance Atlantis. As part of that purchase, Canwest had also been required to pay benefits of $151 million. Canwest's television and newspaper divisions were sold off separately out of bankruptcy starting the following year, beginning a process of "de-convergence" a decade after convergence first visited Canadian media.[58] Its Global Television network was bought by cable company Shaw Communications, which the CRTC allowed to pay a discounted rate of 5 percent in public benefits on some Global assets that it found to be in financial distress.[59] Later that year, BCE bought the 85 percent of CTV it did not already own, de-converging that network from the *Globe and Mail*. BCE argued that it should not have to pay benefits on that deal because it had already done so as part of its original purchase of CTV in 2000 before selling most of CTVglobemedia in 2005. The CRTC rejected that argument and a subsequent one that BCE should be allowed to pay a discounted rate on of some of CTV's assets, as Shaw had, due to their financial distress. The CRTC found that the CTV assets were not distressed and required BCE to pay benefits at the regular rates of 6 percent in radio and 10 percent in television, which totaled $245 million.[60]

In 2012, BCE agreed to pay $3.4 billion for Montreal-based Astral Media and its 85 radio stations, twenty-four cable television channels and two CBC television affiliates.[61] In a surprise move, however, the CRTC denied the application after several other networks objected and some campaigned against it. The CRTC calculated the acquisition would give Bell 42.7 percent of English-language television viewership and ruled that concerns over concentration were not outweighed by the proposed benefits package.[62] The ruling was seen as a victory for consumers, but it turned out to be fleeting. Within a month, after appealing to the federal Cabinet, Bell and Astral re-worked the deal slightly and Bell launched a publicity campaign to promote it, including on social media. It promised to divest a dozen television stations to bring its English-language audience share to 35.7 percent, and to also sell ten radio stations. It proposed a public benefits package worth $174.6 million, 85 percent of which would be "on-screen initiatives." This "second-kick-at-the-can strategy" was "highly unusual," noted Dwayne Winseck of Carleton University. "To the best of my knowledge, nothing like this has ever been done before."[63] The Competition Bureau passed it, however, and the CRTC held a second set of hearings in May 2013. It approved the deal the following month, but not before setting its value at $4.1 billion and insisting on $72 million more from Bell in public benefits payments, bringing the total package to $246.9 million.[64] This made it the largest in history, ahead of two previous Bell packages (see Table 5).

TABLE 5: LARGEST BROADCASTING BENEFITS PACKAGES
SINCE 2000 ($ *millions*)

Buyer	Purchased	Year	Media	Price	Benefits
Bell	Astral	2013	radio, TV	4,100	247
Bell	CTV	2011	radio, TV	2,680	239
Bell	CTV	2000	TV	2,300	230
Shaw	Global	2010	TV	2,047	180
Canwest	Alliance Atlantis	2007	TV	1,512	151
CTV	CHUM	2007	radio, TV	1,700	147
Canwest	WIC	2000	TV	692	82.3
Quebecor	TVA	2001	TV	489	48.9
Rogers	CITY-TV	2007	TV	375	37.5
CTV	TSN	2000	TV	352	35.2

Source: CRTC public notices

Market research

The administrative-critical dichotomy in media research was first drawn by media research pioneer Paul Lazarsfeld in 1941 after a fruitless wartime collaboration with members of the exiled Frankfurt School of critical media scholars from Germany.[65] Administrative researchers who used mostly survey methods usually failed to

consider "crucial issues of institutional structure and power relations," noted William Melody and Robin Mansell of Simon Fraser
University, yet many critical theorists were equally at fault. "For
most administrative research, the existing power structure can
do no wrong; for most critical research, it can do no right."[66] Both
sides, they noted, tended to spend "insufficient effort examining
the specific structural relations of the relevant institutions involved
in a particular research problem." Institutions, they pointed out,
were "not about to knowingly finance research into matters that
could undermine their power." They thus urged policy researchers
to "examine the structure of power relations, if for no other reason
than to know what vested interests are subtly nurturing research
in what directions to achieve what ends."[67] Dallas Smythe and Tran
Van Dinh of Temple University then added another dimension to
the debate.

> We suggest that a third factor is also involved—the ideological orien-
> tation of the researcher. All of us have our predispositions, either to
> criticize and try to change the existing political-economic order, or to
> defend and strengthen it. The frequent pretense of scientific "neutral-
> ity" on this score is a delusion.[68]

Donna Logan made no secret of her ideological opposition to
critics of media ownership concentration. She regularly downplayed the high level of media ownership concentration in Vancouver, where from 2000 until its breakup in 2010 Canwest
owned both English-language daily newspapers, the dominant
television station, and almost all of the non-daily newspapers. In
a 2000 letter to the CRTC supporting the license renewal of CTV
following its merger with the *Globe and Mail*, she dismissed concentration concerns in no uncertain terms. (See Appendix 2 on
pages 132–133.)

> I am particularly concerned by questions that have been raised by the
> Commission with respect to a potential reduction in diversity of edi-
> torial voices arising from media cross-ownership. . . . The claim that
> media mergers result in fewer voices is largely a myth perpetrated by
> the critics of joint ownership.[69]

The integrity of research

As Robert McChesney of the University of Illinois noted in his 2007 book *Communication Revolution*, "when push comes to shove, the integrity of research cannot be determined by who pays for it." The most important barrier preventing the field from embracing a turn to more critical research, he pointed out, was "the wealth and influence" of the corporate sector. "University administrators look to this sector to bankroll their communication programs to the greatest extent possible and will hardly be enthusiastic toward an approach that effectively lessens that possibility," noted McChesney. "Corporate interests are eager to encourage research that supports their agenda."[70]

While public benefits were intended in part to offset the deleterious effects of increased media ownership concentration, the program obviously fell victim to the CRTC's regulatory capture by Canadian broadcasters. As Townley pointed out, the *quid pro quo* of public benefits payments is that "in return, the CRTC accommodates and protects the exercise of market power in . . . advertising markets."[71] The ability of buyers to pass down the cost of benefits payments to consumers, which results in the public paying for them in the long run, enables the shell game of regulatory capture. "Obviously, no . . . station owner would be willing to pay this levy unless it could be recouped from advertisers. Indeed, the excess profits earned on these licences may be many times the . . . levy." Townley concluded that because media owners "can accrue market power by paying [for] it, this is a case of regulatory capture — regulation is for the regulated."[72]

In its 2008 Credibility Gap study, the CMRC reported what it saw as a change in public perceptions of media in Canada since its 2004 Report Card. The original findings, it admitted, had been counter-intuitive. "The relationship between Canadians and their news media wasn't as bad as we thought. Canadians . . . were slightly more positive in general than Americans around key measures of media credibility."[73] Rather than detecting a "significant, largely negative" change in public opinion, however, the credibility gap research likely only just began to measure the level of distrust many Canadians harboured for their news media. Perhaps in response to criticism of its flawed Report Card on Canadian news media, its 2008 survey questions were more comparable to those asked in other countries. As a result, the results tended to be less exculpatory of media ownership.

The CMRC was an obvious example of the CRTC's regulatory capture, illustrating perfectly the type of middle-aged "co-option by industry interests," or even old-aged "bureaucratic senility" described by Fraser. More seriously from a regulatory standpoint, as an agency that specialized in marketing surveys and audience studies, it resulted in an "end run" being made around the CRTC's proscription against the use of public benefits payments for those purposes. It may well have provided Wilton's promised "invaluable information and material for use by the media elites and decision makers." Its administrative focus and lack of critical inquiry, however, prevented it from delivering his promised "ground-breaking research into media issues" that would "foster an unprecedented constructive debate among the general public as to the media's role, now and in the future." Nor did it, as Fletcher promised, "focus on important economic, social and cultural issues," and "produce stimulating and socially important research for public debate." For that, a more critical focus would be required, along with a more arm's-length approach to public benefits funding.

APPENDIX 1

CANADIAN MEDIA RESEARCH CONSORTIUM
CONSORTIUM CANADIEN DE RECHERCHE SUR LES MÉDIAS
UNIVERSITY OF BRITISH COLUMBIA
6388 Crescent Road
Vancouver, BC, Canada V6T 1Z2

Directors

Fred Fletcher
York-Ryerson
Graduate Program
in Communication
and Culture

Florian Sauvageau
Centre d'études
sur les Média
Université de Laval

Donna Logan
The School of
Journalism
University of
British Columbia

Bill Wilton
Canadian
Journalism
Foundation

Michael Cobden
University of
King's College

August 23, 2000

Ursula Menke
Secretary General
CRTC
Ottawa, ON
K1A 0N2

Dear Mrs. Menke:

Re: BCE Acquisition of CTV – Application – 2000 – 15497

The Directors listed on this letterhead represent the newly-formed Canadian Research Media Consortium. We are writing in support of BCE-CTV's proposal to fund its media research and related activities as part of the benefits package in the above application.

The Canadian Media Research Consortium will put Canada on the global map in the leading-edge field of media research. It is a timely initiative aimed at establishing a collaborative network with an integrated pan-Canadian strategy towards research, scholarly training and dissemination. The Consortium's work will promote open discussion, improve the quality of media and journalism, and provide current, topical and useful information to media industry players, policymakers and the Canadian public.

The creation of the Consortium responds to a strong need for concerted media research in Canada. While the technological possibilities of media are rapidly evolving, there is a corollary need for experts and specialists to track and analyse these changes and study the dynamic of their commercial, industrial, social and cultural dimensions.

BCE-CTV's support of the Research Consortium is timely because it will be difficult to finance otherwise. Similar types of media research structures have been established with great success in the United States, where there is a long tradition of research foundations, endowed centres of media scholarship and academic networks working on collaborative projects. Notable examples in the U.S. are the Poynter Institute, Freedom Forum and Harvard's Shorenstein-Baronne Centre. In Canada, while there has been a slight increase in media research in recent years, there are still no major centres or well-developed networks undertaking collaborative research in the area of media and communications. Much of the media research in Canada today is insufficiently multi-disciplinary.

The Consortium would undertake research in media and communication with particular focus on important economic, social and cultural issues related to technological change in media. The work would put particular emphasis on dissemination, i.e. the need to produce stimulating and socially important research for public debate. This will be accomplished through the Internet, lectures, television specials and conferences.

The Directors of the Consortium believe very strongly that Canadian media would benefit greatly from such discourse at this time. Prof. Sauvageau, Prof. Logan and myself would very much like to appear before you to further explain the proposed work of the Consortium and its importance to the industry and the Canadian public.

Yours sincerely,

Fred Fletcher
Professor, Political Science and in Environmental Studies
Director, Joint Graduate Programme in Communication and Culture
York University
C: James Macdonald, BCE Media Inc.
     Trina McQueen, CTV

Telephone: (604)822-6688 Facsimile: (604)822-6707

APPENDIX 2

THE UNIVERSITY OF BRITISH COLUMBIA

THE SCHOOL OF JOURNALISM
Sing Tao Building
6388 Crescent Road
Vancouver, BC, Canada V6T 1Z2
Tel: (604)822-6688
Fax: (604)822-6707
E-mail: journal@interchange.ubc.ca
http://www.journalism.ubc.ca

March 22, 2001

Ms. Ursula Menke
Secretary General
Canadian Radio-television and
  Telecommunications Commission
Ottawa, Ontario
K1A 0N2

Via Facsimile: (819)994-0218 and E-mail

Dear Ms. Menke:

Re: **CTV Television Inc. Station Group Licence Renewal**
      Application #2000-2236-9

I am writing in support of the above-mentioned application.

I am particularly concerned by questions that have been raised by the Commission with respect to a potential reduction in diversity of editorial voices arising from media cross-ownership.

While is it understandable that the commission might wish to discuss this matter, the suggestion that restrictions on co-operation and sharing should be imposed as a condition of licence is disturbing. Not only would it nullify the benefits of joint ownership but it would impose limits on freedom of speech that are clearly unacceptable in a democratic society such as ours.

The claim that media mergers result in fewer voices is largely a myth perpetrated by the critics of joint ownership. In a technological age where media choices are proliferating at an unprecedented rate, through the Internet, cable and regional news specialty channels, it is ludicrous to suggest that there are fewer voices. The landscape is changing, to be sure, but the viewer is better served, not worse.

An eminent media scholar, Roger Fidler, said in his recent book, *Mediamorphosis*, that "common assumptions that the present convergence will lead to fewer forms of communication...are not supported by historic evidence. Everett Rogers and other media scholars have clearly shown that the history of communication is the story of more."

The CRTC already has the authority to hear complaints from the public on journalistic fairness and to make determination on those complaints. It seems clear that further regulation of viewpoints would be a serious infringement on freedom of speech among journalists and journalistic organizations.

I have read the TQS code that is intended to deal with some of the issues raised by media convergence. While the code may or may not be appropriate to the particular circumstances of the companies and the areas served, it is certainly extremely rigid and severe. I believe that it inhibits, rather than encourages good journalism. In any case, given the competitive nature of the English-Canadian journalistic situation, it is clearly beyond anything needed in the licence renewals before you.

Because of the importance of this issue, I would very much like to appear before you to further explain why this sensitive matter must be given careful consideration.

I look forward to hearing favorably from you.

Yours sincerely,

Donna Logan
Director, The School of Journalism
Professor, University of British Columbia

cc: Ms. Trina McQueen, President and C.E.O.
        CTV Inc.
        9 Channel Nine Court
        P.O. Box 9, Station "O"
        Scarborough, Ontario M1S 4B5
        Via Facsimile and Courier: (416)332-5065 and DHL

EIGHT

The Competition Bureau and Journalism's Crisis

If you're looking for a villain to blame for the sorry state of Canadian journalism, look no further than the federal Competition Bureau. It is knee-deep in complicity, particularly for its 2015 rubber stamping (without even holding hearings) of Postmedia Network's purchase of 175 Sun Media newspapers. This was effectively the takeover of the country's second-largest newspaper chain by its largest (seller Quebecor retained three French-language tabloids), yet it was adjudicated in secret by the Competition Bureau. Not only that, but after it announced that its economic analysis absurdly concluded the newspapers in Calgary, Edmonton, and Ottawa didn't compete anyway, the Competition Bureau refused my request for a copy of this taxpayer-funded research.

Once it got the green light for its takeover, Postmedia's announcement in early 2016 that it was merging the newsrooms of its newspapers in those cities was predictable. The shocker is that it would try to do the same thing in Vancouver. When the *Vancouver Sun* and the *Daily Province* formed a partnership in 1957, the Competition Bureau's predecessor, the Restrictive Trade Practices Commission, held hearings both in Ottawa and Vancouver. After declaring the merger an illegal combination between competitors, the Commission buckled to arguments that neither paper might survive without the partnership. It allowed it to go forward, on conditions including that the two newspapers maintain separate newsrooms.

A 2006 Senate report on Canadian news media was sharply critical of the Competition Bureau, which succeeded the RTPC in the mid-1980s, for failing to prevent our stratospheric level of press ownership concentration. It accused the Competition Bureau of nothing short of "neglect" for failing to halt press consolidation. "One challenge is the complete absence of a review mechanism to consider the public interest in news media mergers," it noted. "The result has been extremely high levels of news media concentration in particular cities or regions." Concentration of ownership, the report noted, had "reached levels that few other countries would consider acceptable."[1]

Canada was "unique among developed countries," the 2006 Senate report noted, in not having a forum where mergers of news media organizations could be openly addressed. The way the Competition Bureau and CRTC were set up, it argued, actually inhibited discussion of the public interest in news media mergers. It recommended a new section for the Competition Act to deal with news media mergers and prevent dominance in any market. As the Competition Bureau was unlikely to have the expertise to deal with the public interest in such mergers, it recommended an expert panel conduct the review. It urged limiting media concentration the way some other countries do, by applying a local news "diversity" test in deciding whether to allow a change in ownership. Election of an ardently deregulationist Harper government that year, however, doomed the recommendations.

Postmedia CEO Paul Godfrey argued that taking over Sun Media was necessary for it to compete with Facebook, Google, and other websites that had siphoned off most advertising revenues. In addition to Postmedia's website Canada.com, the deal gave it Sun Media's canoe.ca website, but they were puny Davids against a brace of online Goliaths. They weren't even in the same business.

Google is an online search engine and Facebook is a social network. The only connection they had with Postmedia was that they all made money mostly off advertising.

Postmedia's business was newspapers, and if it really sought to instead become a digital giant, rather than simply dominating newspapers, it was likely on a fool's errand. By adding Sun Media, its share of daily newspaper circulation in Canada rose to 37.6 percent, by my calculations. Even more daunting was its control of the newspaper business in Western Canada, where it reached a 75.4 percent share of circulation in the three westernmost provinces, owning nine of the eleven largest dailies. Newspapers still trade on the perception that new media are killing them. Sure, their revenues have gone down significantly, requiring them to downsize, but they have done so successfully. As I document in my 2014 book *Greatly Exaggerated: The Myth of the Death of Newspapers*, they are still making double-digit profit margins. Even as it was pleading poverty in acquiring Sun Media, its financial statement for the three months ending November 30, 2015 showed Postmedia made a healthy 16.9 percent return on revenue, with earnings of $42.5 million on revenues of $251 million.

The new Trudeau government now has the opportunity to halt the madness. Or it can sit back and watch as one corporation, which is mostly owned by rapacious US hedge funds (in flagrant violation of foreign ownership limits on Canadian media), consolidates almost all of the country's remaining press competition.

NINE

Can Canada's Media Be Fixed?

Remember the nasty shooting war that broke out between Canada's TV networks and cable companies during the recent recession? The networks claimed they were losing money, threatened to shut down money-losing stations, and bombarded viewers with commercials braying "Local TV matters." They claimed to be in dire financial straits and asked Ottawa to force the carriage companies, which were making lush profits despite the economic downturn, to pay them fifty cents per subscriber to rebroadcast over-the-air programs the cable and satellite providers had always carried for free. The cable and satellite companies fired back by threatening to pass along any re-transmission fees to their subscribers and running their own commercials braying "Stop the TV tax." When federal hearings looked into the supposed financial plight of the networks, however, it turned out they were actually still making healthy profits, just not as healthy as before and not nearly as rich as the unregulated cablecos. They were just looking for a bit of wealth re-distribution. In the end, the networks got the right to negotiate what they called "fee for carriage," but in a dramatic reversal of fortune they had all by then been, or were about to be, gobbled up by those very same carriage companies. The Rogers cable conglomerate bought the CITY network in 2007. Shaw cable bought the Global Television network out of bankruptcy in 2010. Bell Canada, which includes satellite television transmission in its vast media holdings, re-acquired a controlling interest in CTV later that year.

These were the death throes of convergence, the media experiment that visited the world at the millennium and found its greatest foothold in Canada, because ours was one of the few countries without limits on television and newspaper companies going into business together. The theory was that all media were converging into one digital medium, but that didn't happen and won't. Global TV's owner, Canwest Global Communications, collapsed under the weight of the debt it incurred buying the country's largest newspaper chain and other media properties. Its television and newspaper assets were sold off separately out of bankruptcy. Quebecor retreated back to a provincial media empire in 2014 when it sold Sun Media, the country's second-largest newspaper chain. So hare-brained was the partnership between newspapers and television that CTV and the *Globe and Mail* voluntarily dissolved their ten-year marriage in 2010, joining a worldwide trend to deconvergence of media.

We are now dealing with the consequences of convergence and picking up the pieces of a media system that has been battered by technological change, regulatory neglect (as the 2006 Senate report on news media termed it), and no small amount of ownership connivance. As a result, we now have levels of ownership concentration and vertical integration — carriage companies owning television networks — that are among the highest in the world. The same few media conglomerates also own most of Canada's radio stations, mobile phone companies, and lucrative internet service providers. The country's largest newspaper chain is mostly owned by US hedge funds, which won the company by buying up distressed Canwest debt for pennies on the dollar. The Harper government turned a blind eye to that flagrant end run around Canada's foreign ownership limits and also presided over the Competition Bureau's rubber-stamping of Postmedia's 2014 purchase of Sun Media.

As a result we have a decimated news media in Canada. An increasing amount of the content found in newspapers and online news media nowadays is not journalism at all but instead "sponsored" content (also known as "native" advertising) disguised as news. Postmedia now owns fifteen of the twenty-one largest English-language newspapers in Canada, including eight of the nine largest in the three westernmost provinces. One could argue that much of their content is thinly-disguised propaganda for one cause or another. BC premier Christy Clark was surprisingly re-elected in 2013 after a front-page ad disguised as a news story in Quebecor's Vancouver commuter tabloid *24 Hours* enthusiastically declared her the "Comeback Kid" two weeks before the election for performing well in a debate. Postmedia ordered its editors to endorse the Harper Conservatives for re-election last fall and subjected readers of several of its dailies to full-page ads on their covers, mere days before the election, warning that voting Liberal would "cost" them. In the end, such naked partisanship may have worked against Harper's re-election. It has certainly worked against Postmedia's reputation, which may never recover.

The remaining chickens of Canada's lax media ownership laws came home to roost in early 2016, when Postmedia announced it would merge the newsrooms of its duplicate dailies in Vancouver, Calgary, Edmonton, and Ottawa. That prompted Parliamentary hearings to seek a solution to the country's crisis in local news coverage, which has been ravaged by mergers, layoffs, and cutbacks by media companies that are again pleading poverty due to plunging ad revenues and heavy debt. But can the country's broken media system even be fixed? An old saying about a horse and a barn would seem to apply here, but with a bit of foresight the evolving media ecosystem could perhaps be nursed back to some semblance of health. It is likely our last best chance to fix Canada's media.

This time it's different

The tragedy of media ownership reform in Canada is that untimely changes in government have thwarted its best opportunities. The

1981 Royal Commission on Newspapers was soon followed by a change in government. By the time the Senate committee that began examining Canada's news media in 2003 issued its report in 2006, the Conservatives had already been elected with a minority government. This time it's different. Instead of heading out of office, the Liberals are just coming in after a decade away. Vancouver MP Hedy Fry promptly convened Heritage Ministry hearings on local news in February 2016, which planned to tour Canada in the fall. A majority Liberal government with a strong mandate to reverse course from Harper's malign deregulationism has an opportunity to re-landscape Canada's media. But the horse is still out of the barn. Can it be reined back in, or would measures to boost the country's emerging digital news media show more foresight? Wise policy moves now might help return Canada's news media to something more resembling the public service journalism idealized in democratic theory. For that to happen, however, higher levels of competition and ownership diversity will somehow have to be arranged. To that end, it would be helpful to rectify past mistakes and avoid repeating them.

Regulatory "neglect"

As the 2006 Senate report on news media pointed out, much of the blame for Canada's media mess can be laid at the feet of two federal regulatory agencies. The CRTC's "public benefits" payments allow the country's few big media conglomerates to basically bribe their way to ever greater corpulence. It has allowed big players like Rogers and Bell to establish dominant market positions as long as they are willing to make sometimes enormous public benefits payments, such as the $230 million that Bell promised in order to secure its $2.3 billion purchase of CTV in 2000. These payments usually went towards the production of Canadian content, but increasingly they ended up in higher education, as when the CTV takeover in 2000 resulted in $3.5 million in funding for a Canadian Media Research Consortium set up by several journalism schools (as discussed in Chapter 7). Ryerson

University had several endowed chairs named after corporations such as Bell and Rogers as a result of their takeover payments (including a Maclean–Hunter Chair for Communications Ethics). Both Western University (as the University of Western Ontario is now known) and UBC are stained by fellowships named after Canwest Global Communications, which also no longer even exists. UBC's graduate school of journalism is housed in the Sing Tao Building, which is named after the Hong Kong newspaper company that founded it. Perhaps not coincidentally, academics seemingly fell all over each other to testify to the benefits that corporate convergence would bring to Canadian journalism at CRTC hearings in 2001.

The Competition Bureau has arguably been even more derelict than the CRTC in its duty to guard against media monopolies. The 2006 Senate report on news media deemed the Competition Bureau a failure when it came to media industry mergers and take-overs because it considers only advertising revenues, not the information needs of Canadians. "The Competition Bureau's operating procedures may be well suited to analysing most markets for goods and services in Canada," it concluded, "but not the news media market." It proposed changes to the Competition Act to deal with media transactions differently, but once again, a change of government, this time to Harper's deregulationist regime, doomed its recommendations.

A measure of the Competition Bureau's negligence is that it failed to even hold hearings into Postmedia's 2014 purchase of Sun Media, investigating it in secret and refusing to release its market analysis. (Believe me, I've asked.) It absurdly concluded that Postmedia being allowed to own both daily newspapers in Calgary, Edmonton, and Ottawa wouldn't harm consumers or even advertisers there because those newspapers didn't compete anyway. It is hard to resist the conclusion that both the Competition Bureau and the CRTC have fallen victim to the well-documented phenomenon of "regulatory capture," acting not in the public interest but instead in the interests of the corporations they regulate.

The Black plague

Canadian journalism, of course, was set on its course to banana republic status in large part by Conrad Black. He engineered a hostile takeover of the historic family-owned Southam newspaper chain in the mid-1990s before renouncing his citizenship in 2000 to take a seat in the UK House of Lords. (Thence to trial for fraud in Chicago and to prison for several years in Florida.) By then head of the third-largest press empire in the world, Black brought a level of political partisanship to Canadian news media that had not been seen since the "party press" era of the nineteenth century. He abhorred the "soft liberal" journalism he felt marked much of Canada's news media and sought to imbue it instead with the hard-headed neo-conservatism he pushed in his newspapers in the US, the UK, and Israel. He founded the *National Post* in 1998 with the expressed intent, as emblazoned on its first front page, to "unite the right" of Canada's fractured conservatives parties. The resulting rightward turn taken by much of the country's news media not only coalesced the country's conservatives, it arguably enabled the Harper decade. Soon neo-conservative politics and neo-liberal economic prescriptions filled the pages of not just the *National Post* but also the once-progressive Southam dailies. The sea change was perhaps most noticeable from the outside. "Your media are not representative of your people, your values," Lawrence Martin reported a European diplomat telling him in a 2003 *Globe and Mail* column headlined "It's not Canadians who've gone to the right, just their media."[1]

Black passed the Southam dailies on to even more meddlesome owners. The Asper family of Winnipeg pushed their own personal hobby horses, including unstinting support for Israel in its conflict with the Palestinians, and constant criticism of the CBC, which they saw as unfair government-subsidized competition for their Global Television network. But the Aspers were even less subtle in their wielding of power than was Black, ordering "national" editorials written at company headquarters to be printed over the objections of many Southam journalists, who valued their local independence. The Aspers also appeared more willing than their predecessors to get rid of writers and editors who did not adhere to the family line—Canwest's firing of *Ottawa Citizen* publisher Russell Mills in 2002, for running an editorial contrary to company policy, was perhaps the defining act of the darkest chapter yet in Canadian journalism history. It all came down in the crash of 2008 after Canwest became over-extended with billions in debt from all its acquisitions. Its bankruptcy promised better ownership because . . . well, it couldn't get much worse, could it?

Vulture capitalists descend

The recent collapse of the newspaper industries in the US and Canada has seen a new type of owner emerge. Hedge funds, faceless and secretive, came into existence in the 1980s in response to worldwide deregulation of financial markets. During the recession, these high-risk, high-reward investors, who were often derided as "vulture" capitalists, began buying up the debt of foundering newspaper companies across North America with the intention of acquiring them cheaply in bankruptcy proceedings.

Calling themselves Postmedia, hedge funds led by New York-based GoldenTree Asset Management and Silver Point Capital bought an estimated 58 percent of Canwest's newspaper division when it went bankrupt. Canadian print media are supposedly subject to a de-facto foreign ownership limit in the form of a tax provision that requires 75 percent Canadian ownership for the expense of advertising in them to be tax deductible. That should have discouraged the hedge funds, but instead they found a loophole by taking most of their ownership in the former Southam newspapers as limited-voting shares. Postmedia set up a two-tier share structure, with "variable" voting rights for foreign stockholders. This way, despite majority American ownership, it claimed that Canadian shareholders controlled it. Their neatest trick, however, was trading in only part of the secured Canwest debt they held, retaining enough that they would be first in line with a claim on the company in the event it went bankrupt again. Not only that, but they were guaranteed to be paid regularly and richly for the debt they held, skimming their take off the top whether business went up, down, or sideways. Harper's government turned a blind eye to all of this financial engineering and then watched as Postmedia bought the Sun Media chain for $315 million in 2014. As a result, the hedge funds were bleeding dry not one but two Canadian newspaper chains due to the hefty interest rates (up to 12.5 percent) on the debt they held. During the three months ended May 31, 2016, for example, Postmedia made interest payments of $18.2 million, or 92 percent of its $19.8 million in operating earnings that quarter.

The internet, of course, was supposed to make all of this irrelevant. Old media were said to be not long for this world once online media took hold. There was only one small problem with that notion. Except for the "killer apps" Google and Facebook, which are not news media at all, online news media have found it hard to make money in the Darwinian world of the internet. In stark contrast to old media such as newspapers and television, where the preferred business model is monopoly, the internet allows anyone to post a website and sell ads on it. Oversupply, along with other doubts about the effectiveness of online advertising, thus drove down online ad rates to a fraction of what legacy media still command. Newspapers and television stations continue to post enviable profit margins, albeit on greatly reduced revenues. Their profits, however, are enabled only by the constant cost cuts they have been forced to make, mostly to their actual reporting staff.

By contrast, the few digital news startups that have emerged in Canada have had to seek revenue from sources other than advertising. Online subscriptions have shown promise at some online publications such as AllNovaScotia in Halifax, which started in 2004 and is said to be profitable with ten thousand subscribers, each paying thirty dollars a month. The Tyee in Vancouver has been providing a progressive slant on the opposite coast since 2003, but it is heavily subsidized by labour unions. If every town in Canada had a similar online news outlet to supplement its dwindling legacy media, however, the local news crisis would be eased considerably. But compared to other countries, significant barriers remain to digital news media succeeding in Canada.

To subsidize or not?

Some have proposed government subsidies as an answer to both keeping old media alive and incubating new media until they can stand on their own, but most journalists are leery of anything that smacks of government influence. This ignores the fact that news media have historically benefited from subsidies ranging from low postal rates to government advertising to free broadcasting licences, which press baron Roy Thomson famously described as "like having a licence to print your own money."

Scandinavian countries have long subsidized their press to stave off the declining competition that has afflicted the newspaper industries in North America. As a result, they continue to enjoy thriving press systems with diversity of both ownership and view-point, plus press freedom rankings that are among the highest in the world, unlike in the US and Canada.

Another model that has been employed in other countries is charitable not-for-profit news media companies. In the US, dozens of digital news startups have emerged since the recession due to laws that allow them to claim non-profit status and accept tax-deductible donations from foundations and individuals. These companies, designated under Section 501(c)(3) of the US tax code, must re-invest any profits they make and may not pay dividends to investors. Online publications such as MinnPost, Voice of San Diego, ProPublica, and the Texas Tribune are thus able to perform valuable public affairs reporting and even investigative journalism that legacy media are now hard-pressed to afford.

According to a recent study by institutes at the University of Oxford and Yale University, however, Canada is one of the few English-speaking countries in which non-profit news media cannot claim charitable status. "The charitable system in Canada is effectively in disarray," observed lawyer Adam Aptowitzer, who noted that jurisdiction over granting charitable status belongs to the provinces, yet Ottawa is in charge of defining charity.

Parliament has been so afraid to discuss the definition of charity that the one and only discussion, which took place in the 1930s, was truncated and left to the Courts because of the difficult political nature of the discussion. (That is, no MP wanted to be seen as disparaging a "good cause"). The key question is why the provinces have decided to abdicate their jurisdiction in this area.[2]

This is obviously one funding avenue in which federal policy leadership could work wonders.

Saving the media

One ambitious new prescription for saving the news media emanates from France and could not only secure ample funding for new media startups but would also make them considerably more democratic than today's corporate media. Economist Julia Cagé proposes a model for news media that is halfway between a foundation and a stock issuing company. A nonprofit media organization would be able to accept tax-deductible donations, in exchange for which it would issue shares of ownership that would not trade publicly. Readers and employees could also buy shares that would enjoy voting rights disproportionate to those of larger shareholders. Power would thus be diffused throughout the organization and not confined to those with the most shares. "The question is not whether the media should be subsidized," writes Cagé in *Saving the Media*. "It is rather whether they should be granted a favorable legal and tax status in recognition of their contribution to democracy."[3] She points to the example of universities as organizations that are able to receive tax-deductible gifts because they play a similar societal role. "The news media provide a public good, just as universities and other contributors to the knowledge economy of the twenty-first century do," argues Cagé. "For that reason they deserve special treatment by the government."[4]

Another possible alternative might be a national network of government-funded digital "mojos" (mobile journalists) covering local communities. But we already have a national network of government-funded journalists. It's called the CBC. Restoring the funding cutbacks endured by the public broadcaster during the Harper decade provides an opportunity to re-orient the government broadcaster away from broadcasting and more toward the online realm. Hyper-local mojos could feed into the national network via the CBC website and also provide basic audio and video for radio and TV. Local CBC news websites could offer a basic service free to all, but also provide access to longer-form journalism and special features to those willing to pay a subscription fee in the often successful "freemium" model.

Once a more diverse and democratic news ecosystem is thriving, all that would be left for government to do is police the worst excesses of what passes for journalism these days. The Federal Trade Commission in the US has already taken publishers to task for potentially misleading readers by presenting native ads in a format that resembles news or feature content. It issued guidelines in late 2015 that require sponsored content to be clearly labeled as advertising. Websites or print publications that fail to adequately distinguish between advertising and journalism risk being prosecuted for deceptive practices.[5] Ottawa needs to similarly protect consumers by drawing clear lines between journalism and hucksterism.

The Toronto School

The Royal Commission on Newspapers was "born out of shock and trauma," its report observed, after long-publishing dailies in Winnipeg and Ottawa were folded by their corporate owners on the same day in 1980, creating two more local monopolies. Its year-long investigation of the Canadian news media also examined the digital alternative that was even then looming on the horizon. "Canada is in a favored position to understand this new technology, to develop it, exploit it, and benefit from it," the Royal Commission report noted.

We have a solid foundation of theoretical studies in modern communications, largely because of the work of the economic historian Harold Innis, who died in 1952, and Marshall McLuhan, the media philosopher, who died in 1980. McLuhan, strongly influenced by Innis, altered mankind's appreciation of the influence of media.[6]

Today considered founders of the so-called Toronto School, after the university where they developed their ideas, Innis and McLuhan revolutionized thinking about media influence in the 1950s and '60s by focusing on their form rather than their content. As McLuhan famously put it, "the medium is the message." Control of any society's dominant medium, Innis realized by examining empires dating back to ancient Egypt, inevitably results in control of its political and economic life. Changes to the dominant medium in a society, according to McLuhan, bring fundamental shifts in social organization and even sensory perception.

Neil Postman, the American scholar who helped revive interest in what came to be called "medium theory" and then "media ecology," pointed to the ability of a dominant medium to influence a society's definition of such concepts as intelligence and even truth. Political discourse, he warned, had sunk to dangerous levels of absurdity under television compared to the more rational regime of the printing press. Few could have foreseen the changes wrought by online media, where search engines, blogs, and social media now rule.

When the wave of convergence washed over Canada at the millennium, few could similarly have predicted how it would reshape the country's media. Regulators who considered in 2001 whether to limit the merging of television and newspapers decided to let it run its course, which unfortunately went straight into the ground. "They prefer to get a good handle on how convergence will develop before trying to regulate it," noted the *Globe and Mail* at the time. "Technology is changing so quickly, they say, that there is no clear indication how cultural diversity will fare."[7] Now that we have a better idea of some of the perils inherent in this brave new media world, it behooves government to finally act in the public interest. Fortunately, when it comes to Canadian news media, there is no shortage of good ideas for doing so.

TEN

Is This the News We Deserve?

Postmedia announced a restructuring of its debt in mid-2016 which, depending on how you looked at it, either bought it some existential breathing room or prolonged its dominance over Canada's newspaper industry. In what amounted to a voluntary mini-bankruptcy, the company shed almost half its $648 million in debt by converting its unsecured bond holders into shareholders. As US hedge funds made up the bulk of both groups and its shares were almost worthless, it seemed suspiciously like a shell game. GoldenTree Asset Management, apparently fed up after six years of holding its northern investment, was replaced as its largest shareholder by New Jersey-based Chatham Asset Management. Americans as a result owned a dizzying 98 percent of Postmedia stock, leading a writer for the Tyee to call for an end to the sham of its supposed Canadian control. "The deal surely shreds the phony claim that Postmedia is a Canadian-controlled company," railed Paul Willcocks, a former publisher of several Canadian dailies. "Who really believes, no matter how elaborate the share structure, that the corporation is Canadian-owned at this point?"[1]

Noting that the Communications, Energy and Paperworkers Union of Canada had tried to force a government review of Postmedia's tax status in 2012, Willcocks suggested the recent changing of the political guard in Ottawa suddenly made such a push more realistic.

> I wouldn't expect great government enthusiasm for a review of Postmedia's tax status. But the Liberal government might be slightly more receptive than the Harper Conservatives. . . . So there is not much to lose by pushing for a federal review of Postmedia's Canadian status.[2]

The Heritage committee holding hearings into media and local communities recessed for the summer in advance of its cross-Canada tour in the fall, but not before farming the problem out to a think tank for further study.

The Public Policy Forum was newly headed by former *Globe and Mail* editor Edward Greenspon. "We're not, if you will, hired by the government," said Greenspon. "But we're doing this in co-operation with the government."[3] Founded in Calgary in 1987, the PPF was designed to "create an independent space where leaders from the private and public sectors could meet regularly to discuss governance and public policy."[4] Its review, according to the Canadian Press, revolved around three questions: "Does the deteriorating state of traditional media put at risk the civic function of journalism and thus the health of democracy? If so, are new digitally based news media filling the gap? If not, is there a role for public policy to help maintain a healthy flow of news and information, and how could it be done least intrusively?"[5] A half-dozen roundtables with "invited experts" were planned, as was polling designed to determine "how Canadians view the news media and its role in democratic society." A concluding symposium was scheduled for the fall.[6] CBC News obtained a Heritage Ministry report under the Access to Information Act which showed the PPF was being paid $270,000 for its study and had a deadline of year's end to deliver it.[7]

Secrecy surrounded the PPF's roundtables, which were held under "Chatham House" rules, according to one participant who nonetheless made his own thoughts public. "My contribution to the debate yesterday (aside from calling Facebook 'the devil') was to recommend a great deal of wait and see," wrote former *Ottawa*

Citizen editor Andrew Potter on the blog In Due Course. "I'm increasingly of the view that we need to just let this process play itself out. The convulsion of news media is a decade old, and it probably has another decade or so to go."[8]

The PPF also had its own investigator in the field for the previous year, awarding a 2015 fellowship sponsored by the Royal Bank to *Economist* correspondent Madelaine Drohan, who studied news media. "Serious journalism in Canada will survive in the digital era," she concluded. "The media outlets providing it will likely be smaller and more specialized, but they will have learned how to have a relationship with their viewers, listeners and readers."[9]

Postmedia's "breathtaking audacity"

Before adjourning for the summer, the Heritage committee heard from a Postmedia delegation that only managed to further inflame resentment toward the company. CEO Paul Godfrey told committee members that unless the government took action, Canada's newspaper industry would suffer even more. "It's ugly," he said. "It will get uglier, based on the present trends that exist today."[10] Citing the recent closure of the minor dailies *Guelph Mercury* (by Torstar) and *Nanaimo Daily News* (by Black Press), Godfrey warned that without government aid, "more drastic measures will need to be taken" by the chains.[11] "In three years," he said, "there will be many more closures in your own communities because of the state of the newspaper industry."[12] He suggested tax incentives allowing ads in Canadian publications to be written off at a higher rate than ads in foreign-owned media such as Google and Facebook. He also asked for government support in the form of increased advertising. "Come back and advertise in our newspapers and on our websites," he pleaded, noting recent government cuts to advertising. "We're asking the government to be an ally, not for a bailout of the Canadian newspaper industry."[13]

That brought a sharp response from Liberal MP Adam Vaughan, himself a former journalist. "There have been no fiercer critics of subsidies to the media than the *Toronto Sun* and the *National Post*," he told Godfrey. Vaughan made it abundantly clear that Postmedia could expect markedly different treatment from the new government than it received under the Harper Conservatives. "Why would we fund a failing business model that's owned by US interests?" he asked rhetorically.[14]

Godfrey also suggested the Heritage Ministry's Aid to Publishers program be expanded from magazines, digital publications, and community newspapers to also include dailies. Noting Godfrey's $1.7 million salary, Shannon Rupp of the Tyee called him for "breathtaking audacity" and fulminated that "when it comes to gall, the champion has to be Postmedia's Paul Godfrey."

> His ever-increasing pay packet tells us that he's doing exactly the job his bosses want: helping US hedge funds strip the Canadian assets for cash. It's clever. Technically, Postmedia is a Canadian-owned company. Which means it can take advantage of all of our so-called cultural protection laws: a mix of tax advantages and grants. . . . But, personally, I object when a corporate CEO starts asking for more government handouts to subsidize his billion-dollar marketing business. Especially in the case of Postmedia, which is putting that cash into the hands of US vulture capitalists.[15]

In September 2016, Postmedia provided an example of what Godfrey meant when he said things would get "uglier." It broke new ground in newspaper consolidation when it closed the newsroom of its Vancouver commuter tabloid *24 Hours*. The newspaper would continue publishing, but it would be filled with content from Postmedia's other dailies—mainly the *Vancouver Sun* and *Province* and the *National Post*. This was a new concept in journalism—a newspaper without a newsroom. Quebecor's *24 Hours* tabloids in Toronto and Vancouver had been included in the 2014 Sun Media acquisition by Postmedia. It promptly laid off half the newsroom staff of its Vancouver edition, which had been the second most-read newspaper in Western Canada behind only the *Vancouver Sun*. "They wrote a lot of content that no one else had," said Erica Bulman, the newspaper's former editor, after the other half were axed. "It was very much a community paper. It was a voice of the community, and those stories aren't going to exist anymore. Now you're going to have three key news outlets in Vancouver that are all providing the same content."[16]

Where are the watchdogs?

The failure of financialized news media to live up to the watchdog role of journalism was never more apparent than in their lack of reporting on the financial engineering that crashed the world economy in 2008. A housing bubble in the US that grew due to the unscrupulous practices of lenders who pushed mortgages on unqualified (i.e., "sub-prime") borrowers went largely unnoticed by journalists. When the bubble burst, the effect was catastrophic, not just in the US but around the world. The business press, according to Dean Starkman in his 2014 book *The Watchdog That Didn't Bark*, was oblivious to impending disaster largely because it had long since abandoned investigative reporting. Cutbacks to journalism by its increasingly corporatized ownership led to a "do more with less" mentality that created a "hamster wheel" for reporters just trying to keep up. Corporate owners such as Rupert Murdoch and Sam Zell, noted Starkman, were hostile to investigative reporting on business in the first place.

Another culprit was the corporate push for a "digital first" approach to news in line with what he called the "future-of-news (FON) consensus," which agreed that all media would soon be online only. The focus by digital media on quantity over quality and the growing preponderance of public relations operatives over journalists, according to Starkman, rendered the internet incapable of accommodating accountability journalism. The growing focus on the internet by media owners and educators, he argued, had thus helped to disable journalism's "great bullshit detector." The internet, of course, was where bullshit reigned supreme. "Investor-oriented, insider-focused journalism — the corporate profiles and features on Wall Street houses and big banks — not only missed the story but was part of the problem, and not a small one."[17]

In Canada, according to Carleton University media economist

Dwayne Winseck, the media "were not only swept up in the financialization of the economy, but [were] on the cutting edge of this process."[18] A dramatic transformation beginning in the latter half of the 1990s, he pointed out, led to a sharp rise in first ownership concentration and then convergence, with disastrous consequences. "Far from being innocents caught up in events not of their making, Quebecor, Canwest, Cogeco, Bell Globemedia, and so on took the lead in fostering the financialization of the media to begin with," noted Winseck, who tracked media ownership through his Canadian Media Concentration Project. "It is this reality that has come back to haunt them."[19] And us.

The best way the vulture capitalists found to profit from declining news media companies, unfortunately for Canadians, was to strip their assets, decimate their journalism, and otherwise suck them dry. Even as the Heritage committee on media and local communities adjourned its hearings for the summer of 2016, foreign investors were being urged to acquire even more of Canada's news media. "Current regulatory support provides a great opportunity for large media companies," noted the American stock website Seeking Alpha in touting investment in Canada's second-largest newspaper publisher.[20] "The company has been greatly undervalued as Torstar's real estate assets alone make up its current market [value]," it noted in May 2016. "A potential acquisition would be able to unlock this shareholder value."[21] Postmedia's purchase of Sun Media was "a big step towards beginning the necessary consolidation in the Canadian market," according to the website. "Regulators were very supportive of the deal which was rather interesting when considering that with this acquisition, Postmedia would control around 30 percent [actually 37.6 percent] of the country's newspaper market."

> With this recent move and the favorable support seen from regulators, the Canadian print industry is a sector that has the potential to see some major consolidation in the following years in an effort to protect established papers facing profitability issues.[22]

In some countries, such as the UK and Australia, a "diversity" or "plurality" test for media mergers and acquisitions prevented corporate dominance of local markets. Even in the US, which lacked such limits, competition regulators kept a close eye on media consolidation and the Department of Justice often stepped in to say no. This was seen as recently as March 2016 in Southern California. The Department of Justice blocked Tribune Publishing, which owned the *San Diego Union-Tribune* and *Los Angeles Times*, from buying the *Orange County Register*, because it would have given it 98 percent of the daily English-language newspaper market in Orange County.[23] A 2016 bid in New Zealand to merge that country's two largest newspaper chains, which were already foreign owned, prompted overwhelming opposition when the competition regulator there solicited public input on whether to approve it. The merger would give the combined company 89 percent of the daily newspapers in New Zealand, but most submissions warned that would be bad for journalism and for democracy. The reaction prompted the Commerce Commission to postpone until 2017 its decision on whether to approve the merger of Fairfax Media and New Zealand Media and Entertainment, and to consider holding public hearings. It's a pity the public doesn't get similar input into media mergers in Canada.

Here a lack of ownership limits has historically been exacerbated not just by the inaction of the Competition Bureau, but also by a political reluctance to enforce other laws. By the twenty-first century, however, government inaction bordered on malfeasance. Allowing US hedge funds to buy a majority of Canada's largest newspaper chain in 2010 was "like turning the blood bank over to Dracula," said John Miller, a professor emeritus at Ryerson. "Hedge funds don't love newspapers," he wrote on his blog The Journalism Doctor. "They love money."[24] Former Vancouver journalist Ian Gill confessed astonishment at the state of Canada's media ownership when he delved into it for his recent book *No News is Bad News*. "I actually didn't expect to discover the degree to which media ownership concentration still beggars belief," he admitted. "Media ownership has become so concentrated it's a wonder your newspaper or television broadcast doesn't come with a health warning."

All this has happened under the noses of regulators who don't do their jobs and reporters who mostly don't do theirs, either. . . . The hollowing out of Canada's media is bad for democracy, and it runs counter to the claim that, in the post-Stephen Harper era, Canada is somehow "back."[25]

The Vancouver school

Gill called on the new Liberal government to provide subsidies for independent digital journalism in order to counter the dominance of foreign-owned corporate media. He advocated for journalism as practiced by news websites like the Tyee and the Vancouver Observer, the latter of which went national in 2015 with considerable investigative resources. Their advocacy journalism focused on energy and environmental issues in what *Alberta Oil* magazine called the "Vancouver school" of journalism.[26] But the number of visitors their combined websites attracted—about a million a month—was dwarfed by those who viewed Postmedia's numerous websites, noted *Alberta Oil*, such as the twelve million unique monthly visitors boasted by the *National Post's* website alone.

As the country's defender of free markets, the *Post* derided the notion of subsidies for Canadian journalism, no matter how sorry its state. Terence Corcoran, its business editor, nominated several advocates of subsidies for an award he called the "Most Pompously Wrongheaded Argument for a Government Bailout of the Newspaper Industry." (He included me among the nominees, even though I had advocated no such thing.) "The dark roots of the idea that governments can and should own, subsidize, licence and otherwise meddle in the business of freedom of the press run deep," wrote Corcoran, raising the spectre of totalitarian control. "The central claim is that the right to freedom belongs to the government and is only bestowed on individuals and groups under licence and forebearance."[27]

Unfortunately, Corcoran included some disinformation in support of his arguments. The Press Ownership Review Board recommended by the Davey report in 1970, he claimed, would have issued licences and guidelines to publications amounting to government interference. The Davey report made no mention of licensing, which is anathema to press freedom. The Press Ownership Review Board, whose job it would have been to approve media mergers and takeovers, was an idea well ahead of its time. Had it been adopted, it would have nipped in the bud the problem of ownership concentration that came to engulf Canada's news media.

Another *National Post* columnist dismissed even the need for an inquiry into the press mess. "Inquiries are generally deemed advisable when seeking to identify the roots of a problem, whereas there is absolutely no mystery about what's going on in the news business these days," wrote Kelly McParland.

> Readers and advertisers won't pay as much for news on screens as they did for news on paper. Which makes the existing order unaffordable. That's it in a nutshell. You could royal commission your way across the country from now until a week next Christmas and it would still come down to that.[28]

Luckily, others realized it wasn't just the cause of the problem that was at issue, but more importantly what to do about it, if anything. Winseck urged merging the CBC and Canada Post into a Canadian Communication Corporation. In addition to its legacy duties, it would also operate a fourth national cell phone network, blanket cities with free wi-fi, extend broadband access to underserved areas, and "create, disseminate and make public art and culture as accessible and enjoyable as possible." For Winseck and most other advocates of breaking the corporate stranglehold on Canadian news media, subsidies were no bogeyman. "We need to consider subsidizing independent journalism in ways that do not just put public money directly into the pockets of the existing newspaper groups that have driven the press into the ground through endless consolidation, inflated asset values and unsustainable debts."[29]

As a long-time journalist, however, I am leery of subsidies because of the possibilities they create for government influence over the news media. Any program of assistance should be well insulated from editorial control, but that doesn't mean tax incentives can't be provided to encourage the establishment and assist the operation of local media outlets dedicated to serving the news needs of Canadians. Such incentives could also render ownership of Canada's existing news media more diverse. Local ownership of news media was one of the first things that fell by the wayside in the rush to consolidation starting in the 1960s and '70s, when absentee chain ownership became the norm. Tax incentives could be provided that would make advertising in locally-owned, independent media more cost effective than in chain-owned publications. Godfrey's suggestion to the Heritage committee of increased tax incentives for ads in supposedly Canadian publications such as his could be modified to instead allow ads in locally-owned media outlets to be written off at a higher rate than other ads. That might encourage the sale of chain-owned dailies to local owners who could make them more responsive to their communities. Any merger or closure of newspapers should be prohibited without first offering them for sale. Subsidies and/ or tax incentives could then be provided to encourage their sale to local owners or even to their employees, as at Victoria's CHEK in 2010.[30]

First, however, the few existing laws protecting our news media have to be enforced, even retroactively, including those limiting foreign media ownership and preventing monopoly control of local markets. The inexplicable entrenching of foreign ownership of Canada's largest newspaper company — and then its second-largest — should be investigated, as should the corporate dealings that have led to a disappearance of newspaper competition in BC. The merging of Postmedia's newsrooms in Vancouver, Calgary, Edmonton, and Ottawa, despite promises to the contrary, and in the case of Vancouver an official long-standing promise, should be put up for reconsideration. If political favouritism by the former Conservative government was in any way involved in approving the decisions that allowed them, the increased consolidation and foreign ownership of our news media should be rolled back.

New directions needed

The problem of corporate influence over Canadian journalism schools finally made it onto the scholarly agenda in 2014 at a conference held at Ryerson University in Toronto titled "Toward 2020: New Directions in Journalism Education." Robert Picard of the Reuters Institute for the Study of Journalism at Oxford was asked by conference organizers to give the keynote address. I suspect they began to regret their invitation as soon as he began to lay into them for what he called "deficient tutelage." Picard lambasted the assembled educators for providing mere vocational training instead of imparting critical thinking skills. A primary reason for journalism education's deficiencies, according to Picard, was that it had long been co-opted by industry. "For decades, journalism programs have been influenced by and aligned with major employers," he told his stunned audience. "Their curricula have been designed to produce news factory workers who can be dropped into a slot at a journalism factory."[31] Actually, Picard went easy on them. Privately, he told me at a conference in 2016 that the situation here was the worst in his considerable experience. "I have never seen journalism education more co-opted by industry than in Canada," he said.

Fortunately, the problem has also come to the notice of some Canadian scholars. The conference at Ryerson included a panel that dissected the latest trend toward teaching "entrepreneurial" journalism. By seeking new ways to serve advertisers and maximize page views, panelists noted, courses in entrepreneurial journalism weakened journalism as a public service while attempting to strengthen it as a business. "In the rush to respond to a virtual collapse of the business model that has for decades supported journalism, we are in danger of abandoning the fundamental principles of journalism," warned Paul Benedetti of Western University. In the published version of his paper, titled "The Big Sellout," Benedetti urged journalism educators to "stand firm against new attempts to appropriate journalism as a commercial enterprise enlisted to

serve the market instead of the public."[32] One such ethical infringement was the trend to "sponsored" content, also known as "native
advertising," in which advertisers paid for content that was pre-
sented as news. "An idea that was anathema to all journalists for
most of the twentieth century—that an advertiser could buy the
services of a reporter and get a story published—was now being
lauded as 'innovative, collaborative,' and 'strategic,'" noted Benedetti, a former investigative reporter for the *Hamilton Spectator*. Under
this new commercial logic, not only was the traditional "church-
state wall" separating editorial content from advertising sales being
disregarded, he pointed out, it was "openly mocked."

> Entrepreneurial journalism, by its very nature, calls for a fusion of
> editorial and business concerns. The pundits don't apologize for
> the perceived need to abandon the wall in the face of dire economic
> reality; they welcome this development as long overdue, a necessary
> adaptation.[33]

The other way journalism schools served media owners was in
their seemingly never-ending quest for the Holy Grail of digital
salvation. Much of their curriculum has been given over to teaching technology in the hopes of discovering the magic digital bul-
let that will somehow "monetize" online content, saving the news
business. Dean Starkman of the *Columbia Journalism Review* blew the
whistle in 2011 on what he called the "future-of-news (FON) consensus" that promoted a "network-driven system of journalism in
which news organizations will play a decreasingly important role."
Under this system, news would increasingly be "assembled, shared,
and to an increasing degree, even gathered," noted Starkman, not
by journalists but by readers. The problem, Starkman pointed
out, was that public service journalism was falling by the wayside amidst all the blogging, tweeting, and social networking. "Its
anti-institutionalism would disempower journalism," he wrote of
the FON consensus led mostly by New York City academics. "Their
vision for replacing it with a networked alternative, or something
else, is hazy at best."[34]

Perhaps the epitome of this trend can be seen where else than at

UBC, where the latest director of the journalism school (and fifth in less than two decades) teaches an "innovative" course in conjunction with the Sauder School of Business. Journalism 520A: Decoding Social Media, which is cross-listed as Commerce 486S, teaches students how to run online promotional campaigns. One group of students in the course even won a Social Media Marketing award in 2013 from the Society for New Communication Research for a campaign they created for *Vancouver* magazine.[35] Taught by Alfred Hermida, a social media expert and former BBC journalist, the course includes such topics as "Handling a social media crisis" and "Psychological triggers and user experience."[36]

Suffice it to say not all journalism educators in Canada are in favour of this trend. According to Sean Holman of Mount Royal College in Calgary, journalism schools need to re-focus on teaching journalism instead of on the technology that is transforming the craft. "Journalism schools need to spend more time teaching their students how to find untold truths," urged Holman. "This means rebalancing our curriculum so students spend, for example, more time learning how to use search engines and spreadsheets rather than video microphones and cameras."

> It means spending more time learning how to come up with good stories than simply how to tell them. It means spending more time learning how to think critically about the world than just recording and publicizing its goings-on. . . . By doing more to teach those critical thinking skills, Canadian journalism schools won't just be saving themselves. They'll be helping to save our profession.[37]

The non-profit solution

In analyzing proposals designed to offset or ameliorate the insidious effects of news media financialization, Núria Almiron noted in 2011 that the proposals "all point in the same direction."[38] That direction is away from for-profit news media to a journalism uncoupled from corporate speculation and financial engineering. "This call can be regarded," she wrote, "as an unprecedented ethical

claim to devote journalism, once and for all, to the public interest."
But doing that, according to Almiron, will require "a mindset shift
away from the old way of thinking about non-profit and the media,
where non-profit becomes a model not just for small and second-
ary media, but for private mainstream media as well."

> We should consider what is harmful in terms of public/social inter-
> ests instead of private/individual interests. We should avoid defining
> public interest in relation to business performance; we already have
> evidence enough to know about the harmful consequences of this
> recurrent relationship throughout the 20th century.[39]

In Canada, a mindset shift is also needed among both federal regulators and journalism educators. News media should no longer be
treated by Ottawa like any other business but instead as a public
service of enormous social and political importance. The Competition Bureau has abdicated its duty to the public in this regard and
should be investigated from top to bottom. Its capture by an industry it is tasked to regulate, as with the CRTC, is patently apparent.
The broadcasting regulator should prohibit journalism schools
from participating in its public benefits program because the temp-
tation to mute any criticism of corporate media takeovers, or even
to advocate for them, is apparently too great for some educators to
resist.

Instead of looking out for the best interests of media owners, in
whose pockets they have thrust their hands so deeply, journalism
educators should advocate for the best practices of journalism and
for the news needs of Canadians. Most journalism educators in
Canada (with a few notable exceptions), have largely given ownership a pass and thus been nothing less than derelict in their duty to
serve the profession and practice of journalism. Our news media
have been transformed as a result of ownership changes over the
past two decades, and not for the better. Perhaps only one in eight
Canadians believe media owners influence the news they receive, as
UBC's Mary Lynn Young told senators when they visited her journalism school in 2005. Canadians need to instead realize that ownership influence over media content is significant and arguably aids

in hegemonic social and political control by the country's elite and now foreign financiers. First it seems most journalism educators in Canada need to wake up to that possibility.

As mentioned in Chapter 9, to a great extent the horse is already out of the barn. Decades of unrestricted consolidation and now foreign ownership have decimated Canada's news media. Canadians need to demand better from their news media and from their government. If they don't, they will inevitably get, as Davey noted, the press they deserve. Bold measures are needed to redress years of official neglect. Canada now has an opportunity to institute some forward-looking media policies. It might be the last chance for any hope of a diverse and independent news media in Canada.

Acknowledgements

I would like to thank everyone who has helped me along the way with my research over the past fifteen years, especially all of the editors and journal staff members I have worked with over the years in publishing my research. While New Star Books publisher Rolf Maurer is a big picture guy, he also did an excellent job of editing my manuscript. Mike Leyne is the details guy who gave it a thorough copy editing before it went off to press. He is also New Star's go-to guy for publicity and he generally keeps the place running. I would like to thank Professor Robert Hackett of Simon Fraser University for his encouragement over the years. We lost my mentor David Spencer of Western University of Ontario to cancer this year, and I for one will miss him. I am grateful to my colleagues at University Canada West for providing me the opportunity to teach in my own country for a change and for assisting me in my research, especially Arthur Coren, David Weins, Bob Rogerson, Bruce Hiebert, Brad O'Hara, Will Carne, Adrian Mitescu, and Carol Thorbes. A big thanks goes out to Vincent Mosco for writing such a kind foreword, and to Robert Picard, Robert Hackett, and Dwayne Winseck for providing their assessment of my research. Thanks to my landlord . . . er, waterlord Michael Goodman and his assistant Omar Lalani for getting rid of the barking dogs next door that almost drove me crazy while writing this book. (It's a short drive.) Thanks to my buddies Doug Cadorette, for taking such an interest in my work and for dragging me out for lunch every so often; Ian Dolling, for providing Friday afternoon relaxation; Cam Birge, for getting me into a couple of hockey pools; and Dave Coutu, for taking me to the occasional Canucks game. Finally, thanks to Hedy Fry for taking the problem of Canada's news media seriously enough to get it on the front burner of the new federal government's agenda.

Notes

NOTES TO INTRODUCTION

1. Paula Simons, "And yes. Before you ask, this was a decision made by the owners of the paper," Twitter, October 15, 2015. Available online at https://twitter.com/paulatics/status/655006911117393921

2. Sean Craig, "Postmedia Told Edmonton Journal to Endorse Jim Prentice, Says Edmonton Journal," Canadaland, May 4, 2015. Available online at http://canadalandshow.com/article/postmedia-told-edmonton-journal-endorse-jim-prentice-says-edmonton-journal

3. James Bradshaw, "Andrew Coyne exits editor role at National Post over endorsement," *Globe and Mail*, October 20, 2015.

4. John Honderich, "Postmedia let down readers by dictating election endorsements," *Toronto Star*, November 9, 2015. Available online at https://www.thestar.com/opinion/commentary/2015/11/09/postmedia-let-down-readers-by-dictating-election-endorsements-honderich.html

5. Jessica Chin, "Postmedia, Sun Front Pages Replaced With Full-Page Political Ads," Huffington Post Canada, October 18, 2015. Available online at http://www.huffingtonpost.ca/2015/10/18/postmedia-front-page-ads_n_8326634.html

6. Geoff Olson, "Strange days: Playboy gets clean, Postmedia gets dirty, Parliament gets new PM," *Vancouver Courier*, October 20, 2015. Available online at http://www.vancourier.com/opinion/strange-days-playboy-gets-clean-postmedia-gets-dirty-parliament-gets-new-pm-1.2091169#sthash.qJErdaCp.dpuf

7. Bradshaw, "Andrew Coyne exits editor role."

8. Andrew Coyne, "Dissenting from the Post endorsement," Twitter, October 19, 2015. Available online at https://twitter.com/acoyne/status/656131496697294848

9. Andrew Coyne, "I don't see public disagreement as confusing," Twitter, October 19, 2015. Available online at https://twitter.com/acoyne/status/656131552972296192

10. Andrew Coyne, "While Postmedia's intervention was unprecedented in my experience," Twitter, October 19, 2015. Available online at https://twitter.com/acoyne/status/656131770245582848

11. Ethan Cox, "Andrew Coyne resigns over censored column," Ricochet, October 19, 2015. Available online at https://ricochet.media/en/684/andrew-coyne-resigns-over-censored-column

12. Ethan Cox, "Margaret Atwood vs. the National Post," Ricochet, August 22, 2015. Available online at https://ricochet.media/en/557/margaret-at-wood-vs-the-national-post

13. Jennifer Pagliaro, "Margaret Atwood's column criticizing Stephen Harper vanishes, then returns to, National Post website," Thestar.com, August 21, 2015. Available online at https://www.thestar.com/news/gta/2015/08/21/margaret-at-woods-column-criticizing-stephen-harper-vanishes-from-national-post-website.html

14. Jeet Heer, "So every Post column must now align with 'the values of the National Post and its readers'?" Twitter, August 21, 2015. Available online at https://twitter.com/HeerJeet/status/634907801580539904

15. Cox, "Andrew Coyne resigns over censored column."

16. John Barber, "Postmedia's support for Conservatives leaves it out of step with the public," TheGuardian.com, November 1, 2015. Available online at http://www.theguardian.com/media/2015/nov/01/election-blow-canada-postmedia-stephen-harper

17. Benjamin Mullin, "Canadian newspapers run huge political ads on front pages," Poynter.org, October 19, 2015. Available online at http://www.poynter.org/2015/canadian-newspapers-run-huge-political-ads-on-front-pages/379543/

18. Paul Benedetti and James Compton, "The sounds of silence: Postmedia buys Sun Newspaper chain and no one heard a thing," Rabble.ca, April 6, 2015. Available online at http://rabble.ca/news/2015/04/sounds-silence-postmedia-buys-sun-newspaper-chain-and-no-one-heard-thing

19. Toronto Star, "US hedge funds strengthen ownership of Canadian papers," *Toronto Star*, October 7, 2014.

20. David Parkinson, "Postmedia deal will force regulator to rethink mandate," *Globe and Mail*, October 6, 2014.

21. Canada, Standing Senate Committee on Transportations and Communications, "Final Report on the Canadian News Media, Volume 1," June 2006, 24. Available online at http://www.parl.gc.ca/content/sen/committee/391/tran/rep/repfinjun06vol1-e.pdf

22. *Ibid.*, 16.

23. *Ibid.*, 17.

24. *Ibid.*, 24.

25. Jacquie McNish and Jacqueline Nelson, "The US hedge funds financing

'Project Canada,'" *Globe and Mail*, October 7, 2014.

26. Marc Edge, "The Never-ending Story: Postmedia, the Competition Bureau, and Press Ownership Concentration in Canada," *Canadian Journal of Media Studies* 14(1), Spring/Summer 2016, 53–81. Available online at http://cjms.fims.uwo.ca/issues/14-01/edge.pdf

27. Competition Bureau, "Competition Bureau will not challenge Postmedia's acquisition of Sun Media," March 25, 2015. Available online at http://www.competitionbureau.gc.ca/eic/site/cb-bc.nsf/eng/03898.html

28. Competition Bureau, "Statement regarding the proposed acquisition by Postmedia Network Inc. of the English-language newspapers of Quebecor Media Inc.," March 25, 2015. Available online at http://www.competitionbureau.gc.ca/eic/site/cb-bc.nsf/eng/03899.html

29. Claire Brownell, "Regulator clears path for $316M sale," *National Post*, March 26, 2015.

30. Ambarish Chandra and Allan Collard-Wexler, "Mergers in Two-Sided Markets: An Application to the Canadian Newspaper Industry," *Journal of Economics & Management Strategy* 18(4), Winter 2009, 1067.

31. *Ibid.*, 1069.

32. Ben Bagdikian, *The Media Monopoly*. Boston: Beacon Press, 1983, 123.

33. Robert R. Kerton "Price Effects of Market Power in the Canadian Newspaper Industry," *Canadian Journal of Economics* 6, November 1973, 605.

34. Stephen Lacy and Todd F. Simon, *The Economics and Regulation of United States Newspapers*. Norwood, NJ: Ablex, 1993, 109.

35. Trevor MacKay, personal communication, undated (letter posted October 9, 2015).

36. Carrie Tait, "Strange bedfellows in Alberta," *Globe and Mail*, January 23, 2016.

37. Antonella Artuso, "Postmedia buys Sun Media's English-language papers, including the Calgary Sun, for $316M," *Calgary Sun*, October 6, 2014.

38. Christine Dobby and James Bradshaw, "Competition Bureau clears way for Postmedia to buy Sun Media papers," *Globe and Mail*, March 26, 2015.

39. Margo Goodhand, Above the Fold," TheWalrus.com, February 4, 2016. Available online at https://thewalrus.ca/above-the-fold/

40. Teresa Tedesco, "How Postmedia met Quebecor," *National Post*, October 7, 2014.

41. John Ivison, "Ottawa likely to see sense in deal," *National Post*, October 7, 2014.

42. *Ibid.*

43. Mark Burgess, "Postmedia's $316-million newspaper deal to maintain segregated markets, newsrooms to offer niche advertising," *Hill Times*, October 10, 2014. Available online at http://www.hilltimes.com/2014/10/10/postmedias-316-million-newspaper-deal-to-maintain-segregated-markets-newsrooms-to-offer-niche-advertising/29915/39915; Mark Burgess, "Surviving the takeover," *Media*, Spring 2015, 13. Available online at http://www.caj.ca/wp-con-

tent/uploads/2015/03/Winter2015_final.pdf

44. Goodhand, "Above the Fold."

45. Conrad Black, "Newspapers must fight back," *National Post*, May 3, 2015.

46. "Experts on the concentration of media ownership," Macleans.ca, October 6, 2014. Available online at http://www.macleans.ca/news/canada/experts-weigh-in-on-concentration-of-canadian-media-ownership/

47. Paul Hunter, "Postmedia's big purchase means more Canadian cities like Vancouver," *Toronto Star*, October 10, 2014.

48. CTV National News, "Postmedia merger," October 6, 2014. Accessed August 9, 2015 from Factiva database.

49. Pete Evans, "Postmedia cuts 90 jobs, merges newsrooms in Vancouver, Edmonton, Calgary, Ottawa," CBC.ca, January 19, 2016. Available online at http://www.cbc.ca/news/business/postmedia-job-cuts-1.3410497

50. Christopher Waddell, "Paper Pusher: Has the death of newsprint been overstated?" *Literary Review of Canada*, May 2015. Available online at http://review-canada.ca/magazine/2015/05/paper-pusher/

51. Marc Edge, *Greatly Exaggerated: The Myth of the Death of Newspapers*. Vancouver: New Star Books, 2014.

52. Ian Gill, *No News is Bad News: Canada's Media Collapse — and What Comes Next*. Vancouver: Greystone Books, 2016, 37.

53. *Ibid.*, 49.

54. *Ibid.*, 18–19 and 3.

55. David Olive, "As long as it continues to live, Postmedia is blight to readers," *Toronto Star*, January 30, 2016.

56. David Olive, "Postmedia and the high price of survival," *Toronto Star*, January 24, 2015.

57. Canada, *The Uncertain Mirror: Report of the Special Senate Committee on Mass Media*, Vol. I, 1970. Ottawa: Information Canada, 80.

58. Toby D. Couture, "Without Favour: The Concentration of Ownership in New Brunswick's Print Media Industry," *Canadian Journal of Communication* 38(1), 2013, 57–81.

59. Canada, Standing Senate Committee on Transportations and Communications, "Final Report on the Canadian News Media, Volume 2," June 2006, 59. Available online at http://www.parl.gc.ca/content/sen/committee/391/tran/rep/repfinjun06vol2-e.pdf

60. See Bruce Livesey, "The Irvings' media monopoly and its consequences," National Observer, July 6, 2016. Available online at http://www.nationalobserver.com/2016/07/06/news/irvings-media-monopoly-and-its-consequences

61. See Erin Steuter, "He Who Pays the Piper Calls the Tune: Investigation of a Canadian Media Monopoly," *Web Journal of Mass Communication Research* 7/4, September 2004. Available online at http://www.scripps.ohiou.edu/wjmcr/vol07/7-4a-b.html; Erin Steuter, "The Irvings Cover Themselves: Media Representations of the Irving Oil Refinery Strike, 1994-1996," *Canadian Journal of Communication* 24/4, 1999. Available online at http://www.cjc-online.ca/index.php/journal/

article/view/1128/1039; Jacques Poitras, *Irving vs. Irving: Canada's Feuding Billionaires And The Stories They Won't Tell.* Toronto: Viking, 2014.

62. Megan Devlin, "Why does Black Press buy and then close small BC papers?" J-source.ca, April 13, 2016. Available online at http://www.j-source.ca/article/why-does-black-press-buy-and-then-close-small-bc-papers

63. Bethany Lindsay, "Nanaimo loses its daily newspaper," *Vancouver Sun*, January 23, 2016.

64. Peter Steven, *About Canada: Media*, Halifax: Fernwood, 2011, 10; 13.

65. Jennifer Ditchburn, "State of Canada's news media focus of Commons committee," *Winnipeg Free Press*, February 17, 2016.

NOTES TO CHAPTER ONE

1. Keith Davey, *The Rainmaker: A Passion for Politics.* Toronto: Stoddart, 1986, 8.

2. Davey, "Preface," in Canada, *The Uncertain Mirror: Report of the Special Senate Committee on Mass Media*, Vol. I. Ottawa: Information Canada, 1970, viii.

3. Ben Bagdikian, *The Media Monopoly.* Boston: Beacon Press, 1983, 99.

4. Canada, *The Uncertain Mirror: Report of the Special Senate Committee on Mass Media*, Vol. I. Ottawa: Information Canada, 1970, 63.

5. *Ibid.*, 4.

6. *Ibid.*

7. *Ibid.*

8. *Ibid.*, 71.

9. Davey, *The Rainmaker*, 153.

10. Canada, Royal Commission on Newspapers, *Report.* Ottawa: Queen's Printer, 1981, 215, 218.

11. Robert Lewis, "Nobody here but us chickens," *Maclean's*, April 27, 1981, 32.

12. Quoted in Robert Lewis, "The pressure on the press," *Maclean's*, August 31, 1981, 30.

13. *Ibid.*

14. Lorne Slotnick, "Monopoly legitimate, Thomson lawyer says," *Globe and Mail*, October 15, 1983.

15. Lorne Slotnick, "Newspaper chains cleared of Combines Act charges," *Globe and Mail*, December 10, 1983.

16. See Marc Edge, *Pacific Press: The Unauthorized Story of Vancouver's Newspaper Monopoly.* Vancouver: New Star Books, 2001, 360–365.

17. Gerald A. Epstein, "Introduction: Financialization and the World Economy," in Epstein, ed., *Financialization and the World Economy.* Cheltenham, UK: Edward Elgar, 2005, 3.

18. Thomas I. Palley, "Financialization: What It Is and Why It Matters." Working Paper No. 525, The Levy Economics Institute, Bard College, Annandale-on-Hudson, NY, December 2007, 2. Available online at http://www.levyinstitute.org/pubs/wp_525.pdf

19. *Ibid.*

20. Núria Almiron, *Journalism in Crisis: Corporate Media and Financialization*. Cresskill, NJ: Hampton Press, 2010, 159.

21. *Ibid.*, 154.

22. *Ibid.*, 174, 175–176.

23. *Ibid.*, 166.

24. Ben Bagdikian, *The Media Monopoly*. Boston: Beacon Press, 1983.

25. Canada, Royal Commission on Newspapers, *Report*, 230.

26. See Allan Bartley, "The regulation of cross-media ownership: The life and short times of PCO 2294," *Canadian Journal of Communication* 13(2), Summer 1988, 45–59.

27. See Marc Edge, "And 'The Wall' Came Tumbling Down in Los Angeles." In Joseph Bernt and Marilyn Greenwald, eds. *The Big Chill: Investigative Reporting in the Current Media Environment*. Ames: Iowa University Press, 2000.

28. See James Ledbetter, "The Slow, Sad Sellout of Journalism School," *Rolling Stone*, October 16, 1997, 73–81; 99–100.

29. Neil Tudiver, *Universities for Sale: Resisting Corporate Control over Canadian Higher Education*. Toronto: James Lorimer, 1999.

30. James Compton, "Sing Tao School of Journalism: What's in a name? Apparently, quite a lot," *Media*, Winter 1998, 23.

31. Daniel Sieberg, "Beware Automatic Reaction Against Concentration, J-School Head Says," *Vancouver Sun*, April 27, 2000.

32. Donna Logan, "What Do the Mega Media Deals Mean for Journalists? Opportunities and Challenges," *Media*, Fall 2000, 15.

33. "Code of conduct the big debate at CRTC hearings," *Regina Leader-Post*, April 26, 2001.

34. Claire Hoy, "CRTC's appointed power hacks," *Hill Times*, May 14, 2001, 6.

35. "Canwest pledges $500,000 to fund visiting journalist program at UBC," *Vancouver Sun*, June 26, 2001.

36. University of British Columbia, "Leading the Media Revolution." Downloaded October 19, 2002 from http://www.journalism.ubc.ca/events_convergence.html.

37. Donna Logan, Interview with Rafe Mair, CKNW radio, Vancouver, June 28, 2002.

38. *Ibid.*

NOTES TO CHAPTER TWO

1. Patrick Nagle, "Charter members mark passing of Southam News," *Globe and Mail*, March 5, 2003.

2. Ben Bagdikian, "Conglomeration, Concentration and the Media," *Journal of Communication* 30(2), Spring 1980, 59–64.

3. Ben Bagdikian, *The Media Monopoly*. Boston: Beacon Press, 1983.

4. Doug Underwood, *When MBAs Rule the Newsroom*. Columbia University Press: New York, 1993.

5. Lou Ureneck, "Newspapers arrive at economic crossroads," *Nieman Reports*, Summer 1999, 11.

6. *Ibid.*

7. Thomas Kunkel and Gene Roberts, *Leaving Readers Behind: The Age of Corporate Journalism*. Fayetteville: University of Arkansas Press, 2001, 6.

8. Gilbert Cranberg, Randall Bezanson and John Soloski, *Taking Stock: Journalism and the Publicly Traded Newspaper Company*. Ames: Iowa State University Press, 2001.

9. Peter J.S. Dunnett, *The World Newspaper Industry*. London: Croom Helm, 1988, 199.

10. Charles Bruce, *News and the Southams*. Toronto: Macmillan, 1968, 204.

11. *Ibid.*, 14.

12. *Ibid*, 207.

13. Harvey Enchin, "Southam's future may unfold today," *Globe and Mail*, August 2, 1985.

14. Bud Jorgensen, "Southam rule set to protect shareholders," *Globe and Mail*, August 9, 1985.

15. Shaun Assael, "Northern Exposure," *NewsInc.*, January 1993, 29–30.

16. John Partridge, "Southam, Torstar avert trial with agreement," *Globe and Mail*, September 20, 1988.

17. Roger Leach, "Fisher faces Southam defence task," *Financial Post*, September 26, 1988.

18. Richard Siklos, *Shades of Black: Conrad Black and the World's Fastest Growing Press Empire*. Toronto: Minerva, 1996, 383.

19. Tim Jones, "That Old Black Magic," *Columbia Journalism Review*, March/April 1998, 40.

20. Erwin Frenkel, *The Press and Politics in Israel: The Jerusalem Post from 1932 to the Present*. Westport, CT: Greenwood Press, 1994.

21. Siklos, *Shades of Black*.

22. *Ibid.*

23. *Ibid.*, 307.

24. *Ibid.*

25. Harvey Enchin, "Financiers running show at Southam," *Globe and Mail*, May 31, 1993.

26. Casey Mahood, "Southam director dismisses scolding by CEO," *Globe and Mail*, March 8, 1996.

27. Siklos, *Shades of Black*.

28. John Miller, *Yesterday's News: Why Canada's Daily Newspapers are Failing Us*. Halifax: Fernwood, 1998, 62.

29. Mark Fitzgerald, "Hollinger gains control of Southam," *Editor & Publisher*, December 7, 1996, 12.

30. Brenda Dalglish, "Hollinger to pay special dividend," *Financial Post*, April 23, 1997.

31. Casey Mahood, "Black fails in quest to take Southam private," *Globe and Mail*, June 24, 1997.

32. Casey Mahood, "Hollinger picks up big Southam block," *Globe and Mail*, August 20, 1998.

33. Brenda Dalglish, "Hollinger bids for rest of Southam," *Globe and Mail*, December 3, 1998.

34. Brenda Dalglish, "Southam accepts Hollinger new bid," *Globe and Mail*, January 7, 1999.

35. Barbara Shecter, "Hollinger swallows Southam: Raises stake to 97%," *National Post*, January 20, 1999.

36. Anthony Wilson-Smith, "War of Words: The gloves are off over circulation claims in the newspaper industry," *Maclean's*, February 8, 1999, 48.

37. Robert Sheppard and Patricia Chisholm, "A Strategic Retreat," *Maclean's*, May 8, 1999, 30.

38. Alan Freeman, "Lord Black on hold: Ottawa blocks bid for peerage," *Globe and Mail*, June 20, 1999.

39. Heather Scoffield, "Black's nationality an issue in newspaper ownership," *Globe and Mail*, June 23, 1999.

40. Guy Abbate, "Court rejects Black's bid to sue PM over peerage," *Globe and Mail*, March 16, 2000.

41. Shawn McCarthy, "Megadeal creates Canada's largest media empire," *Globe and Mail*, August 20, 2000.

42. Conrad Black, "It's a little like reading your own obituary," *National Post*, August 5, 2000.

43. Richard Siklos, "The Napoleon of Newspapers," *Globe and Mail*, August 4, 2000.

44. Keith Damsell and Gayle MacDonald, "Canwest, Hollinger deal in trouble," *Globe and Mail*, November 11, 2000.

45. Keith Damsell, "Canwest reveals revenue strategy," *Globe and Mail*, November 30, 2000.

46. Rob Ferguson, "Thrills and chills of earnings season," *Toronto Star*, July 20, 2001.

47. Keith Damsell, "Asper pledges profit at Post," *Globe and Mail*, August 25, 2001.

48. Dana Flavelle, "Deep cuts at National Post," *Toronto Star*, September 18, 2001.

49. Keith Damsell, "Canwest Global's loss doubles," *Globe and Mail*, November 15, 2001.

50. Oliver Moore, "Canwest abandons Southam sabbatical program," *Globe and Mail*, November 20, 2001.

51. Elizabeth Church, "Southam's national editorial policy comes under fire," *Globe and Mail*, December 7, 2001.

52. John Miller, "How free is our so-called free press?" *Toronto Star*, 26 April, 2002.

53. Aaron J. Moore, "Ownership: A chill in Canada," *Columbia Journalism Review*, March/April 2002, 11.

54. Keith Damsell, "Canwest accused of more meddling," *Globe and Mail*, March 8, 2002.

55. Gordon Pitts, "Canwest posts loss on ad woes," *Globe and Mail*, April 26, 2002.

56. Keith Damsell, "Canwest editorial policy blasted in ad," *Globe and Mail*, June 6, 2002.

57. Keith Damsell, "Canwest Global stock hits a six-year low," *Globe and Mail*, June 6, 2002.

58. Kim Lunman, and Shawn McCarthy, "Sacking of Ottawa publisher draws international criticism," *Globe and Mail*, June 19, 2002.

59. Clifford Krauss, "Canadian Press Freedom Questioned in Publisher's Firing," *New York Times*, June 29, 2002.

60. Keith Damsell, "Canwest takes a beating," *Globe and Mail*, July 10, 2002.

61. Rob Ferguson, "Canwest Global sells East Coast," *Toronto Star*, July 11, 2002.

62. David Estok, "Aspers' views won't disappear, but just take on subtle guise," *Globe and Mail*, October 2, 2002.

63. Rob Ferguson, "Canwest Global shares fall 16% to 52-week low," *Toronto Star*, October 5, 2002.

64. Martin Cash, "Canwest posts $104-M loss," *Winnipeg Free Press*, November 6, 2002.

65. Keith Damsell, "Canwest set to launch news hub," *Globe and Mail*, January 20, 2003.

66. Irwin Block, "Conference features clash over media ownership," *National Post*, February 15, 2003.

NOTES TO CHAPTER THREE

1. Wm. David Sloan, "In Search of Itself: A History of Journalism Education," in Sloan, ed., *Makers of the Media Mind*. Hillsdale, NJ: Lawrence Erlbaum, 1990, 10.

2. Peter Johansen, David H. Weaver and Christopher Dornan, "Journalism Education in the United States and Canada: Not merely clones," *Journalism Studies*, 2001, 473.

3. Slavko Spichal and Colin Sparks, *Journalists for the 21st Century*, Norwood, NJ: Ablex, 1994, 40.

4. Lee Bernard Becker, Tudor Vlad, and Holly Anne Simpson, "2013 Annual Survey of Journalism Mass Communication Enrollments: Enrollments Decline for Third Consecutive Year," *Journalism & Mass Communication Educator* 69(4), 2014, 349–365.

5. Marc Edge, "Professionalism versus pragmatism: Canadians should pay attention to the way the debate over journalism schools played out in the United States," *Media*, Fall/Winter 2003, 10.

6. Johansen, *et. al.*, "Journalism Education in the United States and Canada," 470.

7. Becker, *et. al.*, "2013 Annual Survey of Journalism Mass Communication Enrollments," 356, 360.

8. Leo Charbonneau, "While the journalism industry contracts, journalism programs continue to expand," *University Affairs*, June 27, 2013. Available online at

http://www.universityaffairs.ca/opinion/margin-notes/while-the-journalism-industry-contracts-journalism-programs-continue-to-expand/

9. Johansen, *et. al.*, "Journalism Education in the United States and Canada," 470.

10. Peter Desbarats, "News about the history of news," *Globe and Mail*, June 3, 1989.

11. Quoted in Robert Fulford, "The scoop on j-schools," *Toronto Life*, November 1998, 63.

12. John Fraser, "Journalism: One Last Rant," *Globe and Mail*, October 15, 1994.

13. Robert Fulford, "Just what is the point of j-school?" *National Post*, July 31, 2002.

14. Barbara Amiel, "Best journalism learned on the job, not taught in journalism school," *Vancouver Sun*, May 22, 1998.

15. Allan Fotheringham, "A brief history of misspent youth," *Maclean's*, October 17, 1988.

16. Peter Desbarats, *Guide to Canadian News Media* 2nd ed. Toronto: Harcourt Brace Jovanovich, 1996, 229.

17. *Ibid.*, 231.

18. Jennifer Lewington, "Journalism school saved by one vote," *Globe and Mail*, October 30, 1993.

19. Larry Cornies, "Western's J-school Filed Under Library," *London Free Press*, November 18, 2000.

20. Arthur Siegel, Andrew Osler, Gregory Fouts and Eugene D. Tate, "The beginnings of communication studies in Canada: remembering and narrating the past," *Canadian Journal of Communication*, Winter 2000, 61.

21. Desbarats, *Guide to Canadian News Media*, 233.

22. *Ibid.*, 233.

23. Wilfred H. Kesterton, *A History of Journalism in Canada*. Ottawa: Carleton University Press, 1967, 165.

24. Canada, Royal Commission on Newspapers, *Report*. Ottawa: Minister of Supply and Services Canada, 1981, 155.

25. *Ibid.*, 157.

26. *Ibid.*, 211.

27. Al Sheehan, "Funds urged for journalism schools," *Vancouver Sun*, April 6, 1990.

28. Jes Odam, "Journalism education in BC is weak, report says," *Vancouver Sun*, April 7, 1990.

29. Canada, Royal Commission on Newspapers, *Report*, 153.

30. Jamie Lamb, "The pen is now slightly mightier," *Vancouver Sun*, February 19, 1988.

31. James Compton, "Sing Tao School of Journalism: What's in a name? Apparently, quite a lot," *Media*, Winter 1998, 23.

32. Douglas Quan, "J-school's Asian connection attacked," *Ubyssey*, October 20, 1998.

33. Allan Fotheringham, "When you and I were young, Allan," *Maclean's*,

November 2, 1998, 100.

34. Derek DeCloet, "A $3m link to corruption: fraud allegations against a Communist-friendly Hong Kong publisher tarnish UBC," *British Columbia Report*, April 5, 1999, 39.

35. Andrea Lobo, "J-school on firm ground," *Ubyssey*, November 21, 2000.

36. Natasha Norbjerg, "Journalism students start student union: School re-naming a factor," *Ubyssey*, February 16, 2001.

37. Johansen, *et. al.*, "Journalism Education in the United States and Canada," 476.

38. Peter Desbarats, "Who's on the barricades?" *Globe and Mail*, June 3, 1998.

39. Matthew Sekeres, "Ryerson endowment hinges on BCE deal," *Globe and Mail*, August 15, 2000.

40. "BCE tables $230 million benefits package as part of CTV acquisition," BCE.ca, July 17, 2000. Available online at http://www.bce.ca/news-and-media/releases/show/bce-tables-230-million-benefits-package-as-part-of-ctv-acquistion

41. Terence Corcoran, "At least they should send the money back," *National Post*, May 29, 2001.

42. *Ibid.*

43. *Ibid.*

44. Canwest was required by the CRTC to divest one of the two stations, however, and it chose to sell its original CKVU and retain market-leading BCTV.

45. "Code of conduct the big debate at CRTC hearings," *Regina Leader-Post*, April 26, 2001.

46. *Ibid.*

47. Peter Desbarats, "Get out of our newsrooms," *Globe and Mail*, July 11, 2001.

48. *Ibid.*

49. Desbarats, *Guide to Canadian News Media*, 229.

50. Peter Desbarats, "News about the history of news."

51. Robert O. Blanchard and William G. Christ, *Media Education and the Liberal Arts*. Hillsdale, NJ: Lawrence Erlbaum, 1993, 62.

52. Desbarats, "Who's on the barricades?"

NOTES TO CHAPTER FOUR

1. David Taras, "Does Canadian TV have a future?" *Winnipeg Free Press*, July 6, 2003.

2. Canada, Standing Committee on Canadian Heritage, *Our Cultural Sovereignty: The Second Century Of Canadian Broadcasting*. Ottawa: Queen's Printer, 2003, 405. Available online at http://www.parl.gc.ca/InfoComDoc/37/2/HERI/Studies/Reports/herirp02-e.htm

3. *Ibid.*, 411.

4. Antonia Zerbisias, "Heritage report buried," *Toronto Star*, July 10, 2003.

5. Laura Bracken, "Fate of Lincoln report falls to Martin," *Playback*, November 24, 2003.

6. *Ibid.*

7. Sean Davidson, "Report? What report? Critics warn that media concentration is threatening debate and broadcast reform," *Playback*, January 5, 2004, 1.

8. *Ibid.*

9. Roger Yu, "FCC retains media cross-ownership rules," *USA Today*, August 11, 2016. Available online at http://www.usatoday.com/story/money/2016/08/11/fcc-retains-media-cross-ownership-rules/88584310/

10. See Allan Bartley, "The regulation of cross-media ownership: The life and short times of PCO 2294," *Canadian Journal of Communication*, Summer 1988, 45–59.

11. Michael Lewis, "CRTC approves trust to hold CTV shares: clears way for BCE," *National Post*, March 23, 2000.

12. James Brooke, "Canadian TV Makes a Move Into Papers," *New York Times*, August 1, 2000.

13. Matthew Fraser, "Monty will have his way with CRTC: Regulators will play along with BCE's revised agenda," *National Post*, September 18, 2000.

14. Bertrand Marotte, "Quebecor wins Vidéotron," *Globe and Mail*, September 13, 2000.

15. Patti Summerfield, "Canada's top 12 media companies," *Strategy*, November 17, 2003, 4.

16. Leonard Asper, "Observations on the media, Canada and Winnipeg," *Canadian Speeches*, January/February 2001, 54.

19. Susan Pigg, "CRTC okays merged newsrooms—But management of newspaper and TV operations must be separate," *Toronto Star*, August 3, 2001.

20. Heather Scoffield, "CRTC okays newsroom convergence," *Globe and Mail*, August 3, 2001.

21. *Ibid.*

22. Heather Scoffield, "Writers blast convergence decision," *Globe and Mail*, August 7, 2001.

23. Elizabeth Church, "Southam's national editorial policy comes under fire," *Globe and Mail*, December 7, 2001.

24. David Asper, "Who controls freedom of speech?" *Calgary Herald*, December 14, 2001.

25. I.H. Asper, "So who's watching the CBC? Nothing 'essential' about it," *National Post*, February 27, 2002.

26. "Canwest's anti-CBC campaign gets louder," *Toronto Star*, February 22, 2002.

27. Irwin Block, "Asper blasts CBC, world media as anti-Israel," Vancouver *Province*, October 31, 2002.

28. Joe Paraskevas, "CBC should get out of local news, sports, Asper says," *Vancouver Sun*, March 18, 2003.

29. Ian Jack, "Commons panel to hold hearings on broadcasting," *National Post*, March 1, 2001.

30. Campbell Clark, "Freedom of the press questioned: Essay defending PM prompts opposition MPs' call for inquiry into media ownership," *Globe and Mail*, March 13, 2001.

31. Graham Fraser and Allan Thompson, "Ottawa to study media ownership," *Toronto Star*, March 13, 2001.

32. Ian Jack, "Ottawa drops study of media ownership," *National Post*, March 17, 2001.

33. Heather Scoffield, "Ottawa and the Goliaths: Media giants are converging at breakneck speed. Will regulators be left in the dust?" *Globe and Mail*, March 26, 2001.

34. Ian Jack, "Commons committee to probe media issues," *National Post*, June 22, 2002.

35. Ian Jack, "Committee divided on report," *National Post*, June 6, 2003.

36. Kate Jaimet, "TV protectionists score win at Commons heritage committee: Keep content restrictions," *National Post*, June 10, 2003.

37. Ian Jack, "Give Canadian TV more cash, MPs say: Ottawa told to make decision on cross-media ownership," *National Post*, June 11, 2003.

38. Zerbisias, "Heritage report buried."

39. John McKay, "Report will stand out," *Montreal Gazette*, June 28, 2003.

40. Simon Tuck, "Broadcasting report expected," *Globe and Mail*, May 20, 2003.

41. Brian Preston, "The *Post* and The Coast: How the *Post* dimmed the *Sun*," *Vancouver*, October 1999.

42. Charles Layton, "News Blackout," *American Journalism Review*, December/January 2004, 20.

43. *Ibid*.

44. Gal Beckerman, "Tripping up big media," *Columbia Journalism Review*, November/December 2003, 15.

45. Trudy Lieberman, "You Can't Report What You Don't Pursue," *Columbia Journalism Review*, May/June 2000, 44.

46. *Ibid*.

47. Commission on Freedom of the Press, *A Free and Responsible Press*. Chicago: University of Chicago Press, 1947, 68.

48. *Ibid*., 8.

49. Warren Breed, "Social Control in the News Room," *Social Forces*, May 1955, 326.

50. *Ibid*.

51. Herbert J. Gans, *Deciding What's News*. New York, Random House, 1979, 94.

52. Pamela J. Shoemaker and Stephen D. Reese, *Mediating the Message: Theories of Influences on Mass Media Content*, 2nd ed. White Plains, NY: Longman, 1996, 170.

53. Canada, Royal Commission on Newspapers, *Report*, 219.

NOTES TO CHAPTER FIVE

1. Eulalie O. Grover, *The Folk-lore Readers*. Chicago: Atkinson, Mentzer & Grover, 1916.

2. Mario Rizzo and Glen Whitman, "The Camel's Nose is in the Tent: Rules, Theories, and Slippery Slopes," *UCLA Law Review* 51(2), 2003, 539–592.

3. Rita Zajacz, "Liberating American Communications: Foreign Ownership Regulations from the Radio Act of 1912 to the Radio Act of 1927," *Journal of Broadcasting & Electronic Media* 48(2), 2004, 157–178.

4. C. Ann Hollifield, "Effects of foreign ownership on media content: Thomson papers' coverage of Quebec independence vote," *Newspaper Research Journal* 20(1), 1999, 65.

5. Anthony Giddens, *Runaway World: How Globalization is Reshaping Our Lives.* London: Routledge, 2000.

6. Sylvio Wainsbord and Nancy Morris, "Rethinking Globalization and State Power," in Wainsbord and Morris, eds., *Media and Globalization: Why the State Matters.* Lanham, MD: Rowman & Littlefield, 2001.

7. Jock Given, "Foreign ownership of media and telecommunications: An Australian story," *Media & Arts Law Review* 7(4), 2002, 253–272.

8. Leo Gray, "Foreign ownership of broadcasting: will the real limitation please stand up?" *Communications Law Bulletin* 10(1), 1990, 3.

9. Lesley Hitchens, *Broadcasting Pluralism and Diversity: A Comparative Study of Policy and Regulation.* Oxford: Hart, 2006, 83.

10. David Bowman, *The Captive Press.* Ringwood, Victoria, Australia: Penguin, 1988.

11. Allan Brown, "Newspaper ownership in Australia," *Journal of Media Economics* 6(3), 1993, 49–64.

12. Brigit Griffen-Foley, "The Fairfax, Murdoch and Packer Dynasties in Twentieth-century Australia," *Media History* 8(1), 2002, 89–102.

13. Richard Siklos, *Shades of Black: Conrad Black and the World's Fastest Growing Press Empire.* Toronto: Minerva, 1996.

14. *Ibid.,* 241.

15. Colleen Ryan and Glenn Burge, *Corporate Cannibals: The Taking of Fairfax.* Melbourne: William Heinemann, 1992.

16. William C. Symons, "Conrad Black Likes a Good Fight — And He's Getting One," *Business Week,* December 1, 1991, 118.

17. Mark Westfield, "Coup of the decade goes to Canwest's one-off TEN deal," *The Australian,* 28 January, 1998.

18. Ryan and Burge, *Corporate Cannibals.*

19. Australia, Senate, *Percentage Players: The 1991 and 1993 Fairfax Ownership Decisions.* Canberra: Commonwealth of Australia, 1994.

20. Quoted in Australia, Senate, *Percentage Players,* 103–104.

21. Conrad Black, *A Life in Progress.* Toronto, Key Porter, 1993, 471.

22. Sandra Olsen, "Banker slams media tycoon on PM claims," *Brisbane Courier-Mail,* 12 February, 1994.

23. "Black distorts truth: Hawke," *Brisbane Courier-Mail,* April 12, 1994.

24. L. Clausen, "Hawke spy offer claim," *Brisbane Courier-Mail,* April 22, 1994.

25. *Ibid.*

26. M. Cole, "Insults fly in Black-Hawke stoush," *Brisbane Courier-Mail,* April 25, 1994.

27. Stephanie Raethel, "Black mark against PM: Report hits link," *Brisbane Courier-Mail*, June 10, 1994.

28. Brenda Dalglish, "Black sells Fairfax stake," *Toronto Sun*, December 17, 1996.

29. *Ibid.*

30. Paul W. Taylor, "Third Service, Third Network: The *Canwest* Global System," *Canadian Journal of Communication* 18(4), 1993, 469.

31. *Ibid.*

32. *Ibid.*

33. Matthew Fraser, *Free For All: The Struggle for Dominance on the Digital Frontier.* Toronto: Stoddart, 1999.

34. Margie Comrie and Susan Fountaine, "Retrieving public service broadcasting: Treading a fine line at TVNZ," *Media Culture & Society* 21(1), 2005, 104.

35. Mark Westfield, *The Gatekeepers: The Global Media Battle to Control Australia's Pay TV.* Sydney: Pluto Press, 2000, 105.

36. Marc Edge, *Asper Nation: Canada's Most Dangerous Media Company.* Vancouver: New Star Books, 2007.

37. Westfield, *The Gatekeepers,* 105.

38. Allan Levine, *From Winnipeg to the world: The Canwest Global story.* Winnipeg: Canwest Global Communications, 2002.

39. Kim Sweetman, "Canadian TV boss sees 'no sense' in our media laws," *Adelaide Advertiser,* November 6, 1995.

40. M. Cole, "Canadian TV threat to beam from Fiji," *Brisbane Courier-Mail,* November 6, 1995.

41. Australian Broadcasting Authority, *Investigation Into Control: Canwest Global Communications Corporation/The Ten Group Ltd.* Sydney: Australian Broadcasting Authority, 1995.

42. Rebecca Lang, "TEN's owner in threat to pull out," *Melbourne Herald Sun,* December 7, 1995.

43. "Canwest bullish on float of Ten," *The Australian*, December 19, 1996.

44. Australian Broadcasting Authority, *Investigation Into Control: Canwest Global Communications Corporation/The Ten Group Ltd. Second Investigation.* Sydney: Australian Broadcasting Authority, 1997.

45. Bryan Frith, "Conflicting views put Asper at sixes and sevens on Ten," *The Australian*, May 22, 1997.

46. Clive Mathieson, "Mixed signals," *The Australian*, May 26, 1997.

47. Deborah Brewster, "Right to sack board does not an owner make, Asper claims," *The Australian,* July 18, 1997.

48. Anne Davies, "Canada weighs in to help TV mogul," *Sydney Morning Herald*, May 28, 1997.

49. Clive Mathieson, "Canwest loses court appeal on Ten stake," *Weekend Australian*, August 9, 1997.

50. Deborah Brewster, "Next move in Canwest snakes and ladders," *The Australian*, September 2, 1997.

51. Ivor Ries, "Izzy turns defeat into victory," *Australian Financial Review*, February 26, 1998.

52. Robert Brehl, "Canwest strikes gold with Australian investment," *Globe and Mail*, April 4, 1998.

53. Westfield, "Coup of the decade goes to Canwest's one-off TEN deal."

54. "Asper: A life of sharp contrasts," *The Australian*, October 9, 2003.

55. See Marc Edge, "Cross Ownership," in Wolfgang Donsbach, ed., *International Encyclopedia of Communication*. Oxford: Blackwell, 2008.

56. Given, "Foreign ownership of media and telecommunications."

57. Australia, Productivity Commission, *Broadcasting Inquiry Report*. Melbourne: Productivity Commission, 2000, 324.

58. *Ibid.*, 334.

59. Eric Beecher, "Crumbling Pillars?" *Media International Australia* 122, 2007, 9.

60. Edge, *Asper Nation*.

61. *Ibid.*

62. Tim Arango, "Black Given Prison Term Over Fraud," *New York Times*, December 11, 2007.

63. Neil Shoebridge, "Happy Canwest waits for bounce," *Australian Financial Review*, June 27, 2008.

64. Terry Flew, "Broadcasting and the Social Contract," in Marc Raboy, ed., *Global Media Policy in the New Millennium*. Luton, UK: University of Luton Press, 2001.

NOTES TO CHAPTER SIX

1. Michael O. Wirth, "Issues in Media Convergence," in Alan Albarran and Sylvia Chan-Olmsted, eds., *Handbook of Media Management and Economics*. Mahwah, NJ: Lawrence Erlbaum, 2005, 445.

2. Rich Gordon, "The meanings and implications of convergence," in Kevin Kawamoto, ed., *Digital Journalism: Emerging Media and the Changing Horizons of Journalism*. Lanham, MD: Rowman & Littlefield, 2003.

3. Wirth, "Issues in Media Convergence."

4. Gillian Doyle, "Convergence: 'A unique opportunity to evolve in previously unthought-of ways' or a hoax?" in Chris Marsden and Stefaan Verhulst, eds., *Convergence in European digital TV regulation*. London: Blackstone, 1999; Gillian Doyle, *Media Ownership: The Economics and Politics of Convergence and Concentration in the UK and European Media*. London: Sage, 2002.

5. Kai Hildebrandt, Walter Soderlund and Walter Romanow, "Media Convergence and Canwest Global," in Soderlund and Hildebrandt, eds., *Canadian Newspaper Ownership in the Era of Convergence: Rediscovering Social Responsibility*. Edmonton: University of Alberta Press, 2005; Robert Sparks, Mary Lynn Young and Simon Darnell, "Convergence, corporate restructuring, and Canadian online news, 2000–2003," *Canadian Journal of Communication* 31(2), 2006, 391–423.

6. See Patricia Aufderheide, *Communication Policy and the Public Interest*. New York: Guilford, 1999; Kenneth C. Killebrew, *Managing Media Convergence: Pathways to Journalistic Cooperation*. Ames, IA: Blackwell, 2005; and Jonathan A. Knee, Bruce C. Greenwald and Ava Seave, *The Curse of the Mogul: What's Wrong With the*

World's Leading Media Companies. New York: Portfolio, 2009.

7. See Alec Klein, *Stealing Time: Steve Case, Jerry Levin, and the Collapse of AOL Time Warner.* New York: Simon & Shuster, 2003; John Motavalli, *Bamboozled at the Revolution: How Big Media Lost Billions in the Battle for the Internet.* New York: Viking, 2002; Nina Munk, *Fools Rush In: Steve Case, Jerry Levin, and the Unmaking of AOL Time Warner.* New York: Harper Business, 2004; Kara Swisher and Lisa Dickey, *There Must Be a Pony in Here Somewhere: The AOL Time Warner Debacle and the Quest for a Digital Future.* New York: Crown Business, 2003.

8. A. Michael Noll, "The Myth of Convergence," *International Journal on Media Management* 5(1), 12.

9. See Everett E. Dennis, "Prospects for a Big Idea — Is There a Future for Convergence?" *International Journal on Media Management* 5(1), 2003, 7–11; Stephen Quinn, *Convergent Journalism: The Fundamentals of Multi-Platform Publishing Around the World.* New York: Peter Lang, 2005.

10. See Mark Glaser, "Business Side of Convergence Has Myths, Some Real Benefits," *Online Journalism Review,* May 19, 2004. Available online at http://www.ojr.org/ojr/business/1084948706.php; Castulus Kolo and Patrick Vogt, "Strategies for Growth in the Media and Communications Industry: Does Size Really Matter?" *International Journal on Media Management* 5(4), 2003, 251–261; Gracie Lawson-Borders, *Media Organizations and Convergence: Case Studies of Media Convergence Pioneers.* Mahwah, NJ: Lawrence Erlbaum, 2006.

11. Gordon Pitts, *Kings of Convergence: The Fight for Control of Canada's Media.* Toronto: Doubleday, 2002; David Taras, "The New World of Communications in Canada," in David Taras, Fritz Pannekoek and Maria Bakardjieva, eds., *How Canadians Communicate.* Calgary: University of Calgary Press, 2003.

12. Glaser, "Business Side of Convergence Has Myths, Some Real Benefits;" Gordon, "The meanings and implications of convergence."

13. Bob Garfield, *The Chaos Scenario.* Nashville: Stielstra, 2009; Jonathan W. Palmer and Lars Eriksen, "Digital News: Paper, Broadcast and More Converge on the Internet," *International Journal on Media Management* 1(1), 1999, 31–34.

14. Pitts, *Kings of Convergence.*

15. Rob Ferguson, "Canwest Global sells east coast newspapers — Pressing need for capital overrides convergence strategy," *Toronto Star,* July 11, 2002.

16. Bertrand Marotte, "Quebecor Media taps junk bonds," *Globe and Mail,* June 16, 2001.

17. Bertrand Marotte, "Quebecor Media on credit watch," *Globe and Mail,* September 17, 2002.

18. Robert Gibbens, "Quebecor Media taken off credit watch," *National Post,* February 12, 2003.

19. Sean Silcoff, "Quebecor cutting media division debt," *National Post,* October 10, 2003.

20. Bertrand Marotte, "Cogeco, Bell Globemedia buy TQS from Quebecor," *Globe and Mail,* September 19, 2001.

21. Michael Lewis, "Teachers and Bell take sporting reins," *National Post,* February 12, 2003.

22. Grant Robertson, "Canwest ruling seen as setting precedent," *Globe and Mail*, December 21, 2007.

23. David Olive, "Convergence gets personal at Quebecor," *Toronto Star*, September 12, 2003.

24. Paul Brent, "Quebecor buys Toronto 1 TV station from CHUM," *National Post*, August 21, 2004.

25. Grant Robertson, "Quebecor triumphant in Osprey battle," *Globe and Mail*, August 4, 2007.

26. Grant Robertson and Jacquie McNish, "BGM grabs CHUM for $1.4-billion," *Globe and Mail*, July 13, 2006.

27. Dwayne Winseck, "Media Merger Mania," *Canadian Dimension* 42(1), 2008, 30–33.

28. Antonia Zerbisias, "Just say no to this monstrous media deal," *Toronto Star*, August 7, 2006.

29. Grant Robertson, "Rogers acquires CITY-TV stations for $375-million," *Globe and Mail*, June 12, 2007.

30. Grant Robertson, "Asper defends move to retain Aussie TV," *Globe and Mail*, July 13, 2007.

31. Grant Robertson, "TV network profits at 'crisis' levels," *Globe and Mail*, February 11, 2009.

32. Grant Robertson, "Canwest puts E! up for sale," *Globe and Mail*, February 6, 2009.

33. Grant Robertson, "A week of reckoning for Canadian TV," *Globe and Mail*, August 31, 2009.

34. See Diane Dakers, *CHEK Republic: A Revolution in Local Television*. Victoria, BC: Heritage House, 2014.

35. Grant Robertson, "Canwest sells Australian TV channel," *Globe and Mail*, September 24, 2009.

36. Andrew Willis, "With Australia off its plate, Canwest on to bigger issues," *Globe and Mail*, September 25, 2009.

37. Grant Robertson and Andrew Willis, "The Asper dream ends, the sell-off begins," *Globe and Mail*, October 3, 2009.

38. Susan Krashinsky, "Corus buying CTV specialty channels for $40-million," *Globe and Mail*, July 15, 2009.

39. Richard Blackwell, "CTV cuts 105 positions," *Globe and Mail*, November 28, 2008.

40. Grant Surridge, "CTV sees $100M loss, takes $1.7B writedown," *Montreal Gazette*, February 28, 2009.

41. Matt Hartley, "Broadcasters seek changes for 'broken' industry," *Globe and Mail*, March 4, 2009.

42. David Friend, "CTV axes morning newscasts," *Toronto Star*, March 11, 2009.

43. Krashinsky, "Corus buying CTV specialty channels for $40-million."

44. Jamie Sturgeon and Theresa Tedesco, "CTV rejigs finances to avoid default," *National Post*, September 17, 2009.

45. Susan Krashinsky, "Lights dim for last time at small Manitoba station,"

Globe and Mail, October 3, 2009.

46. Tavia Grant, "CTV Windsor station spared," *Globe and Mail*, July 9, 2009.

47. Greg O'Brien, "Fun with TV numbers as Commission releases BDUs' and broadcasters' aggregate financial data," Carrt.ca, September 29, 2009. Available online at https://cartt.ca/article/fun-tv-numbers-commission-releases-bdus-and-broadcasters-aggregate-financial-data

48. Canada, Canadian Radio-television and Telecommunications Commission, *Communications Monitoring Report*, 2009. Ottawa: CRTC.

49. Francois Shalom, "No holiday cheer at Sun Media," *Montreal Gazette*, December 17, 2008.

50. Aaron Derfel, "Journal de Montréal locks out staff," *Montreal Gazette*, January 25, 2009.

51. Marc Edge, "Le Journal Lockout: Convergence Conquers Workers," The Tyee, March 7, 2011. Available online at http://thetyee.ca/Mediacheck/2011/03/07/LeJournalLockout/

52. David Akin, "Television business model 'broken,'" *Montreal Gazette*, March 11, 2009.

53. Paul Vieira, "Broadcasters argue for more revenue, fewer restrictions," *Montreal Gazette*, April 23, 2009.

54. Rita Trichur, "Carriage-fee necessity exaggerated, Rogers says," *Toronto Star*, April 17, 2009.

55. Kelly Toughill, "Feud roils troubled TV industry," *Toronto Star*, May 16, 2009.

56. Iain Marlow, "Taking on cable giants," *Toronto Star*, October 9, 2009.

57. Grant Robertson and James Bradshaw, "CRTC looks to retool Canadian TV," *Globe and Mail*, February 11, 2009.

58. John Doyle, "We still watch TV. So why are stations going out of business?" *Globe and Mail*, March 10, 2009.

59. Rita Trichur, "Carriage fee fight is on the air," *Toronto Star*, September 14, 2009.

60. Brett Clarkson, "CTV stations face the axe: Cable firms must fork over cash, TV exec says," *Toronto Sun*, October 22, 2009.

61. Susan Krashinsky, "CRTC favours broadcasters in TV shakeup," *Globe and Mail*, March 23, 2010.

62. Robert Picard and Tony Rimmer, "Weathering a recession: Effects of size and diversification on newspaper companies," *Journal of Media Economics*, 12(1), 1999, 1–18; Robert Picard, "Effects of Recessions on Advertising Expenditures: An Exploratory Study of Economic Downturns in Nine Developed Nations," *Journal of Media Economics* 14(1), 2001, 1–14.

63. Raphael Amit and Joshua Livnat, "Diversification Strategies, Business Cycles and Economic Performance," *Strategic Management Journal* 9(2), 1988, 99–110.

64. Sylvia Chan-Olmsted and Byeng-Hee Chang, "Diversification strategy of global media conglomerates: Examining its patterns and determinants," *Journal of Media Economics* 16(4), 2003, 213–33; Jaemin Jung and Sylvia M. Chan-Olmsted, "Impacts of Media Conglomerates' Dual Diversification on Financial Perfor-

mance," *Journal of Media Economics* 18(3), 2005, 183–202.

65. Marc Gunther, "Hard news," *Fortune* 156(3), August 6, 2007, 80–85.

66. David Olive, "Atkinson principles work as Torstar's corporate credo," *Toronto Star*, January 29, 2004.

67. Frank Ahrens, "Newspaper-TV Marriage Shows Signs of Strain," *Washington Post*, January 11, 2007; Leslie Jean Thornton and Susan Keith, "From Convergence to Webvergence: Tracking the Evolution of Print–Broadcast Partnerships Through the Lens of Change Theory," *Journalism & Mass Communication Quarterly* 86 (2), 2009, 257–276.

68. See Marc Edge, "An accidental success story: The forced diversification of Quebecor Media." *Journal of Media Business Studies* 8(3), Fall 2011, 69–87.

69. Kelly Toughill, "CTV: operating profits and job losses," J-Source.ca, March 19, 2009. Available online at http://www.j-source.ca/article/ctv-operating-profits-and-job-losses

70. Dwayne Winseck, "Financialization and the 'Crisis of the Media': The Rise and Fall of (Some) Media Conglomerates in Canada," *Canadian Journal of Communication* 35(2), 2010, 388.

71. *Ibid.*

72. Derek DeCloet, "Don't believe everything they say on TV," *Globe and Mail*, March 15, 2008.

NOTES TO CHAPTER SEVEN

1. See Ernesto Dal Bó, "Regulatory capture: A review," *Oxford Review of Economic Policy* 22(2), 2006, 203–225; Alfred Kahn, *The Economics of Regulation: Principles and Institutions*. New York: John Wiley & Sons, 1971; Jean-Jacques Laffont and Jean Tirole, "The politics of government decision making. A theory of regulatory capture," *Quarterly Journal of Economics* 106(4), 1991, 1089–1127; Michael E. Levine and Jennifer L. Forrence, "Regulatory capture, public interest, and the public agenda: Toward a synthesis," *Journal of Law, Economics and Organization* 6(0), 1990, 167–198; Barry M. Mitnick, *The Political Economy of Regulation: Creating, Designing, and Removing Regulatory Forms*. New York: Columbia University Press, 1980; George Stigler, "The theory of economic regulation," *Bell Journal of Economics and Management Science* 2(1), 1971, 3–21; Tim Wu, *The Master Switch: The Rise and Fall of Information Empires*. New York: Alfred A. Knopf, 2010.

2. Robert B. Horwitz, *The Irony of Regulatory Reform: The Deregulation of American Telecommunications*. New York: Oxford, 1989, 29. Emphasis in original.

3. *Ibid.*, 30.

4. Matthew Fraser, "The man who won't do lunch," *National Post*, June 10, 2000.

5. Herschel Hardin, *Closed Circuits: The Sellout of Canadian Television*. Vancouver: Douglas & McIntyre, 1985; Marc Raboy, *Missed Opportunities: The Story of Canada's Broadcasting Policy*. Montreal: McGill/Queen's University Press, 1990.

6. Canadian Radio-television and Telecommunications Commission, "CRTC Decision 86–367: Applications for authority to transfer effective control of Télé-

Métropole to Power Corporation of Canada," April 18, 1986. Available online at http://www.crtc.gc.ca/eng/archive/1986/DB86-367.HTM

7. *Ibid.*

8. *Ibid.*

9. Laurence J. E. Dunbar and Christian Leblanc, "Review of the regulatory framework for broadcasting services in Canada." Ottawa: CRTC, 2007. Available online at http://www.crtc.gc.ca/eng/publications/reports/dunbarleblanc.htm

10. *Ibid.*

11. *Ibid.*

12. Canadian Radio-television and Telecommunications Commission, "CRTC Decision 1989–110: Background to Decisions CRTC 89-766 to 89-771," September 28, 1989. Available online at http://www.crtc.gc.ca/eng/archive/1989/PB89-110.HTM

13. Canadian Radio-television and Telecommunications Commission, "CRTC Decision 1989–109: Elements assessed by the commission in considering applications for the transfer of ownership or control of broadcasting undertakings," September 28, 1989. Available online at http://www.crtc.gc.ca/eng/archive/1989/PB89-109.htm

14. Canadian Radio-television and Telecommunications Commission, "CRTC Decision 1992–42: Assessment of the impact of the benefits test applied at the time of transfers of ownership or control of broadcasting undertakings," June 15, 1992. Available online at http://www.crtc.gc.ca/eng/archive/1992/PB92-42.htm

15. Canadian Radio-television and Telecommunications Commission, "Public Notice CRTC 1993–68: Application of the benefits test at the time of transfers of ownership or control of broadcasting undertakings," May 26, 1993. Available online at http://www.crtc.gc.ca/eng/archive/1993/PB93-68.HTM

16. Barrie McKenna, "TV station buyers face big pledges: study," *Globe and Mail*, May 26, 1994.

17. Ian Austen, "Does bigger mean better?" *Calgary Herald*, September 14, 1994; Harvey Enchin, "Rogers files $100-million carrot: Promises goodies if CRTC approves MH takeover," *Globe and Mail*, July 23, 1994.

18. Enchin, "Rogers files $100–million carrot."

19. *Ibid.*

20. Canadian Radio-television and Telecommunications Commission, "Decision CRTC 94–923: Rogers Communications Inc.," December 19, 1993. Available online at http://www.crtc.gc.ca/eng/archive/1994/DB94-923.HTM

21. Canadian Radio-television and Telecommunications Commission, "Call for comments on a proposed approach for the regulation of Broadcasting Distribution Undertakings," May 17, 1996. Available online at http://www.crtc.gc.ca/eng/archive/1996/pb96-69.htm

22. Canadian Radio-television and Telecommunications Commission, "Public Notice CRTC 1998–41: Commercial Radio Policy 1998," April 30, 1998. Available online at http://www.crtc.gc.ca/eng/archive/1998/PB98-41.HTM

23. Ira Wagman, "On the policy reflex in Canadian communication studies,"

Canadian Journal of Communication 35(4), 2010, 619–630.

24. Monica Auer, "Is bigger really better? TV and radio ownership policy under review," *Policy Options* 28(8), 2007, 78–83.

25. Matthew Sekeres, "Ryerson endowment hinges on BCE deal," *Globe and Mail*, August 15, 2000.

26. "BCE tables $230 million benefits package as part of CTV acquisition," BCE.ca, July 17, 2000. Available online at http://www.bce.ca/news-and-media/releases/show/bce-tables-230-million-benefits-package-as-part-of-ctv-acquistion

27. Bill Wilton, "In support of BCE/CTV union." [Excerpts from letter dated 24 August, 2000], *National Post*, May 29, 2001.

28. Peter Desbarats, "In support of BCE/CTV union. [Excerpts from letter dated August 24, 2000], *National Post*, May 29, 2001.

29. Fred Fletcher, "Re: BCE Acquisition of CTV–Application–2000–15497." [letter to Ursula Menke, CRTC Secretary General], August 23, 2000.

30. Murray Whyte, "CJF washes hands of donation," *National Post*, May 30, 2001.

31. Peter Desbarats, "Get out of our newsrooms," *Globe and Mail*, July 11, 2001.

32. Frank Luba, "Canwest invests in UBC," *Vancouver Province*, June 26, 2001.

33. Marc Edge, *Asper Nation: Canada's Most Dangerous Media Company.* Vancouver: New Star Books, 2007.

34. Canadian Radio-television and Telecommunications Commission, "Decision CRTC 2000–747 Transfer of effective control of CTV Inc. to BCE Inc.," December 7, 2000. Available online at http://www.crtc.gc.ca/eng/archive/2000/DB2000-747.htm

35. Judy Monchuk, "Canadians believe media easily influenced: Survey," *Kingston Whig-Standard*, June 15, 2004.

36. CRTC, "Transcript of proceedings: TV renewals — CTV/Global across Canada, Volume 7."

37. Canadian Media Research Consortium (CMRC). (2004). Report card on Canadian news media. Downloaded June 7, 2004 from http://www.cmrcccrm.ca/_OLDSITE/english/reportcard2004/01.html

38. *Ibid.*

39. CRTC, "Transcript of proceedings: TV renewals — CTV/Global across Canada, Volume 7."

40. Edge, *Asper Nation*, 257.

41. Canadian Media Research Consortium, "Online Canadians and news study," 2008. Downloaded November 30, 2008 from http://www.cmrcccrm.ca/en/projects/documents/OnlineCanadiansandNewsStudy-CMRC.pdf

42. Canadian Media Research Consortium, "Activities report: June 1, 2007–May 31, 2008," 2008. Downloaded April 20, 2011 from http://www.cmrcccrm.ca/

43. Philip Savage, "Gaps in Canadian media research: CMRC findings," *Canadian Journal of Communication* 33(2), 2008, 291–301.

44. Canadian Media Research Consortium, "The credibility gap: Canadi-

ans and their news media five years later," 2008. Downloaded June 13, 2008 from http://www.cmrcccrm.ca/en/projects/TheCredibilityGapCanadi-ansandTheirNewsMedia.htm

45. Canadian Media Research Consortium, "The state of the media in Canada: A work in progress," 2009. Downloaded August 31, 2012 from http://www.cmrc-ccrm.ca/en/projects/StateoftheMediainCanada.htm

46. Dwayne Winseck, "Financialization and the 'crisis of the media': The rise and fall of (some) media conglomerates in Canada," *Canadian Journal of Communication* 35(2), 2010, 365–393.

47. Florian Sauvageau, Fred Fletcher, Donna Logan and Pierre Juneau, Letter to Diane Rheaume, Secretary General, Canadian Radio-Television and Telecommunications Commission, September 22, 2006. Downloaded September 28, 2006 from http://www.crtcccrm.ca/

48. Canadian Radio-television and Telecommunications Commission, "Public Notice CRTC 2007–53: Determinations regarding certain aspects of the regulatory framework for over-the-air television," May 17, 2007. Available online at http://www.crtc.gc.ca/eng/archive/2007/pb2007-53.htm

49. Canadian Media Research Consortium, "Activities Report: June 1, 2008—December 31, 2009," 2010. Downloaded April 13, 2011 from http://www.cmrcccrm.ca/en/aboutus/documents/Activities_Report_2008_2009_Web.pdf

50. Canadian Media Research Consortium, "Canadian consumers unwilling to pay for news online," 2011. Downloaded April 13, 2011 from http://www.cmrc-ccrm.ca/documents/CMRC_Paywall_Release.pdf

51. Canadian Media Research Consortium, "Canadians value home Internet connection more than other media devices," April 12, 2011. Downloaded from http://mediaresearch.ca/en/projects/documents/CMRCMedia_Devices_April_12.pdf

52. Catherine Murray, "Wellsprings of knowledge: Beyond the CBC policy trap," *Canadian Journal of Communication* 26(1), 2001, 31–53.

53. Peter G.C. Townley, "Sour notes in Canadian media merger assessment: Toward antitrust and cultural harmony," 2003. Acadia University Department of Economics Working Paper 2003-01. Available online at http://papers.ssrn.com/sol3/papers.cfm?abstract_id=400380

54. Dunbar and Leblanc, "Review of the regulatory framework for broadcasting services in Canada."

55. CRTC, "Public Notice CRTC 2007–53."

56. Canadian Radio-television and Telecommunications Commission, "Broadcasting Public Notice CRTC 2008–4: Regulatory policy. Diversity of voices," January 15, 2008. Available online at http://www.crtc.gc.ca/eng/archive/2008/pb2008-4.htm

57. Canadian Radio-television and Telecommunications Commission, "Communications Monitoring Report 2010," 2010. Available online at http://www.crtc.gc.ca/eng/publications/reports/PolicyMonitoring/2010/cmr.htm

58. Marc Edge, "De-convergence and re-convergence in Canadian media," *The

Convergence Newsletter, December 2010. Available online at http://sc.edu/cmcis/archive/convergence/v7no10.html

59. Canadian Radio-television and Telecommunications Commission, "Decision CRTC 2010–782: Change in the effective control of Canwest Global Communications Corp.'s licensed broadcasting subsidiaries," October 22, 2010. Available online at http://www.crtc.gc.ca/eng/archive/2010/2010-782.htm

60. Canadian Radio-television and Telecommunications Commission, "Decision CRTC 2011–163: Change in effective control of CTVglobemedia Inc.'s licensed broadcasting subsidiaries," March 7, 2011. Available online at http://www.crtc.gc.ca/eng/archive/2011/2011-163.htm

61. Canadian Radio-television and Telecommunications Commission, "Broadcasting Notice of Consultation CRTC 2012–370: Notice of hearing," July 10, 2012. Available online at http://crtc.gc.ca/eng/archive/2012/2012-370.htm.

62. Canadian Radio-television and Telecommunications Commission, "Broadcasting Decision CRTC 2012–574," October 18, 2012. Available online at http://www.crtc.gc.ca/eng/archive/2012/2012-574.htm

63. Dwayne Winseck, "On Bell–Astral merger, the CRTC should take its time," *Globe and Mail,* January 29, 2013. Available online at http://www.theglobeandmail.com/technology/digital-culture/on-bell-astral-merger-the-crtc-should-take-its-time/article7947816/

64. Simon Houpt and Sean Silcoff, "Bell's bid for Astral approved," *Globe and Mail,* June 28, 2013.

65. Paul F. Lazarsfeld, "Remarks on administrative and critical research," *Studies in Philosophy and Social Science* 9, 1941, 2–16.

66. William H. Melody and Robin E. Mansell, "The debate over critical vs. administrative research: Circularity or challenge," *Journal of Communication* 33(3), 1983, 110.

67. *Ibid.*, 111.

68. Dallas W. Smythe and Tran Van Dinh, "On critical and administrative research: A new critical analysis," *Journal of Communication* 33(3), 1983, 117.

69. Donna Logan, "Re: CTV Television Inc. station group licence renewal," March 22, 2001. [letter to Ursula Menke, CRTC Secretary General.] Downloaded May 23, 2006 from http://www.crtcccrm.ca/

70. Robert McChesney, *Communication Revolution: Critical Junctures and the Future of Media.* New York: The New Press, 2007.

71. Townley, "Sour notes in Canadian media merger assessment."

72. *Ibid.*

73. CMRC, "The credibility gap."

NQTE TO CHAPTER EIGHT

1. Canada, Standing Senate Committee on Transportations and Communications, *Final Report on the Canadian News Media,* Vol. 1. Ottawa: Senate of Canada, 2006, 63.

NOTES TO CHAPTER NINE

1. Lawrence Martin, "It's not Canadians who've gone to the right, just their media," *Globe and Mail*, January 23, 2003.

2. Adam Aptowitzer, "Canada: The Impact of Charity and Tax Law/Regulation on Not-for-Profit News Organizations," in Robert G. Picard, Valerie Belair-Gagnon and Sofia Ranchordás, eds., *The Impact of Charity and Tax Law/Regulation on Not-For-Profit News Organizations*. Oxford, UK: Reuters Institute for the Study of Journalism, University of Oxford, and the Information Society Project, Yale University, March 2016. Available online at https://reutersinstitute.politics.ox.ac.uk/sites/default/files/The%20impact%20of%20charity%20and%20tax%20law%20regulation%20on%20not%20for%20profit%20news%20organisations_0.pdf

3. Julia Cagé, *Saving the Media: Capitalism, Crowdfunding, and Democracy*. Translated by Arthur Goldhammer. Cambridge, MA: Belknap Press, 2016, 78.

4. *Ibid.*, 133.

5. Federal Trade Commission, "Native Advertising: A Guide for Businesses," December 2015. Available online at https://www.ftc.gov/tips-advice/business-center/guidance/native-advertising-guide-businesses

6. Canada, Royal Commission on Newspapers, *Report*. Ottawa: Queen's Printer, 1981, 211.

7. Heather Scoffield, "Ottawa and the Goliaths: Media giants are converging at breakneck speed. Will regulators be left in the dust?" *Globe and Mail*, March 26, 2001.

NOTES TO CHAPTER TEN

1. Paul Willcocks, "Who Still Believes Postmedia Is Canadian-Controlled?" The Tyee, July 8, 2016. Available online at http://thetyee.ca/Mediacheck/2016/07/08/Who-Believes-Postmedia-Canadian/

2. *Ibid.*

3. Bruce Cheadle, "Public Policy Forum will assess the state of Canada's struggling news industry," Macleans.ca, June 21, 2016. Available online at http://www.macleans.ca/politics/ottawa/liberals-seek-outside-advice-as-they-mull-policy-help-for-news-media/

4. Public Policy Forum, "Our roots," ppforum.ca, undated. Available online at http://www.ppforum.ca/about

5. "Five things to know with Canada's news media industry under public policy review," *Brandon Sun*, June 21, 2016. Available online at http://www.brandonsun.com/national/breaking-news/five-things-to-know-with-canadas-news-media-industry-under-public-policy-review-383860061.html

6. *Ibid.*

7. Dean Beeby, "Ottawa cuts newspaper ad spending amid worries about sector," CBC News, September 1, 2016. http://www.cbc.ca/news/politics/newspapers-canadian-heritage-public-policy-forum-digital-news-gathering-internet-1.3743580

8. Andrew Potter, "What should be done about the state of the news media?" In Due Course, June 28, 2016. Available online at http://induecourse.ca/what-should-be-done-about-the-state-of-the-news-media/

9. Madelaine Drohan, "Does serious journalism have a future in Canada?" Ottawa: Public Policy Forum, 2016. Available online at http://www.ppforum.ca/sites/default/files/PM%20Fellow_March_11_EN_1.pdf

10. James Bradshaw, "Postmedia CEO urges tax breaks to keep ad revenues in Canada," Globe and Mail, May 13, 2016.

11. Marie-Danielle Smith, "Crisis in newspapers 'understated,'" Montreal Gazette, May 13, 2016.

12. Bradshaw, "Postmedia CEO urges tax breaks to keep ad revenues in Canada."

13. Terry Pedwell, "Postmedia head pitches government ad buys," Halifax Chronicle-Herald, May 13, 2016.

14. Ibid.

15. Shannon Rupp, "Postmedia Baron Godfrey's Gobsmacking Audacity," May 28, 2016. Available online at http://thetyee.ca/Opinion/2016/05/28/Godfrey-Gobsmacking-Audacity/

16. Jill Slattery, "24 hrs Vancouver newsroom shut down by Postmedia," Globalnews.ca, September 30, 2016. Available online at http://globalnews.ca/news/2973971/24-hrs-vancouver-newsroom-shut-down-by-postmedia/

17 Dean Starkman, The Watchdog that Didn't Bark: The Financial Crisis and the Disappearance of Investigative Journalism. New York: Columbia Journalism Review Books, 2014, 14.

18 Dwayne Winseck, "Financialization and the 'Crisis of the Media': The Rise and Fall of (Some) Media Conglomerates in Canada," Canadian Journal of Communication 35(2), 2010, 376.

19 Ibid., 386-387.

20 Robert Bezede, "Torstar Corporation—A Top Canadian Newspaper and Prime Acquisition Target," Seeking Alpha, May 31, 2016. Available online at http://seekingalpha.com/article/3978802-torstar-corporation-top-canadian-newspaper-prime-acquisition-target

21 Ibid.

22 Ibid.

23 Andrew Khouri, "US files suit to block Tribune purchase of O.C. Register parent," Los Angeles Times, March 17, 2016.

24 John Miller, "The Hall of Shame," The Journalism Doctor, November 26, 2015. Available online at http://www.thejournalismdoctor.ca/Blog.php/the-hall-of-shame

25 Ian Gill, No News is Bad News: Canada's Media Collapse—And What Comes Next. Vancouver: Greystone Books, 2016, 2–3.

26 Markham Hislop, "The Vancouver School: Inside the BC Media's Anti-Oil Crusade," Alberta Oil, February 2016. Available online at http://www.albertaoil-magazine.com/2016/02/vancouver-observer-the-tyee-energy-projects-bc/

27 Terence Corcoran, "Government to the newspaper industry's rescue? No

thanks," *National Post*, February 6, 2016.

28 Kelly McParland, "The cause of the crisis in newspapers is not a mystery. So why investigate it?" *National Post*, February 3, 2016.

29 Dwayne Winseck, "Modular Media: A radical communication and cultural policy for Canada," *The Monitor*, July/August 2016, 31.

30 See Diane Dakers, *CHEK Republic: A Revolution in Local Television*. Victoria, BC: Heritage House, 2014.

31 Robert G. Picard, "Deficient Tutelage: Challenges of Contemporary Journalism Education," in Gene Allen, Stephanie Craft, Christopher Waddell and Mary Lynn Young, eds., *Toward 2020: New Directions in Journalism Education*, 8. Toronto: Ryerson Journalism Research Centre, 2015. Available online at http://finder.fcad.ryerson.ca/finderadmin/RSJ/Publications/Toward2020/Toward2020NewDirectionsinJournalismEducationFullNov20.pdf

32 Paul Benedetti, "The Big Sellout: A Critical Snapshot of the Rise of 'Entrepreneurial Journalism,'" in *Ibid.*, 94.

33 *Ibid.*, 97.

34 Dean Starkman, "Confidence Game: The limited vision of the news gurus," *Columbia Journalism Review*, November/December 2011, 122–123.

35 "UBC students win international award for social media project," UBC Graduate School of Journalism, undated. Available online at http://www.journalism.ubc.ca/ubc-students-win-international-award-for-social-media-project/

36 See "Course essentials and syllabus," Decoding Social Media 2016 blog, January 4, 2016. Available online at https://blogs.ubc.ca/decodingsocialmedia2016/2016/01/04/syllabus/

37 Sean Holman, "Sacrificing the message for the medium," *Media*, Spring 2016, 12-13. Available online at http://www.caj.ca/wp-content/uploads/2016/05/Media_Spring_2016.pdf

38 Núria Almiron-Roig, "From Financialization to Low and Non-profit: Emerging Media Alternatives for Freedom," *tripleC: Communication, Capitalism & Critique* 9(1), 2011, 57.

39 *Ibid.*, 58.

Bibliography

Núria Almiron, *Journalism in Crisis: Corporate Media and Financialization*. Cresskill, NJ: Hampton Press, 2010.

Núria Almiron-Roig, "From Financialization to Low and Non-profit: Emerging Media Alternatives for Freedom," *tripleC: Communication, Capitalism & Critique* 9(1), 2011, 39–61.

Raphael Amit and Joshua Livnat, "Diversification Strategies, Business Cycles and Economic Performance," *Strategic Management Journal* 9(2), 1988, 99–110.

Adam Aptowitzer, "Canada: The Impact of Charity and Tax Law/Regulation on Not-for-Profit News Organizations," in Robert G. Picard, Valerie Belair-Gagnon and Sofia Ranchordás, eds., *The Impact of Charity and Tax Law/Regulation on Not-For-Profit News Organizations*. Reuters Institute for the Study of Journalism, University of Oxford, and the Information Society Project, Yale University, March 2016.

Leonard Asper, "Observations on the media, Canada and Winnipeg," *Canadian Speeches*, January/February 2001, 54.

Shaun Assael, "Northern Exposure," *NewsInc.*, January 1993, 29–30.

Patricia Aufderheide, *Communication Policy and the Public Interest*. New York: Guilford, 1999.

Monica Auer, "Is bigger really better? TV and radio ownership policy under review," *Policy Options* 28(8), 2007, 78–83.

Australia, Productivity Commission, *Broadcasting Inquiry Report*. Melbourne: Productivity Commission, 2000.

Australia, Senate, *Percentage Players: The 1991 and 1993 Fairfax Ownership Decisions*. Canberra: Commonwealth of Australia, 1994.

Australian Broadcasting Authority, *Investigation Into Control: Canwest Global Communications Corporation/The Ten Group Ltd*. Sydney: Australian Broadcasting Authority, 1995.

————, *Investigation Into Control: Canwest Global Communications Corporation/The Ten Group Ltd. Second Investigation*. Sydney: Australian Broadcasting Authority, 1997.

Ben Bagdikian, "Conglomeration, Concentration and the Media," *Journal of Communication* 30(2), Spring 1980, 59–64.

————, *The Media Monopoly*. Boston: Beacon Press, 1983.

Allan Bartley, "The regulation of cross-media ownership: The life and short times of PCO 2294," *Canadian Journal of Communication* 13(2), Summer 1988, 45–59.

Lee Bernard Becker, Tudor Vlad, and Holly Anne Simpson, "2013 Annual Survey of Journalism Mass Communication Enrollments: Enrollments Decline for Third Consecutive Year," *Journalism & Mass Communication Educator* 69(4), 2014, 349–365.

Gal Beckerman, "Tripping up big media," *Columbia Journalism Review*, November/ December 2003, 15.

Eric Beecher, "Crumbling Pillars?" *Media International Australia* 122, 2007, 9–11.

Paul Benedetti, "The Big Sellout: A Critical Snapshot of the Rise of 'Entrepreneurial Journalism,'" in Gene Allen, Stephanie Craft, Christopher Waddell, and Mary Lynn Young, eds., *Toward 2020: New Directions in Journalism Education*. Toronto: Ryerson Journalism Research Centre, 2015. Available online at http://finder.fcad.ryerson.ca/finderadmin/RSJ/Publications/Toward2020/Toward-2020NewDirectionsinJournalismEducationFullNov20.pdf

Conrad Black, *A Life in Progress*. Toronto, Key Porter, 1993.

Robert O. Blanchard and William G. Christ, *Media Education and the Liberal Arts*. Hillsdale, NJ: Lawrence Erlbaum, 1993.

David Bowman, *The Captive Press*. Ringwood, Victoria, Australia: Penguin, 1988.

Laura Bracken, "Fate of Lincoln report falls to Martin," *Playback*, November 24, 2003.

Warren Breed, "Social Control in the News Room," *Social Forces*, May 1955, 326–335.

Allan Brown, "Newspaper ownership in Australia," *Journal of Media Economics* 6(3), 1993, 49–64.

Charles Bruce, *News and the Southams*. Toronto: Macmillan, 1968.

Mark Burgess, "Postmedia's $316-million newspaper deal to maintain segregated markets, newsrooms to offer niche advertising," *Hill Times*, October 10, 2014. Available online at http://www.hilltimes.com/2014/10/10/postmedias-316-million-newspaper-deal-to-maintain-segregated-markets-newsrooms-to-offer-niche-advertising/29915/39915

————, "Surviving the takeover," *Media*, Spring 2015, 13. Available online at http://www.caj.ca/wp-content/uploads/2015/03/Winter2015_final.pdf

Julia Cagé, *Saving the Media: Capitalism, Crowdfunding, and Democracy*. Translated by Arthur Goldhammer. Cambridge, MA: Belknap Press, 2016.

Canada, Canadian Radio-Television and Telecommunications Commission, *Communications Monitoring Report*, 2009. Ottawa: CRTC.

————, Royal Commission on Newspapers, *Report*. Ottawa: Queen's Printer, 1981.

————, Standing Committee on Canadian Heritage, *Our Cultural Sovereignty: The Second Century Of Canadian Broadcasting* (Ottawa: Queen's Printer), 2003. Available online at http://www.parl.gc.ca/InfoComDoc/37/2/HERI/Studies/Reports/herirp02-e.htm

———, Standing Senate Committee on Transportations and Communications, *Final Report on the Canadian News Media*, Vol. 1, June 2006. Available online at http://www.parl.gc.ca/content/sen/committee/391/tran/rep/repfinjun06vol1-e.pdf

———, *The Uncertain Mirror: Report of the Special Senate Committee on Mass Media*, Vol. I, 1970. Ottawa: Information Canada.

Sylvia Chan-Olmsted and Byeng-Hee Chang, "Diversification strategy of global media conglomerates: Examining its patterns and determinants," *Journal of Media Economics* 16(4), 2003, 213–233.

Ambarish Chandra and Allan Collard-Wexler, "Mergers in Two-Sided Markets: An Application to the Canadian Newspaper Industry," *Journal of Economics & Management Strategy* 18(4), Winter 2009, 1045–1070.

Leo Charbonneau, "While the journalism industry contracts, journalism programs continue to expand," *University Affairs*, June 27, 2013. Available online at http://www.universityaffairs.ca/opinion/margin-notes/while-the-journalism-industry-contracts-journalism-programs-continue-to-expand/

Commission on Freedom of the Press, *A Free and Responsible Press*. Chicago: University of Chicago Press, 1947.

James Compton, "Sing Tao School of Journalism: What's in a name? Apparently, quite a lot," *Media*, Winter 1998, 23–24.

Margie Comrie and Susan Fountaine, "Retrieving public service broadcasting: Treading a fine line at TVNZ," *Media Culture & Society* 21(1), 2005, 101–118.

Toby D. Couture, "Without Favour: The Concentration of Ownership in New Brunswick's Print Media Industry," *Canadian Journal of Communication* 38/1, 2013, 57–81.

Gilbert Cranberg, Randall Bezanson and John Soloski, *Taking Stock: Journalism and the Publicly Traded Newspaper Company*. Ames: Iowa State University Press, 2001.

Diane Dakers, *CHEK Republic: A Revolution in Local Television*. Victoria, BC: Heritage House, 2014.

Ernesto Dal Bó, "Regulatory capture: A review," *Oxford Review of Economic Policy* 22(2), 2006, 203–225.

Keith Davey, *The Rainmaker: A Passion for Politics*. Toronto: Stoddart, 1986.

Sean Davidson, "Report? What report? Critics warn that media concentration is threatening debate and broadcast reform," *Playback*, January 5, 2004, 1.

Derek DeCloet, "A $3m link to corruption: fraud allegations against a Communist-friendly Hong Kong publisher tarnish UBC," *British Columbia Report*, April 5, 1999, 39.

Everett E. Dennis, "Prospects for a Big Idea — Is There a Future for Convergence?" *International Journal on Media Management* 5(1), 2003, 7–11.

Peter Desbarats, *Guide to Canadian News Media*, 2nd ed. Toronto: Harcourt Brace Jovanovich, 1996.

Gillian Doyle, "Convergence: 'A unique opportunity to evolve in previously unthought-of ways' or a hoax?" in Chris Marsden and Stefaan Verhulst, eds.,

Convergence in European Digital TV Regulation. London: Blackstone, 1999.

————, *Media Ownership: The Economics and Politics of Convergence and Concentration in the UK and European Media*. London: Sage, 2002.

Madelaine Drohan, "Does serious journalism have a future in Canada?" Ottawa: Public Policy Forum, 2016. Available online at http://www.ppforum.ca/sites/default/files/PM%20Fellow_March_11_EN_1.pdf

Peter J.S. Dunnett, *The World Newspaper Industry*. London: Croom Helm, 1988.

Marc Edge, "And 'The Wall' Came Tumbling Down in Los Angeles." In Joseph Bernt and Marilyn Greenwald, eds. *The Big Chill: Investigative Reporting in the Current Media Environment*. Ames: Iowa University Press, 2000.

————, *Pacific Press: The Unauthorized Story of Vancouver's Newspaper Monopoly*. Vancouver: New Star Books, 2001.

————, "The Press We Deserve: A Legacy of Unheeded Warnings," *Textual Studies in Canada*, Fall 2002, 9–19.

————, "Professionalism versus pragmatism: Canadians should pay attention to the way the debate over journalism schools played out in the United States," *Media*, Fall/Winter 2003, 10–12.

————, *Asper Nation: Canada's Most Dangerous Media Company*. Vancouver: New Star Books, 2007.

————, "Cross Ownership," in Wolfgang Donsbach, ed., *International Encyclopedia of Communication*. Oxford: Blackwell, 2008.

————, "An accidental success story: The forced diversification of Quebecor Media." *Journal of Media Business Studies* 8(3), Fall 2011, 69–87.

————, *Greatly Exaggerated: The Myth of the Death of Newspapers*. Vancouver: New Star Books, 2014.

————, "The Never-ending Story: Postmedia, the Competition Bureau, and Press Ownership Concentration in Canada," *Canadian Journal of Media Studies* 14(1), Spring/Summer 2016, 53–81. Available online at http://cjms.fims.uwo.ca/issues/14-01/edge.pdf

Mark Fitzgerald, "Hollinger gains control of Southam," *Editor & Publisher*, December 7, 1996, 12.

Terry Flew, "Broadcasting and the Social Contract," in Marc Raboy, ed., *Global Media Policy in the New Millennium*. Luton, UK: University of Luton Press, 2001.

Erwin Frenkel, *The Press and Politics in Israel: The Jerusalem Post from 1932 to the Present*. Westport, CT: Greenwood Press, 1994.

Robert Fulford, "The scoop on j-schools," *Toronto Life*, November 1998, 63.

Gerald A. Epstein, "Introduction: Financialization and the World Economy," in Epstein, ed., *Financialization and the World Economy*. Cheltenham, UK: Edward Elgar, 2005.

Brigit Griffen-Foley, "The Fairfax, Murdoch and Packer Dynasties in Twentieth-century Australia," *Media History* 8(1), 2002, 89–102.

Allan Fotheringham, "A brief history of misspent youth," *Maclean's*, October 17, 1988, 68.

————, "When you and I were young, Allan," *Maclean's*, November 2, 1998, 100.

Matthew Fraser, *Free For All: The Struggle for Dominance on the Digital Frontier*.

Toronto: Stoddart, 1999.

Herbert J. Gans, *Deciding What's News*. New York, Random House, 1979.

Bob Garfield, *The Chaos Scenario*. Nashville: Stielstra, 2009.

Anthony Giddens, *Runaway World: How Globalization is Reshaping Our Lives*. London: Routledge, 2000.

Ian Gill, *No News is Bad News: Canada's Media Collapse — And What Comes Next*. Vancouver: Greystone Books, 2016.

Jock Given, "Foreign ownership of media and telecommunications: An Australian story," *Media & Arts Law Review* 7(4), 2002, 253–272.

Mark Glaser, "Business Side of Convergence Has Myths, Some Real Benefits," *Online Journalism Review*, May 19, 2004. Available online at http://www.ojr.org/ojr/business/1084948706.php

Rich Gordon, "The meanings and implications of convergence," in Kevin Kawamoto, ed., *Digital Journalism: Emerging Media and the Changing Horizons of Journalism*. Lanham, MD: Rowman & Littlefield, 2003.

Leo Gray, "Foreign ownership of broadcasting: will the real limitation please stand up?" *Communications Law Bulletin* 10(1), 1990, 3–5.

Eulalie O. Grover, *The Folk-lore Readers*. Chicago: Atkinson, Mentzer & Grover, 1916.

Marc Gunther, "Hard news," *Fortune* 156(3), August 6, 2007, 80–85.

Herschel Hardin, *Closed Circuits: The Sellout of Canadian Television*. Vancouver: Douglas & McIntyre, 1985.

Markham Hislop, "The Vancouver School: Inside The B.C. Media's Anti-Oil Crusade," *Alberta Oil*, February 2016. Available online at http://www.albertaoil-magazine.com/2016/02/vancouver-observer-the-tyee-energy-projects-bc/

Lesley Hitchens, *Broadcasting Pluralism and Diversity: A Comparative Study of Policy and Regulation*. Oxford: Hart, 2006.

C. Ann Hollifield, "Effects of foreign ownership on media content: Thomson papers' coverage of Quebec independence vote," *Newspaper Research Journal* 20(1), 1999, 65–82.

Sean Holman, "Sacrificing the message for the medium," *Media*, Spring 2016, 12–13. Available online at http://www.caj.ca/wp-content/uploads/2016/05/Media_Spring_2016.pdf

Robert Britt Horwitz, *The Irony of Regulatory Reform: The Deregulation of American Telecommunications*, Oxford University Press, New York, 1989.

Claire Hoy, "CRTC's appointed power hacks," *Hill Times*, May 14, 2001, 6.

Peter Johansen, David H. Weaver and Christopher Dornan, "Journalism Education in the United States and Canada: not merely clones," *Journalism Studies*, 2001, 469–483.

Tim Jones, "That Old Black Magic," *Columbia Journalism Review*, March/April 1998, 40.

Jaemin Jung and Sylvia M. Chan-Olmsted, "Impacts of Media Conglomerates' Dual Diversification on Financial Performance," *Journal of Media Economics* 18(3), 2005, 183–202.

Alfred Kahn, *The Economics of Regulation: Principles and Institutions*. New York: John Wiley & Sons, 1971.

Robert R. Kerton, "Price Effects of Market Power in the Canadian Newspaper Industry," *Canadian Journal of Economics* 6, November 1973, 602-606.

Wilfred H. Kesterton, *A History of Journalism in Canada*. Ottawa: Carleton University Press, 1967.

Kenneth C. Killebrew, *Managing Media Convergence: Pathways to Journalistic Cooperation*. Ames, Iowa: Blackwell, 2005.

Alec Klein, *Stealing Time: Steve Case, Jerry Levin, and the Collapse of AOL Time Warner*. New York: Simon & Shuster, 2003.

Jonathan A. Knee, Bruce C. Greenwald, and Ava Seave, *The Curse of the Mogul: What's Wrong With the World's Leading Media Companies*. New York: Portfolio, 2009.

Castulus Kolo and Patrick Vogt, "Strategies for Growth in the Media and Communications Industry: Does Size Really Matter?" *International Journal on Media Management* 5(4), 2003, 251–261.

Thomas Kunkel and Gene Roberts, eds., *Leaving Readers Behind: The Age of Corporate Journalism*. Fayetteville: University of Arkansas Press, 2001.

Stephen Lacy and Todd F. Simon, *The Economics and Regulation of United States Newspapers*. Norwood, NJ: Ablex, 1993.

Jacques Laffont and Jean Tirole, "The politics of government decision making. A theory of regulatory capture," *Quarterly Journal of Economics* 106(4), 1991, 1089–1127.

Gracie Lawson-Borders, *Media Organizations and Convergence: Case Studies of Media Convergence Pioneers*. Mahwah, NJ: Lawrence Erlbaum, 2006.

Charles Layton, "News Blackout," *American Journalism Review*, December/January 2004, 20.

Paul F. Lazarsfeld, "Remarks on administrative and critical research," *Studies in Philosophy and Social Science* 9, 1941, 2–16.

James Ledbetter, "The Slow, Sad Sellout of Journalism School," *Rolling Stone*, October 16, 1997, 73–81; 99–100.

Allan Levine, *From Winnipeg to the World: The Canwest Global Story*. Winnipeg: Canwest Global Communications, 2002.

Michael E. Levine and Jennifer L. Forrence, "Regulatory capture, public interest, and the public agenda: Toward a synthesis," *Journal of Law, Economics and Organization* 6(0), 1990, 167–198.

Robert Lewis, "Nobody Here But Us Chickens," *Maclean's*, April 27, 1981, 32.

———, "The pressure on the press," *Maclean's*, August 31, 1981, 30.

Trudy Lieberman, "You Can't Report What You Don't Pursue," *Columbia Journalism Review*, May/June 2000, 44.

Donna Logan, "What Do the Mega Media Deals Mean for Journalists? Opportunities and Challenges," *Media*, Fall 2000, 15.

Robert McChesney, *Communication Revolution: Critical Junctures and the Future of Media*. New York: The New Press, 2007.

William H. Melody and Robin E. Mansell, "The debate over critical vs. administrative research: Circularity or challenge," *Journal of Communication* 33(3), 1983,

103–116.

John Miller, *Yesterday's News: Why Canada's Daily Newspapers are Failing Us*, Halifax: Fernwood, 1998.

Barry M. Mitnick, *The Political Economy of Regulation: Creating, Designing, and Removing Regulatory Forms*. New York: Columbia University Press, 1980.

John Motavalli, *Bamboozled at the Revolution: How Big Media Lost Billions in the Battle for the Internet*. New York: Viking, 2002.

Aaron J. Moore, "Ownership: A chill in Canada," *Columbia Journalism Review*, March/April 2002, 11.

Nina Munk, *Fools Rush In: Steve Case, Jerry Levin, and the Unmaking of AOL Time Warner*. New York: Harper Business, 2004.

Catherine Murray, "Wellsprings of knowledge: Beyond the CBC policy trap," *Canadian Journal of Communication* 26(1), 2001, 31–53.

A. Michael Noll, "The Myth of Convergence," *International Journal on Media Management* 5(1), 12–13.

Jonathan W. Palmer and Lars Eriksen, "Digital News: Paper, Broadcast and More Converge on the Internet," *International Journal on Media Management* 1(1), 1999, 31–34.

Robert Picard, "Effects of Recessions on Advertising Expenditures: An Exploratory Study of Economic Downturns in Nine Developed Nations," *Journal of Media Economics* 14(1), 2001, 1–14.

Robert G. Picard, "Deficient Tutelage: Challenges of Contemporary Journalism Education," in Gene Allen, Stephanie Craft, Christopher Waddell, and Mary Lynn Young, eds., *Toward 2020: New Directions in Journalism Education*, 8. Toronto: Ryerson Journalism Research Centre, 2015. Available online at http://finder.fcad.ryerson.ca/finderadmin/RSJ/Publications/Toward2020/Toward-2020NewDirectionsinJournalismEducationFullNov20.pdf

Robert Picard and Tony Rimmer, "Weathering a recession: Effects of size and diversification on newspaper companies," *Journal of Media Economics*, 12(1), 1999, 1–18.

Gordon Pitts, *Kings of Convergence: The Fight for Control of Canada's Media*. Toronto: Doubleday, 2002.

Jacques Poitras, *Irving vs. Irving: Canada's Feuding Billionaires And The Stories They Won't Tell*. Toronto: Viking, 2014.

Brian Preston, "The *Post* And The Coast: How the *Post* dimmed the *Sun*," *Vancouver*, October 1999.

Stephen Quinn, *Convergent Journalism: The Fundamentals of Multi-Platform Publishing Around the World*. New York: Peter Lang, 2005.

Marc Raboy, *Missed Opportunities: The Story of Canada's Broadcasting Policy*. Montreal: McGill/Queen's University Press, 1990.

Mario Rizzo and Glen Whitman, "The Camel's Nose is in the Tent: Rules, Theories, and Slippery Slopes," *UCLA Law Review* 51(2), 2003, 539–592.

Colleen Ryan and Glenn Burge, *Corporate Cannibals: The Taking of Fairfax*. Melbourne: William Heinemann, 1992.

Philip Savage, "Gaps in Canadian media research: CMRC findings," *Canadian*

Journal of Communication 33(2), 2008, 291–301.

Robert Sheppard and Patricia Chisholm, "A Strategic Retreat," *Maclean's*, May 8, 1999, 30.

Pamela J. Shoemaker and Stephen D. Reese, *Mediating the Message: Theories of Influences on Mass Media Content* 2nd ed. White Plains, NY: Longman, 1996.

Arthur Siegel, Andrew Osler, Gregory Fouts, and Eugene D. Tate, "The beginnings of communication studies in Canada: remembering and narrating the past," *Canadian Journal of Communication*, Winter 2000, 61–103.

Richard Siklos, *Shades of Black: Conrad Black and the World's Fastest Growing Press Empire*. Toronto: Minerva, 1996.

David Sloan, "In Search of Itself: A History of Journalism Education," in Sloan, ed., *Makers of the Media Mind*. Hillsdale, NJ: Lawrence Erlbaum, 1990.

Dallas W. Smythe and Tran Van Dinh, "On critical and administrative research: A new critical analysis," *Journal of Communication* 33(3), 1983, 117–127.

Walter Soderlund and Kai Hildebrandt, eds., *Canadian Newspaper Ownership in the Era of Convergence: Rediscovering Social Responsibility*. Edmonton: University of Alberta Press, 2005.

Robert Sparks, Mary Lynn Young and Simon Darnell, "Convergence, corporate restructuring, and Canadian online news, 2000–2003," *Canadian Journal of Communication* 31(2), 2006, 391–423.

Slavko Spichal and Colin Sparks, *Journalists for the 21st Century*, Norwood, NJ: Ablex, 1994.

Dean Starkman, "Confidence Game: The limited vision of the news gurus," *Columbia Journalism Review* 50(4), November/December 2011, 122–123.

———, *The Watchdog That Didn't Bark: The Financial Crisis and the Disappearance of Investigative Journalism*. New York: Columbia Journalism Review Books, 2014.

Erin Steuter, "He Who Pays the Piper Calls the Tune: Investigation of a Canadian Media Monopoly," *Web Journal of Mass Communication Research* 7/4, September 2004. Available online at http://www.scripps.ohiou.edu/wjmcr/vol07/7-4a-b.html

——— "The Irvings Cover Themselves: Media Representations of the Irving Oil Refinery Strike, 1994-1996," *Canadian Journal of Communication* 24/4, 1999. Available online at http://www.cjc-online.ca/index.php/journal/article/view/1128/1039

Peter Steven, *About Canada: Media*. Halifax: Fernwood, 2011.

George Stigler, "The theory of economic regulation," *Bell Journal of Economics and Management Science* 2(1), 1971, 3–21.

Patti Summerfield, "Canada's top 12 media companies," *Strategy*, November 17, 2003, 4.

Kara Swisher and Lisa Dickey, *There Must Be a Pony in Here Somewhere: The AOL Time Warner Debacle and the Quest for a Digital Future*. New York: Crown Business, 2003.

William C. Symons, "Conrad Black Likes a Good Fight—And He's Getting One," *Business Week*, December 1, 1991, 118.

David Taras, "The New World of Communications in Canada," in David Taras, Fritz Pannekoek and Maria Bakardjieva, eds., *How Canadians Communicate*. Calgary: University of Calgary Press, 2003.

Paul W. Taylor, "Third Service, Third Network: The Canwest Global System," *Canadian Journal of Communication* 18(4), 1993, 469–477.

Leslie Jean Thornton and Susan Keith, "From Convergence to Webvergence: Tracking the Evolution of Print-Broadcast Partnerships Through the Lens of Change Theory," *Journalism & Mass Communication Quarterly* 86 (2), 2009, 257–276.

Neil Tudiver, *Universities for Sale: Resisting Corporate Control over Canadian Higher Education*. Toronto: James Lorimer, 1999.

Doug Underwood, *When MBAs Rule the Newsroom*. Columbia University Press: New York, 1993.

Lou Ureneck, "Newspapers arrive at economic crossroads," *Nieman Reports*, Summer, 3–11.

Christopher Waddell, "Paper Pusher: Has the death of newsprint been overstated?" *Literary Review of Canada*, May 2015. Available online at http://review-canada.ca/magazine/2015/05/paper-pusher/

Ira Wagman, "On the policy reflex in Canadian communication studies," *Canadian Journal of Communication* 35(4), 2010, 619–630.

Sylvio Wainsbord and Nancy Morris, eds., *Media and Globalization: Why the State Matters*. Lanham, MD: Rowman & Littlefield, 2001.

Mark Westfield, *The Gatekeepers: The Global Media Battle to Control Australia's Pay TV*. Sydney: Pluto Press, 2000.

Anthony Wilson-Smith, "War of Words: The gloves are off over circulation claims in the newspaper industry," *Maclean's*, February 8, 1999, 48.

Dwayne Winseck, "Media Merger Mania," *Canadian Dimension* 42(1), 2008, 30–33.

———, "Financialization and the 'Crisis of the Media': The Rise and Fall of (Some) Media Conglomerates in Canada," *Canadian Journal of Communication* 35(2), 2010, 365–393.

———, "Modular Media: A radical communication and cultural policy for Canada," *The Monitor*, July/August 2016, 25–31.

Michael O. Wirth, "Issues in Media Convergence," in Alan Albarran and Sylvia Chan-Olmsted, eds., *Handbook of Media Management and Economics*. Mahwah, NJ: Lawrence Erlbaum, 2005, 445.

Tim Wu, *The Master Switch: The Rise and Fall of Information Empires*. New York: Alfred A. Knopf, 2010.

Rita Zajacz, "Liberating American Communications: Foreign Ownership Regulations from the Radio Act of 1912 to the Radio Act of 1927," *Journal of Broadcasting & Electronic Media* 48(2), 2004, 157–178.

Index